I'M STILL STANDING

I'M STILL STANDING

How One Woman's Brushes with Death Taught Her How To Live

. . .

Kelly Standing

Standing Media, LLC

Chicago, Illinois

Published by
Standing Media, LLC
Chicago, Illinois
www.ImStillStandingBook.com

Publisher's Cataloging-in-Publication Data
Standing, Kelly.

I'm still standing : how one woman's brushes with death taught her how to
live / by Kelly Standing. – Chicago, Ill. : Standing Media, LLC, 2012.

p. ; cm.

ISBN13: 978-0-9852745-0-4

1. Standing, Kelly. 2. Women—United States—Biography. 3. Near-death
experiences. 4. Mothers and daughters. 5. Spirituality. 6. Weight loss. I. Title.

CT275.S73 S73 2012
920.720973—dc22   2011960310

FIRST EDITION

Project coordination by Jenkins Group, Inc.
www.BookPublishing.com

Interior design by Heather Shaw

Printed in the United States of America
16 15 14 13 12 · 5 4 3 2 1

For Cathy Standing Dunkin —

the most outstanding, upstanding, understanding
Standing. You are the glue, Seestor. You are the glue.

*"If you don't get what you want,
find a way to love what you get anyway."*

CONTENTS ...

STANDING at the Microphone ...

Photo by Robert Joseph Kessler

Still STANDING on Chicago's Magnificent Mile ... my kind of town.

DON'T SKIP THIS!!! IT'S IMPORTANT!

Greetings, Reader:

Look out! This book won't read like most other books—perhaps not like *any* other book —and not just because it's an autobiography.

By definition, I guess an autobiography would capture one distinct life, in this case, *my* life.

If you stick with me to the end of this book, you will discover how it looks, feels, sounds and even how it smells and tastes ... to be struck by lightning ... to be hit by a car ... to survive a mass murder ... to have a major organ removed and, contrary to medical precedent, to have that organ grow *back*! (For a long time, I wondered whether that organ would know when to *stop* growing ... or ... would it just keep *on* regenerating and pop out of my ear some night over dinner?! I'm happy to report no such phenomenon has occurred ... at least not *yet*.)

Stick with me to the end of this book, and you'll discover what it feels like to die ... to go into the *"Bright Light"* and live to tell. On a less harrowing note, you'll find out how it feels to *lose* 110 pounds—almost a whole person (granted, one of those *skinny* people most of us might like to squash like a bug), but still, I lost one and *gained* a whole new perspective *un*related to how I look. If you stick with me, at least you'll discover how all those memorable events looked, felt, sounded, smelled and even tasted to *me*.

That *alone* makes this book different from other books, but when I say *"different,"* I mean different in terms of format, not just content. Most books contain periods, breaks between paragraphs and chapters to indicate pauses. Mine will, too. That qualifies as conventional, common, expected, ordinary. I should warn you, however, about some *un*conventional, *un*expected and *not*-so-ordinary keystrokes you'll encounter on the following pages. You see ... for a long time, I wrote speeches for a living—corporate speeches, nothing political, so don't blame *me* for any promises made or broken by your least favorite lawmaker. I wrote this book as a speechwriter ... for your *ear*, not for your *eye*.

Sure, I write with all the obvious devices—commas, periods, question and quotation marks—but for *this* book, for *my* book, I invoke the more obscure tools of my speechwriter's trade, as well. You'll find this book full of atypical grammar, stage direction, conversational language, parenthetical facial expressions and gestures I invite you to imagine. You'll find hyphens where they don't normally belong. I use more than the customary amount of alliteration, again, because I write for the *ear*, not for the *eye*. I use numerals (1, 2, 3) instead of spelling out numbers (one, two, three) because speakers find numerals easier to see on a script or a screen. Devices some would *outlaw* on a *printed* page we allow and encourage in a *spoken* presentation. Where I would pause *briefly* in my story if I were delivering it as a *speech*, you'll find those mini-pauses spelled out ... with ellipses (...). Where I would take a *longer*, weightier pause, at the end of a silly or serious thought, for example, you'll find [PAUSE] inserted into the text in all caps, the way it would appear in a script.

I tell my clients, "When you come to the word [PAUSE] in your script, count to 3 in your head s-l-o-w-l-y—1 ... 2 ... 3. It will feel like an *eternity* to *you*, but it sounds very natural to your *audience*."

As a reader of this book, when *you* come to the word [PAUSE], take 3 seconds. That way, you'll experience my story the way a member of an audience might—engaging a few more senses, enjoying it more ... or at least differently. When you come to a syllable or an entire word I would deliver emphatically, you'll find that syllable or word in all caps and/or italicized for emphasis, just the way I would capitalize or italicize for a client. I formatted my text the way it would appear on a TelePrompTer. Sometimes, in this *book*—this *"speech"* you will *see* instead of *hear*—you'll notice I even choreograph my tone of voice and facial expressions, reminding myself to [SMIRK] or to [SNEER] or to speak in a [HIGH-PITCHED] voice when the story calls for those devices.

Where you *see* that, imagine it. Stress the words or syllables. Make the faces. Hear the voices. Have a little fun with it. Who cares if the guy next to you on the plane stares? Who cares if your mate thinks you're nuts and wonders why you keep looking up from your book and pondering as you read? Who knows, my funky format might spark a conversation, prompt a question or jog a memory. Nothing wrong with *that*. Books are supposed to make us stop and think, right? I just make it easier ... by providing obvious "stop signs" throughout my text. But don't let *me* push you around. If you just want to read in your *own* way with your *own* inflection, obviously, you're free to ignore or overrule my format at any point.

I've heard the journalistic wisdom that says, *"If you have to explain a piece of writing— using a lot of italics, all caps or too many exclamation points in an attempt to control your reader—then the writing isn't very strong."* I agree with that ... to a point. Other kinds of writers can trust their readers to add the inflection or the pauses where they belong. As a speechwriter, sorry, but I can't trust you. Speechwriters can't afford that luxury. People rarely *see* our words in print. Our words don't linger on a page; they hang in the air for a few seconds ... then evaporate into the speaker's next line. We get *one shot* to ensure that the words we write come out of the speaker's mouth and go into the listener's ear the way we intend. We accomplish that with a script—a marked-up, odd-looking, often-ignored but painstakingly prepared pile of paper or series of lines on a prompter.

Photo by Jeff Brown

If you don't *like* my format at first, give it a chance. I suspect you'll get used to it. Let yourself *hear* this book with your *ears. Hear* my story. I *could* deliver it in a more typical way, but this format looks, sounds and feels more like *me* ... and ... it will let you in on a few of the behind-the-scenes secrets of my profession. For example, we speechwriters craft even our ad libs. Those seemingly spontaneous one-liners you find funniest of *all*? We may spend *hours* refining and rehearsing them.

Yes, most books contain commas, periods, breaks between paragraphs and chapters to indicate pauses, and mine will, too. That qualifies as conventional, common, expected, ordinary. Most people who know me well would tell you I'm *none* of those things.

Good, bad or indifferent, I tend to strike people as *unc*onventional, *unc*ommon, *une*xpected and anything *but* ordinary. Sometimes they like that about me; sometimes they don't.

As for me, I tend to like *every*one, at least at first. Truth be told, in the past, I tended to keep *on* liking people long after they had given me ample reason to stop. I was like that proverbial little kid frantically digging away in a pile of manure. When a puzzled onlooker asks, *"What are you DOing?!"* the confident kid replies, *"There's GOTTA be a pony in here SOMEwhere!"* I spent a substantial chunk of my life digging for ponies that weren't there. This might be a good time to tell you I've changed some of the names in this book to protect the ... pony snatchers.

I want to be quick to add that, despite all that disappointing digging that led me to the *wrong* people, I unearthed a lot of the *right* people, too—more all the time. The Universe has seen fit to surround me with an amazing assortment of bright, authentic, articulate, funny, loyal and loving friends, colleagues and family members. I don't mean a *little* bit bright or a *little* bit funny or a *little* bit loyal. I mean eye-poppingly bright, jaw-droppingly funny, hand-holding, bum-kicking, spackle-for-your-cracks, umbrellas-in-your-drink kind of people. Sure, I've felt the sting and the stench of the manure, but I got the garden to go with it.

On this subject, my dad once told me, *"Kell, you and I always look for the good in other people, and it always surprises us when we realize it isn't there."* He added, *"Sure, we get hurt sometimes, but I wouldn't want to live any other way."*

I agree. I'm happy to report that, like me, my dad got a garden, too, including 55 happy, harmonious, often hilarious years—and counting—with my mom. You won't be*lieve* how my dad convinced me to see poop storms as parties, to see the possibilities in my pain—good thing, considering all the manure that hit my fan over the years. My mom says my dad is *"wired differently."* She's right. He shared his inspired, uncommon, unwavering optimism early and often. I *needed* it, and I'm grateful.

I have witnessed a peculiar speech-writing/speech-giving/speech-receiving phenomenon. Right or wrong, like it or not, sacred or secular, audience members make every message their own. Speakers and speechwriters can't control that. I can't explain it, but I *have* witnessed the power of it throughout my career. Speakers stand on a stage, or in a pulpit, or in a TV studio and talk about *one* thing, but audience members walk away having heard something *else entirely.*

I *like* that. It makes me feel like we're collaborating—the Universe, my audience members and I—crafting the message *together*—and I don't have to carry the whole weight, share my office space or split my fees.

I've seen it countless times. It happens *every*where speakers speak. Church members file out of sanctuaries and stop to congratulate pastors on a job well done. *"I loved your sermon!"* they gush, genuinely grateful for the message, not just blowing smoke up the pastor's holy skivvies. *Smart* pastors with their egos in check respond, *"You loved my sermon? Thank you. ... What part?"* In return, members often say something like, *"I felt like you were talking right to me when you said ..."* Then they finish their compliment with a quote the pastor didn't deliver, a thought the pastor absolutely did NOT express ... at least not *consciously.* Those kinds of unintended, unauthorized, spontaneous rewrites happen in listeners' heads and hearts during those 3-second pauses I mentioned, *if* the speaker remembers to deliver them—1 ... 2 ... 3.

It might appear there's a lot of poop hittin' a lot of fans these days. Taking a few 3-second pauses won't deflect the poop or unplug the fan, but it might help us breathe. I'm an expert. Trust me; as one who hasn't always been sure where her next breath was coming from, I say, *"Take 'em while you can GET 'em."* Try not to blow past the pauses in my text. Where you see a "..." or a "[PAUSE]," honor it. Be still. Breathe.

I feel less Zen and more tightly wound than that makes me sound.

In language, as in life, timing is everything. At the end of jokes, at the end of good or bad financial forecasts, at the end of a compelling sales pitch, the 3-second pause makes audience members laugh harder, concentrate better and *buy* more. I'm not sure I'm *"selling"* any*thing in these pages, but if my story suggests a way to overcome adversity (without spawning addictions, prescriptions or afflictions), why not give yourself 3 seconds to let the laugh or the lesson sink in?

As I see it, in some ways this autobiography isn't about *me*. The value of a story like mine isn't in how or even how well I *tell* it; the value of *my* story lies in how it connects or clashes with *your* story.

My book invites you to experience my story from *both* sides of the microphone. Why? Because, while you "hear" *my* memories in *my* voice with *my* inflection, I have no doubt your *own* memories will bubble to the surface ... in *your* voice ... *if* you let them—new ones, old ones, happy ones, crappy ones—and you might just see them in a new way. You might find peace where you once felt panic. You might see possibilities where you once saw only pain ... *if* you give those memories 3 ... little ... seconds. After all, like me, you're still standing. *That's* why my autobiography isn't just about me; in 3 seconds, you'll make it about *you*!

CHAPTER 1

STANDING at the End of My Rope ...

As a child, my sister, Cathy, had a birthmark right in the middle of her tummy. You may not care to *know* that. *She* may not care to *have* you know it, but *her* nudity becomes essential to the plot of *my* story, so you ... and *she* ... will just have to bear (or bare) with me, so to speak.

Have you ever *noticed* ... the firstborn in a family inherits a great deal of power? Oh, I don't mean money or possessions. I'm talking about the currency that matters most in *child*hood. *I* would call that power *"naming rights."* By sheer accident of *birth*, firstborns get to tell future siblings what's *what*. ... They get to decide *how* things will *work* in that particular *family* ... how everyone should *feel* about what he or she gets or *doesn't* get. [PINCH LIPS AND SQUINT W/ BITTER EXPRESSION] [PAUSE]

Back in the 1960s, my sister and her friends jump rope *end*lessly in our neighborhood. *E*veryone wants to jump; *no* one wants to turn the *rope*, so they prey on the little kids—*me*, in par*t*icular—and give us important-sounding *ti*tles to get us to do the *dir*ty work. At 6, I *d*esperately want to be part of any game they play. They *know* that. One afternoon, after shooing me away re*peat*edly from their grown-up pursuit of hide-and-seek and *hop*scotch, they switch to jumping *rope*. They call me over enthusiastically.

"Kelly, c'mere!"

[POUTING/SUSPICIOUS] *"Why?"*

"Just c'mere."

"What do you want?"

"We want you to play with us."

"You do not."

"Yes, we do. You get to jump rope with us."

[ABANDONING ALL SKEPTICISM] *"Really?"*

"Mmmmmhmmmm."

Sucker! I should see the *next* part coming, but my heart leaps at the thought of being included. My heart did a *lot* of leaping. ... It still *does* ... leaving my *head* somewhere *else*, occasionally up my *bum*, I'm afraid. Often, in the *past*, I couldn't tell when other people didn't *have* my best *in*terests at *heart*. I certainly don't *see* it on *this* particular day. ...

I walk up the *drive*way to find Cathy and her friends tying one end of the jump rope to the handle on our grandmother's garage door—perfect *rope*-turning height. They hand *me* the *oth*er end of the rope. They *do* it in an almost cere*mon*ial way, as if they are bestowing some grand gift, like an Oscar statuette *or*, even *bett*er, a Bomb Pop from the *ice*-cream man.

"Here ..." they say, *"*YOU *get to be ...* [HUSHED/AWE-STRUCK TONE] *the EVer-ender!"*

They say it as if I were joining some secret soc*i*ety.

I extract my head from my bum long enough to ask ... *skep*tically, *"EVer-ender? What's THAT?"*

[HIGH/CHIRPY, LIKE AN AUTO-SHOP CLERK SOFT-SOAPING A *BIG* ESTIMATE ...] *"It means you get to turn the rope ... for-ev-er.* [EYES WIDE W/ ENVIOUS EXPRESSION] *Get it? Ever-ender!"*

Then, as I re*call*, they fake an argument in *front* of me and wonder aloud to each other whether I can *han*dle the role of ... [REVER-ENT] *ever-ender ... or ...* whether they'll have to call someone *else* ... someone *old*er ... someone *smart*er ... someone more capable of executing the delicate intricacies of ... [HUSHED/REVERENT] *ev-er-ending.* They use what feels like an almost magical, intoxicating kind of charm to get me to fight for a job I hadn't known ex*i*sted 30 seconds *ear*lier and one I wouldn't have wanted at *all* but for their slimy, seductive sales pitch. They look out from their high-level huddle, and someone finally says, *"Oh, let her TRY.* [SKEPTICAL, SIZING ME UP] *She MIGHT be OK."*

I find *that* insulting. How hard can it *be*?! They aren't asking me to defuse a *bomb*! I have to turn my arm from wrist to shoulder in a big arc in front of my *body ... end*lessly. [DOLTISH] *"Duh!"*

Still, they all seem more encou*rag*ing than ins*ul*ting. I *des*perately want to prove I'm up to the task. Before I *know* it, they have put me *lit*erally at the end of my rope. What a *pre*view! I don't know it *then,* but I will find myself in that position—at the end of my rope—*liter-*ally or *fig*uratively—on and off for the next 40+ years.

I run home that night for *din*ner ... all breathless and happy about my elevated *sta*tus ... *still* not *re*alizing I have a jump-rope-re*la*ted *job ...* that will *nev*er allow me ... to *jump.* [PAUSE]. I *burst* through the door and brag excitedly, *"Mommy, we were jump roping at Man-nie's, and they let ME be ...* [REVERENT] *the ever-ender!"*

"The WHAT?"

"The ever-ender. [IMPATIENTLY SUPERIOR TONE] *You know. They tie one end of the rope to the garage, then ...* [TOUCH MY OWN CHEST, BATTING BASHFUL EYELASHES] *the ever-ender turns the other end while the girls get to jump."*

My mom breaks the code *instantly,* just as Cathy slithers through the door a few steps be*hind* me. She shoots Cathy a *"you-little-stink-er"* look that tells me those girls have roped me into something less *grand* than I have *imagined.* (Then a*gain,* my mom's a firstborn, *too,* so I'm not sure, but maybe I detect a glimmer of *"That's-my-girl!"* in her expression, as *well.* Hmmm.)

I think my mom may have proposed a system whereby, every so *often,* even *"ever-enders"* get to jump, but ... as I re*call* ... she never shows up to *monitor* or en*force* that policy. It becomes a law on the books everyone ignores without *penalty* ... like the one that says Chicago politicians can't put their *family* members on the *pay*roll. *Still,* I *could* put a stop to it my*self* by re*fus*ing to take my place at the end of that *rope,* but I want *so* fiercely to be among the *big* girls ... I'll suffer almost *any* humiliation to bask even for a *moment* in their greatness. ... I'm afraid *that* pathetic pattern repeats itself more than once over the next 40+ years, *too.*

Don't hear me casting my birthmark-besmirched sister, Cathy, as a cruel, controlling, ma*nip*ulative older sibling. Not at *all!* Even though we fought frequently and she *did* qualify as a *bossy*-knick-ers at times, I think our struggles had *more* to do with mismatched *interests,* person*ali*ties and *energy* than with *serious, sour* sibling rivalry. I saw Cathy as off-the-charts *smart* (always *was,* always *will* be). I remember her as *quiet, always* well-coiffed, poised, polished and well behaved but with a sweet, subtle sense of humor (even mirth) you might *miss* if you judged her *book* ... *only* by its *cover.*

I thought of my*self* as off-the-charts smart, *too,* but in a *different way. Both* our parents have genius IQs, by the way. No pressure *there!* Even with *all* those smarts swirling around our *gene* pool, I could *not* have mastered Cathy's quiet, poised or well-behaved qualities even if you promised me a factory *full* of brand-new Bar-bie dolls and a lifetime sup*ply* of Bomb Pops.

More often than *not,* Cathy attempts to pro*tect* me from the slings and arrows of childhood, not to in*flict* them. She attempts to ex-clude me *only* as much as *any* privacy-seeking older sister might.

I admit to being the *too*-perky, com*pet*itive, in*vas*ive, *in*-your-face, *spot*light-seeking sibling most firstborns *dread*, but Cathy generally handles it (and *me*) with *grace*. That would be her *way*. As a *todd*ler, I once ran down the middle of our street stark *naked*, apparently just for the *sheer joy* of a *naked romp*. Proper Cathy comes trailing *af*-ter me with a blanket. She throws it over my *head* ... to protect *me* ... *and* our good *name*. Cathy had power and purpose and good instincts and knew how to use them. She still *does*.

Standing goes streaking in style.

Yes, firstborns bestow taunts and titles and *nick*names. My Uncle *Herb*, the firstborn in *his* family, leans over his baby brother's crib, tickling my dad under the chin, saying, *"Kibby, Kibby, Kibby,"* which later becomes *"Kippy"* and then *"Kip"* ... the name my dad goes on to use personally and professionally his whole *life*. Not a bad choice for a kid with two *Eng*lish *imm*igrant *par*ents. You'll find a fair num-ber of *"Kips"* on *that* side of the Atlantic. People as*sume* my dad got that name as an outgrowth of his English *anc*estry but *no*. Thanks to those firstborn *"naming rights,"* he goes from *God*frey (his *given* name) to *Kip* before his first *birth*day, with nothing *Brit* ab*out* it.

I'd say Uncle Herb did him a *favor*. Even though it *still* ranks as an *odd name*, I suspect kids would treat a *Kip far* more kindly on the playground than they might treat a [EXAGGERATED, LOW FORMAL TONE] *"GODfrey."* I think if *I'd* known him back then, even *I* would have kicked his little English bum ... and *I'm* just an ... [GRADE-SCHOOL SNEER] ever-end*er*.

Beside *Kip*, Uncle Herb gave my dad *another* nickname that stuck; he called him a *"ruin-er."* As baby brothers sometimes *do*, my dad would knock over Uncle Herb's carefully constructed *sky*scraper of *blocks* ... or smash a cardboard *car* it had taken Uncle Herb *hours* to con*struct*, and, according to family *lore*, Uncle Herb would wail indignantly, *"Kibby's a ruiner. Kibby's a ruiner."* [POUT] To this *day*,

Uncle Herb and "Kippy."

that ranks as the most *scath*ing insult one can hurl in my family. In *my* family, when you mess up *big*, look *out*! We'll brand *you* ... a *"ruiner."*

As the older sibling and first *grand*child, my sister, *Cathy*, got the *same "naming rights"* Uncle Herb had wielded both fortunate-ly and fiercely in *his* day. *"Kip"?* ... Fortunate. *"Ruiner"?* ... Fierce. Instead of calling our mom's mom *"GRANDmother,"* the al-most *ele*gant, old-*fash*ioned title she would have pre*ferred*, Cathy dubs our grandmother *"Mannie."* No one *knows why*, but it catches on, as undesired nicknames of-ten do. That threw our very prop-er, do-everything-according-to-Emily-Post grandmother into an ex-asperated tizzy, until, finally, she throws in the towel when 4 *more* grandchildren and even her own *friends* start calling her Mannie ... *and* we threaten to change it to *"GRANNY"* as a *com*promise. Hav-ing *no* desire to invite comparisons between her*self* and *"Granny CLAMpett,"* a hillbilly TV *i*con of the time, she decides to cut her nickname losses and even starts signing our *birth*day cards, *"Lots of love, Mannie."* Quite a coup! Behold the power of firstborn nam-ing rights. [PAUSE]

Which brings me back to the birthmark on Cathy's *tum*my. *She* gets to name *that, too*, as part of *her* firstborn naming rights. *She* gets to tell me and the *oth*er kids in the neighborhood what it *means* ... to have a con*spic*uous, *odd*ly shaped, half-dollar-sized *brown* birth-mark right out there where your 1960s two-piece swimming suit can't *hide* it.

Smart cookie, my sister. As the future public-relations maven she would one day be*come*, she knows she has to take her message to the street pre*emp*tively ... get the *word* out about her birthmark be*fore* someone *else* defines the situation in less *flat*tering *terms*. Rather than *wait* to hear her birthmark cast as a *blem*ish or as an embarrassment ... with cool confidence and a degree of self-assurance not usually *found* in an *8*-year-old, Cathy announces, [OFF-HANDEDLY] *"Only the COOLEST kids have BIRTHmarks."*

I think, even at the *time,* her strategy struck me as a *smart* one. I stand back in awe, watching her work the crowd, the way I would *one* day watch her work rooms filled with high-powered executives. It seems she has figured out *long* before she outs her own *birth*mark ... that a taunt *will come* ... *some*day ... and be*fore* that day ar*rives, she* delivers her *brill*iant re*butt*al.

"Only the COOLest kids have BIRTHmarks." She delivers that line *so* con*vinc*ingly I be*lieve* her. We *all* believe her and start searching our *own* bodies for similar evidence of ... *"coolness."* With that *one* *cas*ual   don't-care-if-you-agree-with-me/can't-believe-you-don't-al-ready-*know*-this line, *"Only the COOLest kids have BIRTHmarks,"* Cathy becomes the spin doctor of Fernbrook *Drive.* [PAUSE] ...

We have a *"mass"* of kids on Fernbrook Drive. I mean *"mass"* nu-merically *and* the*o*logically. It seems Cathy and I are 2 of the *very* few *P*rotestant kids on a street *filled* with *Cath*olics. In *those* days, St. Louis Catholics have what *we* consider *huge* families—at least 6 kids in every tiny 2- or 3-bedroom house on our *block.* They turn their garages into bedrooms and stack the kids in double and triple sets of *bunk* beds.

We *love* having so many playmates nearby, e*s*pecially since *we* don't have to share a bedroom our*selves.* The Catholic families of-ten joke that *they* have all the *kids* ... and *we* have all the *toys.* True. In *fact,* more than *once,* our little Catholic friends tell us, *"My mom says YOU'RE going to HELL, but it's OK if I play with your TOYS."*

What?! This confuses ... well, it confuses the *hell* out of me. I say, *"Mom, I'm not even allowed to SAY that word ...* [WHISPER] *h-e-l-l. How do they know I'm GOing there?"* [PAUSE]

NOTE: IF YOU SKIPPED THE INTRODUCTION AND WONDER WHY I FILLED THIS BOOK WITH WONKY WORDS, ALL CAPS AND ODD PUNCTUATION, PLEASE HEAD BACK TO PAGE x FOR A LITTLE CONTEXT. IT 'SPLAINS EVERYTHING.

CHAPTER 2

STANDING between a Bully and a Baby Doll ...

Along with the *"masses,"* we have a genuine *"ruiner"* in our neighborhood growing up— *Danny Beck*ett (not his real name). [MIMIC SINISTER VILLAIN MUSIC HERE.] *DUNT DUNT DUN NUH!*

As I re*call*, Danny doesn't spend a lot of time in the *hood*, but he plays his villainous role memorably when he graces (or *dis*graces) us with his *presence*. He swaggers through whatever game we little kids have going, *flick*ing us out of his *way*, always sneering. I remember him as dirty and dark and *brood*ing. Looking *back*, he was probably just *lonely*, maybe even misunder*stood*, but, even though he was only 12 years *old*, he scared the *poop* out of us.

Mattel's Baby Pattaburp.

I don't remember what I *did* to attract Danny's negative at*ten*tion this par*ticular day*. For *some* reason, I sit out by my*self*, separated from the *herd*, so to speak, playing under a tree ... with a *jump* rope and my *favorite* doll ... Baby *Patt*aburp.

Eventually, I prefer *bicycles* to *baby* dolls, but, in her *day*, on *that* day in 1966, I consider Baby Pattaburp peachy per*fection*. She is the technological toy *marvel* of the *mid*-1960s—with molded plastic arms, legs and *head* attached to a soft, padded cotton *body*. Mattel does a *good* job matching the peachy complexion of her *plastic* parts to the peach-colored cotton *fabric* of her *body*. They give her limbs and a head that droops, *"like a real baby."* They cleverly install a *mech*anism into Baby Pattaburp's cotton *body* so you can hold her to your *shoul*der, *"like a real baby,"* pat her *back*, *"like a real baby,"* and, *eventually, "like a real baby,"* she will ... burp. *Some*times it might take *10* pats to produce a burp, sometimes 25. I *love* that about her—so *life*like and unpre*dic*table, *"like a real baby."*

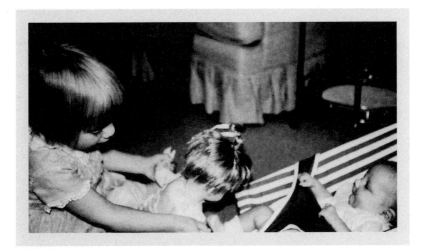

My "real baby" meets my real baby cousin, Jill.

Danny Beckett must find her fascinating, *too*. He *probably* considers him*self* the best burp-er on the block and feels compelled to assess his compe*ti*tion. For what*ever* reason, he approaches in rare form and unleashes what I *hope* is his worst. I *mean* ... I hope what he did to *me* that day was the worst thing he *ever* did to *any*one. If *not*, I suspect he moved from Fernbrook Drive to one (or a *series*) of America's maximum-security correctional institutions shortly there*after*. [PAUSE]

First, against my *frantic* protes*ta*tions, Danny throws my sweet, perfectly peachy Baby Pattaburp into the *creek* that runs behind our *neigh*borhood. *Then*, perhaps to shut me *up*, he uses my *own* jump rope to *hang* me from that tree ... by my *neck*. [PAUSE] ... *Then* ... he *leaves*! [PAUSE]

So there I *am, hang*ing there, at the end of my *own* jump rope ... giving a whole new, *truly sin*ister meaning to the title *"ever-ender"*! It feels *odd*, almost *out* of body, *not* because I can't *feel* the rope twisting a painful burn into my 6-year-old *skin*. I *can*. I feel *that*. I feel my tongue catching and *click*ing. I hear the sound of a poorly clearing drain coming from my own *throat*. [CHUG, CLICK, GLUG] I feel my lungs clutching *so hard* in my *chest* it makes my *stomach* lurch. *Oddly*, I feel each of my internal organs dis*tinctly*, even the non-*respiratory* ones, as if my lungs have gone diving ... diving *franti*cally beneath my ribs and past my stomach *deep* into my gullet ... searching throughout the *"neighborhood"* for any scrap of *air*. I feel the need to *gag*, but I don't throw *up*. I *can't*. The urge to retch feels *so* strong but utterly *stifled* at the same *time*. Danny's inexorable noose does double *duty*, cocking my *chin up* but keeping my stomach contents *down*.

In the midst of all that *physical commotion*, when I *say* it feels *"out of body,"* I *don't* mean I can't *feel* my *body*. I can. I *don't* mean I feel as if I've *left* my body, eit*her*. I *haven't*. I wouldn't find out how *that* feels until 23 years *later*. *No*, when I say it feels *"out of body,"* I mean that, while I *do* feel all that *unfamiliar*, *truly* life-threatening in*tensity* ... oddly, miraculously ... what I do *not* feel ... is *fear*. In fact, as I re*call*, the *first* thing I think to myself after Danny's departure sounds almost *calm*, ana*lytical* and matter of *fact*, something like, *"This can't be good."*

After *that*, perhaps because my brain would *one* day become a *journalist's* brain, I start asking rapid-fire *questions* ... and answering them ... in my *head*:

Q: *"What's HAPpening?!"*

A: *"You're hanging from a tree. You can't BREATHE."*

Q: *"Where's he GOing?!! ... Why did Danny DO this?"*

A: *"Don't know. ... Can't worry about that NOW."*

I carry on a conversation ... a conversation with someone (or some*thing*) familiar. ... I don't have *time* to wonder who or what.

Q: *"How are we gonna get OUT of this?"*

A: *"Try pulling the rope off your NECK and over your HEAD."* ...

I feel blindly for the rope, unable to look *down* because the noose keeps my little chin hoisted at an un*natural* angle in the *air*. I claw at the rope with the fingers of my *left* hand.

"I can't! It's too TIGHT. He doubled it up."

Q: *"Can you reach the tree with your HAND? Try pushing against the TRUNK."*

I struggle to reach, make contact and push against the *tree* with the fingertips of my *right hand*.

A: *"No! Stop! That just makes the rope TIGHTer!"*

I lose contact with the bark of the tree and swing out, tethered only by the *rope*. I gag. I grope for the tree again with my right hand, flailing *wildly*. I suspect my childish, herky-jerky *movements* look like Patty Duke portraying Helen *Keller* in *The Miracle Worker*. Like *Helen, I* need a miracle in that moment, *too*.

At *that* point, my rapid-fire questions to myself become rapid-fire com*mands*: *"Use your toes! Stand on your TOES. Touch the tree with your fingertips. Try to BALance."* That *works*, if only *briefly*, but at least that new, precarious position allows me to draw *one* labored, *long*-overdue *breath*. [DRAW IN DEEP BREATH]

Still, I do *not* feel *fear* ... and, oddly, I do *not* feel a*lone*. In *fact*, I feel a comforting *Presence*. I hear a collaborative, calming *voice* confirming, *"You are NOT alone. EVerything will be all right."* It may sound *crazy*, but I think that Presence even comforts me with a little *pun*, saying, *"Just hang IN there."* [PAUSE] I had felt that comforting, al-most-visceral Presence be*fore* in less *dire* circumstances and would feel it a*gain*, *often*, throughout my *life*. I would hear that certain *voice* at least 2 more times, as *well*.

How *long* did I gasp and twist under that *tree* limb? I have *no* idea. How does a 6-year-old measure or re*member time*? How would *any*-one at *any* age measure time under *those* circumstances? If you asked me to*day*, *"HOW long did you HANG there?"* ... I guess I would *have* to say, *"Long eNOUGH."*

In ad*dition* to the comforting *"Presence"* I feel in those traumatic moments, the Universe provides an *un*expected, more ma*terial* dis-*trac*tion as *well* ... in the *form* ... of Baby *Patt*aburp. From my admit-tedly perilous *vantage* point under the *tree* limb, I can see that Dan-ny the delinquent ruiner has thrown Baby Pattaburp *facedown* in that creek. I re*member*, in that bizarre *moment*, fearing as much for *her* safety as I do for my *own*. I *guess*, in my *mind*, all that *burp*ing, *"like a real baby,"* has blurred the line between baby *doll* and *baby*.

While *I* might be hanging from a *tree*, Baby Pattaburp lay sprawled there, up to her *plastic eyeballs* in muck and stinky water from our *storm* sewer. Something tells me *she* has drawn the shorter *straw*. After *all*, *I'm* only *choking*. *She* is *drowning*! At least *I* can hold *my* head above *water*. *She* is a helpless *baby*. I am her *mother*—an *older*, *wiser*, *hell*-bound ever-ender. [PAUSE]

I remember this *so clearly*. I had on a pair of those little red Keds with round rubber *toes* that were so *very* popular in the mid-'60s. Leave it to *me* to remember my *shoes*!

My family lives on a block of Fernbrook Drive that forms a U with another *street*, *Shell*burne. To*gether*, they connect our neighbor-hood to a *major* street, Laclede Station Road, in 2 spots. Our house is on *one* end of Fernbrook, and the *tree* is in the *middle*, at the bottom of the *U*. My dad *always*, *always* comes home from work the *easiest*, most *logical way*, by pulling *off* of Laclede Station and *onto* Fernbrook Drive from the *top* of the U, nearest our *house*. He *never* takes the Shellburne side—too many kids a*round* whom he'd have to *navigate* on *that* side of the U. By *some* stroke of Divine inter*vention*, he *changes* his *course* that day. He comes home the *other* way—the *Shell*burne way—and just *happens* to see something hanging from that *tree*—me! Whew!

He says he sees me *dangling* there *only* because the toes of those little red Keds peek out from beneath the limbs and leaves of that *tree*. [PAUSE] I'm *pretty* sure I had to lobby *hard* to *get* those red Keds in the *first* place. In *those* days, most kids wore *white* Keds; perhaps because the Catholic moms on our block could toss them into the washing machine with some *bleach* and save them for all those inevitable, *heaven*-bound *siblings*.

In *any* event, now that I *think* about it, perhaps I owe my *life*long affinity for *shoes* to that harrowing *event*. I admit I have a *"thing"* for shoes. Like a cost-conscious *version* of the Carrie *Bradshaw* char-acter from *Sex in the City*, I recently had my condo designer devote an en*tire* floor-to-ceiling *closet* ... to *shoes*. I even tacked up a quote inside the shoe-closet *door*. It reads:

"One shoe can change your life." —Cinderella

I be*lieve* that. I owe my *life*, and Nordstrom owes one of its *best* *cus*tomers ... to *Keds* ... even though I'm *not* sure they ever even *sold* Keds at *Nord*strom. [PAUSE]

My *dad* may have a *"thing"* for shoes, *too.* At least he has a *"thing"* for taking care of his *things*—be they shoes, tools, cars, whatever. Throughout elementary school, *every* Sunday night, my dad invites me into a ritual he has for preparing for the work week a*head.* With a little more pomp and *cir*cumstance and *cere*mony than is abso-*lute*ly *ne*cessary, he spreads out a piece of newspaper on our living room *floor,* takes an ancient but me*ticu*lously arranged *shoe-*shine kit off the shelf of our hall closet, sets his salesman's wingtips out on the *news*paper and proceeds to shine them to a *high gloss.* He *claims* his hands are too big and clumsy to perform the *very* impor-tant *last* step of the shining *process.* He *claims* he *"needs" my* tiny mitts to *fin*ish the job.

I suspect my participation actually *add*ed several minutes to the task and even wore some of the gloss *off* his wingtips, but I *also* think he knew that the time I spent with him on those Sunday nights made my *heart swell* and my *eyes* sparkle with *pride.*

I think he *also* knew that our Sunday night ritual planted the seeds of values he and my mom considered imp*ort*ant: *work* ethic, proper care and *main*tenance, attention to *de*tail, looking one's *best* with-*out* spending a lot of *mon*ey. He showed me how to slide my hand into each shoe ... just *so* ... how to buff the toes with just the right brush and just the right *num*ber of brush strokes ... with just the right amount of *pol*ish ... in just the right *way.*

He produces silly *sound* ef*fects* to *go* with all that polishing and gives funny *names* to *each* stage of the *process: "marnishing"* and *"platining."* He hums as we work and makes up silly songs about where those shoes will *go,* what they will *see* and all the people they will *meet.* To this *day,* if I open one of those small round metal con-tainers of *shoe* polish, my mood and self-confidence *soar* just from that *happy, waxy smell.* [PAUSE]

Yes, I'd say my dad and I *both* have a ... *"thing"* for shoes—*his* related to main*tain*ing them, *mine* more about ac*quir*ing them. Our fam-ily didn't have a lot of money in those days, and any extra money we *did* have went into a kitty my parents set aside for a far-off but *much*-anticipated trip to *Eng*land to meet my dad's *rel*atives and to celebrate all things *English*. *That goal* made Kip a happily thrifty *fellow*, squeezing every shilling 'til it *screamed* ... which makes his actions *later* in this story all the *more* remar*k*able *and* memo*r*able.

Uncle Herb may have dubbed my dad a *"RUiner,"* but Uncle Herb couldn't have been more *wrong*. As you'll soon *see*, on *this* day my dad *a*ctually qualifies as the *"ANti-ruiner"* ... the *fix*er ... a nickname he'll deserve *many* times throughout my *life*.

On this fateful *day*, for *some* reason he can't re*call*, my dad chooses *not* to take his customary route *home*. In*stead*, he glances casually to his right as he rounds that *un*conventional curve toward home, ready to kick *off* those wingtips at the end of a long *week*. Some vague but insistent *some*thing urges him to *pause*. ... He proceeds *past* the *tree* (and *me*) but glances a*gain*, now almost over his *shoul*-der. He *blinks*, trying to *fo*cus. He *squints*. He slows to a stop, *still* trying to make sense of the *scene*. He sees a *little* pair ... of *red Keds*.

Reality sets in. He throws the car into *park*, flings open his door ... realizing those Keds are connected to a pair of *legs*, connected to a little *body*, connected to a *tree* limb, and that *body* belongs to his *daugh*ter, struggling and twisting just barely off the *ground*. In a *flash*, he bolts across the lawn, grabs me around my *legs* with both *arms* and hoists me up to take the pressure off my *neck*. He shifts my weight onto one of his shoulders while he unties the *rope* and lowers it off the limb with his other *hand*. [PAUSE]

At the sight of my *dad*, once standing firmly on my own two *feet* ... finally able to *breathe* ... the fear I *did*n't feel ar*rives* ... in a *flood*. All my pent-up *panic bursts* out of me. I start *wailing—hard!* My dad can't get his head around what must have led to the out*rage*ous cir-cumstances he sees be*fore* him. He unwinds the rope from around my *neck*, checks for broken bones and blood and gently tilts my head to inspect my *neck*. I wobble a little, going limp but still *stand*-ing ... still *wailing*. He sees sub*stan*tial rope burns but can *tell*, mi-raculously, I have *no serious in*juries. I straighten up, taking fast, deep breaths now, and I keep *wailing—*hard, *agonizing* wails!

He *desperately tries to calm me down so I can tell him what *hap*-pened.

"Are you HURT?"

Frustrated that he doesn't understand but unable to *speak*, I shake my head back and forth *v*iolently, tears *stream*ing down my cheeks. *F*inally, I choke out a stuttered, *"N ... n ... nnn ... no!"* Inconsolable wailing re*sum*es.

"What IS it?! What's the MATter?! TELL me!" Again, he checks for serious *in*juries. I jerk my head away from him and try to convey that I *don't* want him to focus on my *n*eck.

What would a parent *think*? He must wonder whether *Cath*y's hanging from some *oth*er tree somewhere.

I wail on. In a brilliant burst of parenting, in *d*esperation, my dad lowers his voice to a *whis*per so I *have* to quiet down to *hear* him, and he says *v*ery s-l-o-w-l-y [WHISPER]: *"Calm down ... and TELL me ... what's the MATter?"*

At *last* I can form full *sent*ences. I point to the creek, and I say, *"It's Baby PATtaburp, Daddy. She's DROWNing! SAVE her, Daddy! SAVE her!"*

Then my dad did a most re*mark*able thing, one of *man*y remarkable things he would do that day and evening. *First*, with*out* hesit*ation*, he wades into that creek and plucks my mucky, *w*ater-logged *doll* out of the *scum*, with *no* apparent thought about his best business suit and those salesman's *wing*tips. He just plunges *right* in, budget be damned!

Now, 4 decades *l*ater, my memories get a little *murk*y. When my dad demands to know who *did* this to me, I must rat out Danny *Beck*ett ... because I *do* remember my dad charging up to the Beck-ett's *h*ouse, with *m*e tucked under *one* arm and Baby Pattaburp's no-*long*er-perfectly-peachy body dripping under the *oth*er, one of us on each *hip*, both positioned face*down*, able to see his squishy *wing*tips. *Some*how, I know my dad carries my *jump* rope, too, as part of his surreal Friday night *welc*ome-*home bun*dle. I remember looking and feeling like awkward *cargo* ... bouncing and slipping on my dad's *hip*, watching my jump rope's *wood*en handles sway at uneven lengths and hearing them clack *int*o each other ... as my dad took purposeful strides toward *Danny's house*. With what I would characterize as re*mark*able re*straint*, my dad pounds on the Beck-etts' *door*. I had never *seen* Danny's *f*ather; none of us *dared* go close enough to their *house* ... to see *what* else or *who* else might *live* there.

I vaguely remember a *big, .burly late*-middle-aged *white*-haired *man* opening the door. As I re*call*, he wore one of those thin white wife-beater *undershirts* that exposed his hairy chest, but, a*gain*, I don't remember this part very *clearly*. As the door swings *open*, we get a pungent whiff of the Becketts' *home*. I remember it smelling like you'd ex*pect* the home of a world-class *ruiner to smell*—like *sour* sweat, *stale* beer and a *vague* hint of overworked *air* freshener. ... From my perch under my dad's *arm*, he seems e*normous*, filling the door frame. My face dangles almost *"eyeball-to-eyeball"* with Mr. Beckett's beer-swollen *belly* button.

Using 3 *very* compelling visual *aids*—a soggy Baby Pattaburp, *my* jump rope and *me*—my dad tells him how he *found* me, *surely* expecting Danny's dad to share his *outrage*. In*stead*, the belligerent Mr. Beckett says, *"Well, I guess that means you better keep YOUR kid away from MY kid, DOESn't it?!"* [PAUSE]

With *that*, he takes *one* step *back* and slams the door in all *3* of our *faces*. He doesn't slam it *hard*, as I re*call*, just in a con*temp*tuous, dis*mis*sive way that says, *"Don't BOTHer ME with YOUR problems."* I find *him* spookier than Danny on his worst day, and I oughta know about Danny's *worst day*. ... Perhaps Mr. *Beck*ett qualifies as the ruiner to end *all* ruiners ... the ruiner who ruined ... *Danny*. [PAUSE]

My *mom* had encountered Mr. Beckett once be*fore* and hadn't fared any *better*. She remembers their lawn as perpetually overgrown and the house as untidy and unin*vit*ing, but she approached *anyway* ... as she circled our block collecting for some *charity*. Surprisingly, she recalls Mr. Beckett gave her a *whole dol*lar. She started to tear a receipt stub from her *book*let, and he said, [GRUFF, SMUG, AMUSED] *"Don't BOTHer. I'm gonna put it down as $50, anyway."* Charming!

Now I *wonder* ... were the Becketts one of the few *Protestant* families on our block? Were *they* the reason *all* those Catholic moms be*lieved* what early 1960s Church *doc*trine *told* them—that we were *all* destined for *hell*? If Danny and his *dad* served as their Protestant *poster* boys, *that* would explain a *lot*! [PAUSE]

I ad*mire* my dad for staying true to his Eagle Scout virtues, then and *always* ... for keeping a clear *head* about what *really mat*tered to him in that scenario—*me*. He shakes off Mr. Beckett's boorish re*ac*tion and takes us *home—me* and Baby *Pat*taburp.

From there, *un*like Mr. *Beck*ett, my dad fires on *every* parenting cylinder he *has*. [PAUSE]

I remain inconso*lable* about Baby Pattaburp's *treat*ment and condition. The cotton batting in her body has soaked up every malodorous microorganism our sewer can cough *up*. She comes out of the creek *caked* with mud. She won't burp, no matter *how* many pats we give her tortured, squishy little back.

My dad takes it as a *chal*lenge—*man* against *muck*. He displays an almost chirpy *optimism*. *"She'll be fine; YOU'LL see. We just need to get her cleaned up, and she'll be as good as NEW."*

He takes us down to the washing machine in our *basement*, makes a *big* show of setting the knobs *carefully* and adding the soap and the softener very pre*cisely*. (I suppose one uses the *gentle* cycle when washing babies who have just cheated *death*.) He keeps repeating, *"She'll be fine."* He closes the *lid* and says with the same mirth I had seen *so* often from my English *grand*father, *"It won't be long NOW."*

My dad sets up a little play *stool* in front of our washing machine so I can sit and listen as the washer works its *magic*. He asks me to a*lert* him when the cycles *stop*. I *dutifully wait*, like a nervous *mom*my in an *e*mergency room. When the cycle *stops*, my dad *carefully* lifts her out of the washer, as if he's cradling a *real* baby. She *still* has stains all over the *cloth* parts of her *body*, which my father cleverly pretends not to *see* and *most* of which he successfully *hides* with his big daddy *hands*. He lifts her to his *nose*, takes an exaggerated *whiff* then declares, *"Mmmm. Downy FRESH!"*

He won't hand her *off* to me just *yet* ... says she needs just a *few* minutes of *fluff*ing to get her *in*nards back in order. He *o*pens the *dry*er, carefully places Baby Pattaburp in*side* and talks about all the *fun* she'll *have*, tumbling around in that *dry*er drum. He scoots my stool the few feet to the *right* so I can monitor *every* soggy *som*ersault. Her plastic parts make a tre*men*dous noise—*budda-bump, budda-bump, budda-bump!*

When it comes time for the reunion of mother and *child*, my dad reaches in to find Baby Pattaburp's face, elbows and feet barked up and *melt*ed a bit by the heat of the *dry*er. *Whoops!* NEXT time, tumble dry *LOW*. The batting in her body has puffed up to quad*ruple* its *nor*mal *size*. That makes her limbs stick straight *out* instead of *droop*ing, like the ... *"real baby"* Mattel had *ad*vertised.

My dad holds Baby Pattaburp at arm's length from me. He kneads her little body back into shape, *know*ing she will never burp a*gain*, trying to figure out how to help me see *all* the day's events ... *and this* dis*fig*ured *doll* ... in a *positive* *light*.

Once a*gain*, he lifts Baby Pattaburp to his *nose*, takes another big *sniff* and sighs, *"Mmmm. She sure SMELLS better ... better than EVer!"*

Un*convinced, I say, *"Yeah, but she's RUined, Daddy! She has brown stains all over her BODy."*

He looks *shocked*. He holds Baby Pattaburp out in *front* of him for a fresh in*spection*, as if he's *missed* something. He acts as if he *truly* hasn't *noticed* the stains. Still holding her out of my *reach*, he cradles my doll's *head* with his *left* hand and her *body* with his *right*. He really makes me be*lieve* that ... who she *is* ... matters *more* to him than how she *looks* ... or what she can *do* for us. (That holds true for my dad with *real* people, *too*, by the way.)

He takes a mildly *scold*ing tone with me, *"Oh, Kelly ... she's not RUined."* He speaks *soft*ly, *slow*ly looking back and forth between me and the doll. *"She's not RUined,"* he repeats, pressing *me* to see what *he* sees.

If we had had the phrase *"WTF"* in those days, I might have thought, *"WTF, Dad?! ... I'm standing right HERE, and I can see with my own EYES she's RUined. Danny Beckett is a RUiner ... the king of ALL ruiners."* I try *hard* to cling to my *anger.

My dad perse*veres. *"Oh, NO, she's not RUined."* He pauses, looking a*gain* from *me* to the *doll* and *back* again. He raises Baby Pattaburp just above his own *face*, like baby Simba, held above the herds in *The Lion King*. My dad's careful choreography gets my eyes to follow my puffy, *barked*-up *baby* doll into the *air*. The gentle way he *holds* her and the kind way he *speaks* about her make me think *I*

have to be *careful* not to hurt her *feel*ings ... not to make her self-
*cons*cious about her ... [WHISPER] stains. He implies I need to
re*mem*ber all *she* has *been* through that day ... (all *SHE* has been
through!) ... and find it in my heart to for*give* her if she doesn't seem
quite like her*self* ... if she doesn't seem ... *per*fect anymore. [PAUSE]

Then my dad delivers a line that will change my life ... and my *out*-
look ... forever.

"You are the luckiest little girl on the BLOCK," he says, *"... because
YOU ... have a doll ... with BIRTHmarks."* [PAUSE]

I *gasp*. My eyes grow wide. I start to reach for my doll, giving him
*inst*ant credit for his in*spired* observation.

"How cool must a kid BE," I wonder, *"if she has a DOLL with birthmarks? ANYbody can have a SISter with a birthmark, but a DOLL
with birthmarks??! NO one has THAT. No one but ME!"* ... Well
played, Dad! [PAUSE]

My dad has just delivered a little well-timed spin doctoring of his
own. In that *mom*ent, with his *out*look ... a 6-year-old victim of a
violent crime ... becomes the *"luckiest little girl on the BLOCK"* ...
blemishes become *"birthmarks"* ... a damaged *doll* becomes a *sta*-
tus symbol ... *all* because my *quick*-thinking, wingtip-*wear*ing, Don
Quixote's–*sword*–wielding *dad* ... lives his *Eagle* Scout virtues ...
and invokes the wisdom from the *streets* ... *"ONly the COOLest kids
... have BIRTHmarks."*

My dad must think he's just made the biggest sale of his *life*. I almost buy the line he has so *bril*liantly shoveled my way ... almost.
Then, my wary smile abruptly gives way to *tears*.

[ABRUPTLY] *"Nope. She's RUined, Daddy. She's RUined!"*

"WHAT?! Why?! What do you MEAN?!" Is he losing the sale *after
all*?

I voice my objection. He must have forgotten: *"She can't BURP anymore."*

Again, in that simul*tan*eously *scold*ing and *com*forting *tone*, my
dad's expression says, *"Oh, is THAT all? I thought it was something*

SERious." Then, he says, "Oh, KELly, she's not RUined." Then he pauses for a long moment, which *forces* me to speak *next.*

"She's NOT?"

"No. ... God knows that a baby who can't burp needs EXtra CARE ... and that's why ... God sent THIS baby ... to YOU." [PAUSE]

I gasp.

With *that,* he gently lowers my doll into my *awe*-struck, *out*-stretched *arms* and, in that *mo*ment, gives birth to the the*ology* and the phi*lo*sophy I will *live* by ... forever *after.*

Simply, that episode taught me that if I don't get what I want, I should find a way to love what I get *anyway* ... to find the *good* even in something very, very *bad.* That episode taught me I can see the world not as it *is* but as it *could* be. Just because *other* people might call something a *"stain,"* I can see it *differently. I* don't have to ac*cept* their vocabulary. *I* can call it something *else.* ... That episode taught me that people's scars make them *more* beautiful, *more* precious, *not less* so. I can ig*nore* the *ru*iners. I can *choose* to call bad things good things ... and *mean* it. That became a kind of *"naming rights"* I didn't *have* to be a *first*born to *claim.*

Keds to the rescue in 1966. (If this page were in color, you'd see that my Keds are bright red.)

Yes, only the coolest kids have birthmarks ... and only the coolest *dads* can help them *see* that. [PAUSE]

CHAPTER 3

STANDING at Attention ...

Speaking of *cool dads*, my father had one of his *own*, Herbert Henry Standing, the cutest, most *humble*, *wittiest* little Englishman *ever* to wield a *walking* stick. He waddled like Charlie Chaplin—*looked* like him, *too*—had that same kind of mirth in his *aspect* ... same narrow little *Hitler mustache* on his *lip*. (That mustache gave *some* men a dapper *look* ... Charlie *Chaplin* and my *grandfather*, to name *2* ... until Adolf *Hitler ruined* it for the rest of the male *population*.) People say I have my Grandpa Standing's *eyes* and a *little* bit of his *sparkle*. Once I turned *50*, I started getting his mu*stache*, too. ... *Kidding!* ... Just seein' if you're still a*wake*.

I remember my grandfather wearing a *tidy*, *tailored bus*iness suit almost *all* the *time*, but he wasn't afraid to get his *hands* dirty, particularly *gardening*. It seems to me he flitted a lot ... like *I* do ... interested in a lot of *things*, *not* comfortable sitting still for very *long*. He struck me as thrifty and a little bit im*patient* but never with *me*, only with my *grand*mother, Gladys Alice Roberts Standing, and only once in a *great while*. (Their naturalization papers show *she* outweighed *him* by 4 pounds—130 to 126!)

They were *cute* together, like British *"Bickersons."* In reti*re*ment, they lived along the Meramec River in Missouri in a house on *stilts*, built as a summer *cott*age, but *they* used it year-*round*, quirky folks that they were. They went to bed be*fore dark*, got *up* before the *sun*. Then, they would sit in the dark drinking their morning *tea*. I didn't ... *get* it. If you were just going to keep the lights *off* and if you needed a *beverage* to keep you a*wake* before the rest of the world even opened its *eyes*, why not stay in *BED*? As I *said*, quirky, but I *loved* them ... *and* ... their English *accents*.

As a child, I announce, *"Your house SMELLS funny."* Once I go to *Eng*land in 1968, I realize their house smells ... like *Eng*land, not that the whole *country* shares *one* scent, but my grandparents have English habits, English hobbies and, un*fortunately*, English *recipes*, so, good or *bad*, they smell ... *well* ... *English*.

I always found life at their house *odd* ... but very enter*tain*ing. Be*fore* our *vis*its, Grandma Standing would glue pairs of shiny faceted buttons in the crevices of several *random rocks*. They looked like little misshapen *creatures* with sparkly eyes and no *bod*ies. She would *hide* them on their beach, for Cathy and me to dis*cov*er, making us think we had unearthed a *treas*ure.

Tea time with our English grandparents ... and their dog, Tiny.

Over tea every afternoon, Grandpa Standing tells silly *stor*ies about our new rock *"friends"* ... about the fairies in his *gar*den ... fish on his *line* ... family back in *Eng*land. He isn't a *"pull-my-finger"* kind of grandpa—too buttoned-up for *that*. Even *bett*er, he's a *"pull-my-heartstrings"* and *"tickle-my-funny-bone"* kind of grandpa—the only kind I ever *knew*, since my *mom's* dad died the year before I was *born*.

I'm told I'm a lot like *him*, too—Wesley Irving *Hart*nagel. I understand I have *him* to thank for my *writ*ing skill. I think my mom deserves *more* of the credit, though. And let's not forget the University of Missouri School of Journalism. [MOCK SALUTE] Isn't it funny how relatives try to carve us *up* into offshoots of our *ances*tors? That's OK with *me*; I *like* knowing from whence I come, and I really *do* see my Grandpa Standing staring back at me from the *mir*ror sometimes ... with*out* the mustache, of course.

While I knew Grandpa Standing only as an older Charlie Chaplin *look*-alike, I knew—and anyone could *tell*—there was more to him than silly stories told over *tea*. Underneath that merrymaking ... beat the heart of a brave and *solid* citizen—a Royal Flying Corps pilot made of *very* stern stuff, a war *hero*.

He didn't share much of *that* story with *me*, but I *do* know he flew a bi-wing Sopwith Camel (like the one Charlie Brown's *Snoopy* flies) with the White Russians against the *Bol*sheviks in WW*I*. He ends up stuck for 5 *months*, *fro*zen in, *un*able to get back to *Lon*don after the war ended, missing his family but making the *best* of it. Appar-ently, the going gets pretty *rough*, but my grandfather clings to a single word that becomes our family *mot*to: "Perse-VERE!"

Herbert Henry Standing

My dad follows in *his* father's military footsteps on the *A*merican side of *"the Pond." He* goes through Air Force ROTC training at the University of Missouri before heading to South Korea in 1957. Stationed in Osan as an ac*coun*ting of-ficer, he misses the birth of my *sis*ter and the first 4 months of her *life*.

Always the *joke*ster, when my mom sends my dad a *tele*gram in *Kor*ea to tell him she's ex*pec*ting, he cables back:

"Dear Mrs. Standing:

I'm very happy to hear that you're going to have a BAby, but I fail to see how this concerns ME. By the way ... do I KNOW you?" [SMILE]

My dad tells the Korean kids his name is "Fiddle-dee-dee." When they learn his real name, they think it's "Lt. DING-Ding" instead of "STAN-ding."

Over *time*, with frequent letters *home*, my dad re*deems* himself. Months *later*, when Cathy arrives, he comes through with a sin*cere* less-is-more response:

"Wonderful job. Father fine. ALL my love, KIP"

When my dad returns from Ko*rea*, he and my mom spend a year in *their* equivalent of my *grand*father's Siberia—living on an *Air* Force base in *Platts*burgh, New *York*, in a 47-by-8-foot *trailer*, where they dry my sister's diapers on the *radiators* (im*agine!) and sub*sist* on next to *noth*ing.

My mom *hates* it. At *one* point, she can hear 10-month-old Cathy SCREAMING but can't *find* her. She looks *every*where, which should take no time at *all*. There are only so many places to *look* ... in the tin can they call *home*. Still *scream*ing, Cathy has her *stump*ed. *Fi*nally, my mom realizes Cathy must have fallen out of the perpetu-ally faulty trailer *door* (which opens *out*). She finds Cathy on her hands and knees up to her *el*bows in *snow* ... and MAD! My mom plucks her *out*, dries her *off*, and they *both* have a good, long *cry*. In *fact*, my dad describes that year in Plattsburgh as *"the year your mother CRIED."*

My family takes patriotism and military service *very* seriously. Like *all* military families, my parents and grandparents made a lot of *sac*rifices—abandoning their con*nec*tions and creature comforts to serve their *coun*tries. Even *so*, humble to the *core*, my dad claims he *"didn't do much,"* compared with the folks who flew missions under *fire.*

He says, *"I felt like I had a 'JOB' with the Air Force, versus the kind of commitment COM-bat service reQUIRES. I think those who have really been in combat—in harm's WAY—are the ones who deserve to be honored, as opposed to what I did—service with-OUT combat."* For that reason, my dad rarely

Good times in a trailer ... or not.

stands for recognition at public ceremonies when a speaker invites veterans to *stand.* (Hmmm. Mr. Standing won't *stand.*)

As with *most* vices or virtues taken to the ex*treme,* the standard of humility my father set serves as both a *bea*con and a *blud*geon as my *own* story unfolds. My dad *al*most always laces *his* humility and service to others with healthy self-e*steem;* at times, *I* don't get that recipe quite *right*—settling for humility at the ex*pense* of my self-esteem in*stead* of striking a *bal*ance. At times I have em*braced* my dad's model. At times I have had to *un*learn it ... or ... add *to* it. [PAUSE]

In 2009, I take my parents to Chicago's Pritzker Military Library, where Ryan Yantis, a military hero in his *own* right and PML's executive director at the *time,* attempts to set my dad *straight* about the significance of his *service,* saying, *"As a payroll officer, YOU made a DIFFerence. Morale would have been PREtty low if those flyers weren't getting PAID. And you were in harm's way whether you SEE it that way or NOT. Transporting cash is DANgerous DUty."* He adds, *"Only 3% of the people in the Air Force actually FLY the PLANES. The OTHer 97% keep them UP there. YOU were one of the GOOD guys."*

One of the good guys, in*deed!*

As you read my story from here on *out,* if you wonder where I get my determi*na*tion, my *quirk*iness, my occasional *sil*liness ... you don't have to look very far up my family tree to find *out.* I love the unconventional mix of ... mirth and might ... among the men in my family. They're *strong,* pro*found*ly patriotic and senti*men*tal.

It seems only fitting that my naturalized U.S. citizen grandfather ... who raised and inspired 2 U.S. Air Force veterans, died on Memorial Day 1976. At the end of my grandfather's difficult *ill*ness, my father leaned in, and Grandpa Standing whispered his *last* word: *"Persevere!"*

CHAPTER 4

STANDING at the Scene of an Accident ...

My mother, Lois Hartnagel Standing, doesn't have many phobias, but the one she *does* have may rank as the mother of *ALL* phobias ... the fear she will outlive one of her children. Early and often, she said, *"You MUST outlive me. ... You MUST outlive me."*

I found that *puzzling* and more than a little disconcerting. As a *kid*, I didn't want to *think* about the order in which my family members *"must" die*. Death hadn't crept onto my *radar* screen ... well ... except perhaps sub*cons*ciously ... pre-*verb*ally ... in the form of my many life-threatening *fevers* as an *inf*ant and the few toddler *ac*cidents that sent me to the *em*ergency room for *min*or *stitch*es.

It almost seems as if my mother experienced my *birth* ... with *death* on her mind. In fact, as it turns out, she *did*. Her father died very suddenly the year before I was *born*, and her beloved grandmother and then her even-*more*-beloved grand*fath*er *all* died within the same *year*. ... I came along in the midst of her profound grief.

They say babies pick up some pretty big clues about their moms in the *womb*. While my mom was happy in a *lot* of ways about a *lot* of things in 1960, as the little bun in her *oven*, I don't think I could have missed her *sorrow*, too. I think, at least subconsciously, I always felt like I was the kid who was supposed to make my mom *feel* better ... to keep her enter*tained* and, in *some* ways, to take *care* of her. I could be *wrong*, and she might disa*gree*, but that's how I *felt*.

From the *start*, I brought my mother face-to-face with her greatest fear, something for which I think she found it increasingly difficult to for*give* me. Oh, she might deny that characterization ... might not even have a conscious *aw*areness of it, but I sensed her fear even before I could *speak*. It seems my many brushes with death frequently put me at cross-purposes with my mother—her *fear* versus my fear*lessness*—even though, at the same *time*, we have many of the same *tal*ents, many of the same *tastes* and the same goofy nose and receding *chin*.

If nothing *else*, at least in 1966, it seems I had a nose for danger and had to keep that chin *up* … in the face of a bully, a bad driver and 2, count 'em, 2 brushes with death. …

I remember the powder-blue snowsuit I wore that year. It came embroidered with what would *now* qualify as a *vin*tage snowman motif, featuring stylized silver and white snowflakes dancing around a snowman wearing *red* mittens on arms made of *sticks*.

I *really loved* that snowsuit. I *loved* that my mom bought it in *blue*, an atypically *boy*ish color for that generation. I liked looking like a bit of a *tom*boy, but the embroidery gave my snowsuit a feminine splash I craved at *that* age, *too*.

I think I may have loved that snowsuit *most* … because *I* wore it *first*. It ranked as a rare season, in*deed*, when *my* growth spurts and my *sis*ter's hand-me-down sizes didn't match *up*. I *rev*eled when that happened.

My *grand*mother, Mannie, made many of our clothes, not the home-madey, backwoods, almost-em*bar*rassing kind Dolly Parton says *she* endured and/or embraced as a child but beautifully tailored suits for *trav*el and charming dresses for *school*. Mannie added special touches—covered buttons, satiny linings, plaids perfectly lined up at the *seams* and difficult darts that made them look *bet*ter than *store*-bought. She made matching outfits for us *all the time*, often using the *same* pattern for *both* of us but in *con*trasting *fab*rics.

That worked *fine* for *Cathy. She* wore her *gold* corduroy suit for 2 years while *I* wore the *same* suit in *green* corduroy. *Then,* Cathy moved *on* to something *new* and more *fash*ionable, while *I* got stuck with Cathy's *gold* one for 2 MORE *YEARS*!

Even *worse*, as a firstborn her*self*, Mannie *some*times showed *no* imagi*na*tion and no com*pas*sion at *all*, stitching *both* our dresses out of the exact *same* fabric—pure agony for the Standing sibling more eager to stand *out* than to blend *in*. It felt like I never grew *out* of *any*thing, just *into* the same flippin' thing in a bigger *size*. Grrr!

That year, that *wonderful year, some*how the stars or the snowflakes aligned, and, along with my red *Keds*, that snowsuit was *all mine*. This hand-me-down-induced variety of sibling rivalry further explains why my *usually non*-ad*dic*tive personality allows me at least that *one "soft addiction"*—shopping for clothes and shoes, usually at *Nord*strom but often at Target and Marshall's, *too*.

I wasn't as happy about dressing alike as I appear.

Yes, I *loved* my 1966 snowsuit and would grow to love it even *more* on this particular *day*. St. Louis snows didn't come along every *day* or even every *year*, and when we *did* get snow, it didn't *last* ... always turning to slush or disappearing before we felt ready to come *in* from the *cold*.

That day, when Mother Nature blessed us with a fresh white *blan*ket, along with the elusive *"snow day"* off school, we *re*veled in it ... but went to school *any*way, *not* for the three *Rs. No*, we headed this particular winter *back* to our elementary school on a *snow* day to take advantage of what we *thought* would be a thrilling but as-yet *un*discovered *sled*ding hill. We thought we'd have that unblemished blanket all to our*selves*. After *all,* who would be *bril*liant enough (or *stu*pid enough) to head to *school* on a *snow* day?

We probably would have arrived to find a BUNCH of kids *al*ready sledding on *"our"* hill ... *but* ... we never make it to *school.* ...

We didn't *have* the high-tech wicking, thermo-insulated *fa*brics we appreciate to*day.* In*stead,* manufacturers made the snow duds of the '60s out of what *felt* like twin-bed *mat*tresses, *so* thick we could barely bend our *limbs.* We tromped around with arms extended like friendly, frosty, *sleep*walking *Frank*ensteins. Getting *dressed* for sledding took longer than the sledding it*self.* Our grandmother innovated by adding a fairly *new* invention to our winter layers—Baggies *in*side our boots and *mit*tens, which may have kept snow from melting *through* to our *skin* but which *al*so made us sweat and slip *in*side our *clothes.*

Cathy had a friend named Lynn Goin, which sounded like *"Going"* (thereby making Lynn a*noth*er lucky kid blessed with a gerund for a last name—one Standing and one Going). They *gen*erously agreed to allow me to tag a*long* on their sledding expe*di*tion, so my beloved snowsuit had places to *go,* people to *see,* hills to *con*quer. If I could have moved at *all* inside that suit, I would have twitched with hyperactive ex*cite*ment.

Our trek to school strikes me as long *now.* Most kids to*day* take a bus or parents drop them *off* if they live as far from school as *we* did. We roughed it in our south suburban St. Louis *school* district. I won't claim we walked uphill both *ways,* but I *do* think the daily walks we took to and from school kept all those Hostess Twinkies and fruit pies we ate *af*ter school from turning into childhood obesity.

Walking that distance wrapped in the e*quiv*alent of a Serta Perfect *Sleep*er makes the going even *rough*er. Cathy and Lynn take turns dragging our sled be*hind* them while *I* forge a few steps a*head.* Cathy and I have an unspoken agreement when she is with her friends. I can be near*by* but *not next* to them (un*less,* of course, I'm at my *post* turning a *jump* rope as an *"EVer-ender").* On *this* day, on that *busy* street, our arm's-length arrangement *suits* me. I usually buzz around at a much higher rate of speed, *any*way. Winter or summer, I run ahead of the other kids until almost out of *sight,* as a kind of *self*-appointed *scout*, and *then* circle back to make sure I'm not *mis*sing anything back in the *pack.*

We *al*most make it to that coveted sledding spot. We round the last corner and can see the school on the horizon, just over a slight hill. I turn back to shout to Cathy and Lynn, *"We're almost there! I SEE it! Do you SEE it?"*

Just *then*, a car comes over that small rise and its 17-year-old driver loses control on the slick *pave*ment. He heads straight for *me* and my powder-blue *snow*suit.

I watch the grill and bumper of his car get *clos*er and *clos*er ... as if in slow *motion*. I stand there ... *frozen*, as in *motion*less, *not* as in *frosty. No*, I feel toasty warm in*side* my *"MATTress."* The weight of it keeps my feet in my Baggied boots *firm*ly *plant*ed.

I can't back *up* ... can't move at *all*, and I don't realize *why* until a few seconds *later*. I watch the center of the car hit the center of my *chest*—just to the left of the embroidered *snow*man.

Eventually I realize I can't *move* ... because I'm standing ... with my back di*rect*ly in front of a *road* sign. Wouldn't it be *ironic* if that sign reads, *"Slippery When Wet"*? I don't re*mem*ber.

Despite what I'm *sure* is frantic braking and attempts to swerve on the part of that teenage *driv*er, his car plows right *into* me. The speed and force of the collision bend *me*, my *snow*suit *and* that *road* sign *right* over *back*ward. We all come to a *stop*, with me ending up in an *awk*ward, *uninten*tional *back*bend, with my arms flailing at my *sides* like the *robot* from *Lost in Space* ... and my *eyes* flung *wide* open in sur*prise*. [EYES WIDE, EXCITED]

Oddly, I am *not* a*fraid*, not even at the point of im*pact*. As the scene un*folds*, I have a very clear sense that this situation will turn out more *icy* than *dicey*. I *know* ... absolutely *know*, I won't *die*. Even be*fore* the car *hits* me, I know it won't *hurt* me. I don't know *how* I know it, but I *do*. In that *moment*, I feel the same Presence I have felt almost since *birth*, a *"you-are-not-alone"* Presence or Spirit that shows up more viscerally on *some* days than *other*s but shows up often, on good days and *bad* days, *ordin*ary and *extra*ordinary days, *nev*er far away, *al*ways present on *some* level. It hovers and hangs out with me as a calm, *reassuring Presence*. It gets my attention and slows me *down* like *noth*ing *else* (always *has* and still *does*).

A *"normal"* person might experience fear or trauma or even *ter*ror under those circumstances. *I* experience the unexpected approaching *grill* of that car ... and the danger it pre*sents* ... as ... pure ex*cite*ment. *That's* the way I have experienced *most* of my brushes with danger and death—with a sense of wonder and wanting to know *more* ... wanting to see how events will play *out* ... *rarely* a*fraid* and, in *fact*, often *fearless* about *out*comes. I don't mean *that* in a *braggy* way. It makes me more *puzz*led than *proud*.

I *love* new stuff—new places, new experiences, new shoes ... especially new shoes.

I've just started to understand *why* I experience injuries and accidents the way I do. It has taken a LOT of introspection and conver*sation*; YEARS of Bible study and prayer; YEARS of therapy; more prayer; LOTS of re*flec*tion and inconsistent, *occas*ional *medit*ation; LOTS of reading; Still *more* prayer; LOTS of time pursuing conventional and *un*conventional means to understand ... *me*. Bottom *line*, I discovered most *re*cently that, at *some* point, *very* early *on*— maybe even in the womb but definitely shortly *out* of the *oven*, so to speak— I must have experienced some early traumas as *"good"* things ... as ex*cit*ing, di*strac*ting, enter*tain*ing things, even be*fore* my dad turned Danny Beckett's *bad* intentions into good (or at least *better*) *head*lines.

Brent Baum, a pioneer in the science of *mem*ory resolution, recently suggested to me that perhaps all the early drama in my life—several life-threatening fevers as an *inf*ant, facial stitches *twice* at age 2, jarring early trips to the ER—may have imprinted a message on my psyche in *child*hood that spurred me to seek *out* or at*tract* that kind of trauma (or *oth*er kinds of drama) for most of the rest of my *life* ... over and *over*. Could be.

I don't disa*gree* with him. I *also* think my traumas made for good *stories*, and I lived in a family of *great* storytellers ... great storytellers and willing *lis*teners, so I heard about and, in essence, re*lived* all of the poop storms of my life OVER and OVER in their re-telling, to the point that I must have started to attract precisely what my mom dreaded *most*—(other than Cathy or me dying before *she* did)—accidents. It appears, some experts would *say*, in some wonky twist of psychology, theology and physics, she may actually have programmed them to happen ... by telling me vivid, articulate, completely detailed stories about my earliest, most harrowing experiences.

Having said that, I think of my mom's ability to remember and re-tell our childhoods as one the greatest gifts she gave my sister and me. She made us know ourselves. Isn't that what adopted kids crave ... part of the reason they go searching for birth parents? My mom told us about ages and events we could not possibly consciously remember. She told us what we wore, down to the tiniest detail. She told us what our facial expressions and even what our posture in various situations told her and told others about us. She painted such vivid, colorful, entertaining pictures of the settings of our early lives ... and in a factual, not a fanciful, way.

My mom has an ability I inherited and passed on to my own daughter, a kind of phonographic memory, an ability to capture and recall certain kinds of dramatic dialogue verbatim, complete with accents and inflection, if necessary. While my dad may have an undeserved nickname, "RUiner," I think my mom deserves a more flattering nickname, too, "NOticer" ... or ... "RememberER." She got and passed *on* the journalist's gene that flows through our family veins—the gene that can notice, remember and re*tell* an event in vivid *de*tail.

For a *long* time, I wasn't sure what I actually re*mem*bered and what I *"remembered"* through my mom's *stor*ies. *Now,* after much psychological work of seeking and listening to my *"inner child,"* I have a clearer sense of where my mom's *stor*ies *end* and where my *own* recollections be*gin.* I experience the foundation my mom provided as a deep, *rich* well of self-*knowl*edge—better than any financial or material legacy she could *leave* me. [PAUSE]

I value that legacy—the chronicle of my early life my mom provided—*so* much that I tried to *du*plicate it for my own *daugh*ter. Along with my *moth*er, I became a *"noticer"* for my daughter and shared vivid memories of *her* life as an infant and *tod*dler ... with *her.*

Now back to the *ac*cident ...

So there I *am,* bent over backward in my powder-blue *snow*suit, not able to *move,* conducting a 6-year-old's version of triage on my*self.*

"Still breathing?" ... "Check."

"Still standing?" ... "Check ... SORT OF."

"Snowsuit unharmed?" ... "CHECK."

"Any blood?" ... "NOPE."

"Broken bones?" ... "NEGative."

"OK, then ..." [VERY MATTER OF FACTLY] *"Will someone PLEASE get me out from between this car and this SIGN? I have SLEDding to do!"*

I can *tell* by the expression on the face of the terrified *driv*er ... my chances of hitting that hill have just come to a screeching (or, more accurately, slipping and sliding) *halt.* I can tell from Cathy's and *Lynn's* faces, *too,* that, *some*how, they fear we are gonna get in *BIG* trouble for this. That doesn't make *sense* to me. What did *we* do?!

The driver bolts from his car, blinks *hard* and realizes I'm not only a*live* but also scratch-*free.* He breathes an e*nor*mous sigh of relief. [BIG SIGH] Even if *my* life doesn't flash before *my* eyes, it appears *his* life flashed before *his* eyes and has gone *on* to lodge in his *throat*. He looks *stark* white. His eyes *bulge*. He bends forward and puts both hands on his *knees*, as if he might throw *up*. The cold air makes it even *more* obvious that he's panting hard as he *rights* himself and helps *un-pin* me from between my frosty rock and a *hard* place.

You gotta love a snowsuit that takes a lickin' and keeps on lookin' cute as a *button*—literally not a smudge nor a scratch nor a *stitch* out of *place*.

The *driver*, the one closest to grown *up* in our group, tries to take charge, in *spite* of his shaky hands and quivering *lip*.

"Where do you LIVE?" he asks, still breathing hard.

"We can't TELL you. You're a STRANGER."

"Well, I think I better get you HOME. Where do you LIVE?"

"We can't TELL you. You're a STRANGER."

"I KNOW ... but we need to tell your parents what HAPpened." Then, as if imagining the scene with my parents, he gasps, *"Oh, GOD!"*

We re*fuse* to tell him our names or addresses, which leaves the poor kid com*ple*tely at a loss as to how to pro*ceed*. He can't just pull a*way* and *leave* us there on the side of the *road*. *Ob*viously, we have no such *thing* as a *cell* phone.

He manages to get us to tell him we live on Fernbrook *Drive*, a little more than a mile away from the scene of our *no*-harm, *no*-foul ac-cident.

We stand now in lightly falling *snow—all si*lent—trying to figure a way *out* of this *im*passe. It seems like a long moment before *any* of us *speaks*, one of those eerily quiet moments in the snow when you can practically hear your own *heart*beat. [PAUSE] I'm *pretty* sure we could still hear *his* heartbeat even above a snowplow if one scraped and rumbled *by*. No such *luck*. We just look into each oth-ers' *faces* with *what-do-we-do-NOW* puzzlement on *all sides*.

Finally, with our collective heart rates returning to *nor*mal and our breathing back in a healthier *range*, Lynn takes a better look at the driver and realizes she *KNOWS* him. He's been to her *house* ... to see her older *brother*. *That* breaks the *ice*. We decide he's *only* a stranger once re*moved*, so it *MIGHT* be OK to accept a ride in his car back to our *house*.

All *3* of us pile into the back seat ... wide like *most* back seats of that day but *not* wide enough to comfortably accommodate *3* little girls wrapped in mattress-thick *snow*suits. I guess he puts our sled into his *trunk*. Cathy seems concerned and ana*ly*tical about it all, wondering, *"What will Mommy and DADdy say about all this? Whose FAULT is this? Will they blame ME? How safe are we in the back seat of a car driven by a guy who just ran off the road and hit my little SISter? Who should do the talking when we get HOME?"* I suspect she decides *she* should be our *spoke*sperson. *GOOD CALL.*

Fortunately—or *un*fortunately for our teenage chauf*feur*—my parents are home, *both* of them snowed *in*, I think. They hear the car in the *drive*way and greet us at the door with startled ex*press*ions. The driver shows *so* much integrity and *cour*age. He walks *right* up and identifies himself. Then he says, *"I ... um ... I ... hit your daughter ... with my CAR."*

With *that*, my stunned parents look frantically at the 3 of us, looking like 3 mini–*Mich*elin Men, *still* trying to pile out of the back *seat*. They can see *in*stantly we're good as *new*.

"You hit our DAUGHter? ... Which ONE?!"

Given my *track* record, I should respond, *"Which one do you THINK?!"* I'm not sure, even by *then*, we had told him our *names*, so he just *points* at *me*. I stand there so ex*cit*ed, nodding my head proudly, as if to say, *"It's TRUE! He hit me with his car. Can you be-LIEVE it?! Can you beLIEVE my good FORtune??!"*

My parents drop to their knees and feel up and down my insu*lat*ed arms and *legs* ... checking to see whether I *tru*ly have emerged from the accident as *un*scathed as I *seem*.

I find it all *thrill*ing. I know this will become a story we will tell for the rest of our *lives*. And, *hey*, if there's no *blood*, no one gets *hurt* and you look cute as can *be* in the latest *fash*ions ... fashions un*sul*lied by an older *sib*ling, no *less* ... *well*, days don't *get* much better than *that*.

No, St. Louis snows don't come every day or even every *year*, but *that* year, *that* day, the snow *did* fall ... and *I* fell ... *back*ward ... but ended up still STANDING ... with something more enduring than gold, something more valuable to me than *mu*tual funds or *mon*ey. *I* had ... a good *story*.

CHAPTER 5

WithSTANDING the Advances of an Eagle Scout ...

My mom and dad don't seem like they should *go* together ... they're more like a hockey skate and a *feath*er duster ... like a tractor and a ban*a*na ... like one of those bright *orange traffic* cones and a certificate of de*po*sit. No apparent con*nec*tion yet, *some*how, to*geth*er, they not only make their relationship *work*; they make *magic*.

They *did*n't make magic at first *sight*, however. Truth be *told*, my mother found my father re*pul*sive on their first *date*. He had to let a whole *year* pass ... allowing her bad memories to *fade* ... before she granted him a *second* chance.

*Un*like my *moth*er, I had just the *op*posite experience in my *own* courtship and eventual marriage. I found myself smitten from the *start*—silly and starry-eyed almost right a*way*—NOT re*pulsed* ... at least not *tho*roughly repulsed, until 21½ years *la*ter, that is.

I relate the following series of stories from my *parents'* relationship, in *part*, because people gasp when anyone in my family *tells* them. Women *swoon. Men groan.* Yes, men *groan*, but they *also* laugh ... and ... in *places*, even *tough* guys fight back *tears.* In *places*, audience members find this story *jaw*-dropping. One woman ran up to me after I delivered this story in a speech several *years* ago. She clutched my arm in*sis*tently and said, *"That BETter be TRUE! It's TRUE, isn't it?! TELL me it's TRUE."* ... [PAUSE] It *is.* [PAUSE]

I don't in*clude* this story *just* for ef*fect* ... *just* to generate swoons or groans or *snif*fles. I *also* relate this par*ti*cular story from my parents' *part*nership because it explains a *lot* about my *own* relationships. This story recalls better than *any* other how I grew up believing married people should *treat* each other. This story relates some of my early im*pres*sions about how and why men and women take *on* or cast *off* certain roles in a relationship.

Still, *this* story isn't about *me*; it belongs to my *parents*, so, for the *most* part, I'll tell it in words *they* provided. [PAUSE]

My parents tell the story the way couples who have lived and loved a *long time* tell their stories—each chiming *in*, remembering the details *dif*ferently and correcting the *oth*er if the facts stray too far into fiction. They *both* contributed to the following version and consider it true e*nough*, though each feels it portrays the other too *kind*ly. *See? I told* you ... a hockey skate and a feather duster. [PAUSE]

Make no mis*take*; in the hockey-skate/feather-duster com*pari*son, my *mom* plays the *hockey* skate. In the tractor/banana comparison, *she* plays the *tractor.* Like a bright-orange *traf*fic cone, my *dad* clears the *way* and makes the traffic flow *smooth*ly, while my *mom* steers, sets the speed, chooses the *lane*, outlines the *terms.* There you *go* ... certificate of de*pos*it.

My mom wore the *pants*uit in our family, so to speak—stricter and more *se*rious than our dad ... very funny in her own right but more ... *Ger*man about it. She *"worked outside the home" way* ahead of most moms of the early '60s, from the time I was 2. My *dad* wore the pants, *too*, but *un*like *most* men of his generation, *he* wore those pants as more of a *part*ner to my mom than as the sole pro*vid*er for his *fam*ily. He seemed *soft*er, *sil*lier and *much* more sentimental than my *mom*.

My dad *jokes, "Your mother agrees that I make all the REALLY im-PORtant decisions in our marriage. ... In 55 YEARS, we haven't had a single REALLY important deCIsion to MAKE."* That arrangement emerged on their first *date* and has endured forever *after*.

I had never heard the story of their first date, not until we took them back to their college town and the site of that first date to celebrate a wedding anniversary, their 49th. They remarked at the time about how improbable their long-STANDING marriage was ... given their relationship's rocky start. [PAUSE]

By his junior year in college, my Eagle Scout father decided his Boy Scout virtues weren't getting him what he wanted with the ladies. By then, following the Boy Scout Law—being "trustworthy, loyal, helpful, friendly, courteous, kind, obedient, cheerful, thrifty, brave, clean and reverent"—felt restrictive and highly overrated, too clean-cut, even for the 1950s.

My dad had always strived to be what his mum called a "GOOD BOY," who didn't go around with [INSERT ENGLISH ACCENT] "nasty girls." Unfortunately, "Mum" hadn't provided a definition to go with that "nasty-girl" label, so my dad admits to some confusion about how one distinguishes the "nasty" girls from the ... keepers.

Perhaps thanks to 2 years in the Lambda Chi Alpha fraternity house at the University of Missouri, with young men whose mums had issued no such cautions ... or ... with young men who threw their mums' cautions to the wind, Kippy came to appreciate (or at least to imagine) some ... new "virtues" he'd like to ... embrace, shall we say. At least for one night, he determined he would take a new tack. Unfortunately for my mother (and for him), he decided to test drive his new virtues on his first date with her—then Lois Hartnagel—a "nice girl" who never had and never would suffer fools gladly. Hockey skate ... feather duster.

To hear them both tell it, my dad turned over his new ... fig leaf ... only once and for only one night. Otherwise, I might never have been Standing at all, much less "STILL Standing."

They went on a double date that first time out ... to the Coronado Club, a happenin' spot where all the coolest coeds *rocked* around the *clock* in 1954. At the end of the *evening*, Lois and Kip head to the parking lot to *meet* the other couple at the *car*. My parents arrive *first*, no other couple in *sight*. My dad must take that as some sort of *sign* ... a sign that the time has ar*rived* to ... make his *move*. Once in the back seat of their friend's *car*, my mother remembers my father as ... *"all hands."*

She is *NOT* ... amused. *Still* ... she claims she rebuffed him po*litely* ... the *first* time. Note: My mom tells *this* part of this story with a dis*gust*ed look on her face, her nose wrinkled up as if she smells something *foul*, eyes rolling and one cheek drawn into a sideways *sneer*. [DEMONSTRATE] Lois can make a *great* repulsed face. *This* part of this *story trigg*ers it.

My mom doesn't *do* things she doesn't want to *do*. I ad*mire* that about her. I sometimes wish she had passed *on* what*ever* gene or *gen*ius it takes ... to say *no* and stand *by* it. At various times through-out *my* life, sometimes for *dec*ades at a *stretch*, I have said yes to all *kinds* of things I didn't want to do ... some of which ended comi-cally, others di*sas*trously. At *times*, I have qualified as a pa*thet*ic people-pleaser. I did *not* get that *can't-say-no* tendency from my *moth*er. Oh, she *pleases* people—as a *host*ess, as a *col*league, as a *sound*ing board—but, un*like me*, she *nev*er loses sight of her own needs and, un*like me*, *nev*er appears to suffer any *guilt* when she says *no*. [PAUSE]

Back to our *story*, already in *prog*ress ... in the *friend's* back *SEAT* ...

I suppose you can't blame a guy for *try*ing, but if he hopes to unleash his inner James Dean for the *first time* on some poor, unsuspect-ing coed, Kip chooses the *wrong* bobby-soxer. My *mom*, speaking as if she were the German judge at an Olympic *event*, remembers his approach as ... *"clumsy"* ... *"UNinspired"* ... *"OFF-putting"* ... and ... *"rePULsive."* Ouch! In short, she *stands* her ground against Kip *Stand*ing. ...

Still, he doesn't want to give up too *quick*ly. That wouldn't speak well of his Boy Scout *train*ing. It wouldn't speak well of his stand-ing as a ... *Stand*ing. After *all*, his family motto re*mains "Persevere!"* His ever-present English *up*bringing *urges* him to ... *"Keep calm and carry on!"*

Bobby-soxer Lois Hartnagel.

*O*verestimating his *charm*, Kip con*vin*ces himself [CHEERFUL PEP-TALK TONE], *"She's just playing hard to GET."* So he makes a*noth*er *pass*, de*ter*mined, *this* time, to show how *suave* he can be. ... Ap*par*ently, my dad finds it a slippery slope from suave ... to *smarmy*. He doesn't grasp the *diff*erence and proceeds ... with*out* caution.

Look *out!* That makes Lois *an*gry. She *push*es him a*way*, leans back and looks at him as if he has *lost* ... his *mind* ... and will lose some- thing *else* if he doesn't back *off!*

He seems genuinely sur*prised* by her rebuff and pretends *previous* girls—*all* the girls—*wel*come this pushy ap*proach.* With *that,* in one *fi*nal attempt to test his ... tes*tosterone* ... to marshal his *manhood* ... Kip unleashes a brazen, bad-boy phrase his sweet inner *Boy* Scout can't *quite* pull *off*, a phrase that has *haunt*ed him *ever since.* Trying hard to sound *sexy* but coming *off* more as ... *creepy*, he pulls my mom toward him and says in a breathy tone 3 octaves *lower* than his normal *voice*, [LOW] *"WhatzaMATter, BAY-bee?!"* [PAUSE]

She *doesn't* find him suave. She *doesn't* feel *threat*ened. She's *not* "playing" hard to get. She *is* hard to get. Lois draws back and at- tempts to shed him the way you might cast off a reeking, mildewed *beach* towel. She delivers a firm and *un*friendly 3-word *response,* *"TAKE ... ME ... HOME!"* [PAUSE]

CHAPTER 6

STANDING in Love ...

Throughout my childhood and even well into my 40s, I would occasionally hear my mom re*buke* my *dad* for some misbe*hav*ior by scolding him mildly with her jaw slightly clenched and her eyes narrowed to *slits*.

"KIP," she'd say, [IMPATIENT SIGH] ... *"You're having a* [MOCKING] *'WhatzaMATter-Bay-bee?' MOment."*

I never knew what that *meant*, but I could *tell* ... by the abrupt change in my dad's *posture* and the look of *shame* on his *face* ... that *he* knew what it meant and the phrase packed a *hum*bling though slightly *humorous punch*. Hockey skate ... feather duster. Tractor ... banana. Traffic cone ... certificate of de*posit*.

To *really* understand the weight of the *rest* of this *chron*icle, you have to understand *3* things:

First, my dad *loves* making my mom *happy*. Perhaps in *part* he hopes to make up for that inauspicious be*gin*ning, but anyone can *see* it's *more* than that, *much* more. My father has devoted his *life*, not just a little *bit* of it, not just his *wak*ing hours or his *non-work*ing hours, not with a when-I-get-a*round*-to-it or when-I-happen-to-*think*-of-it or when-I-want-something-in-re*turn*-for-it attitude but with a *happily self*less, *whole*-hearted, *full*-throated, nothing-*else*-matters-more-on-this-*earth* attitude—he has devoted his *life* to that *one* mission, to making my mother *happy*. Remark*ably*, he *did* that *while* pursuing a *secondary* mission—a successful career in *sales*. [PAUSE]

I read once that the *greatest* gift a man can give his *child*ren ... is to love their *mother*. [PAUSE] Our father has *given* us that incom*parable gift*. And, our *mother* ... makes it worth his *while* ... filling his life—*our* lives—with tra*ditions* and attention to *details* he never even i*mag*ined would *matter* to him but *now* realizes he wouldn't want to live with*out*. [PAUSE]

43

Second, Lois and Kip have pro*found*ly different person*al*ities and *in*terests. *She* reads and collects *books, loves* a good glass of *wine* and *doesn't* like to get ... *dirty. He's* dys*lex*ic, reads *on*ly the *fun*ny papers, collects *tools,* loves to camp and to joke about bodily *func*-tions—and *yet ... some*how ... *each* feeds the part of the *oth*er that's *starv*ing. In a *sense,* it seems my mom loves my *dad* for what he *does,* and my dad loves my *mom* for what and how she *is.* ... That first date a*side, he's* all about the *Boy* Scout thing—*ser*vice, *du*ty and self-*sac*rifice. And *she's* all about ... *grace* notes, *crea*ture *com*forts and hospi*tal*ity—about creating an a*ston*ishingly beautiful *home;* about appreciating literature, culture and *art;* and about mak-ing and preserving vivid *mem*ories ... by entertaining family and friends often and *well.*

One might *won*der whether this qualifies as *true op*posite at*trac*-tion. Do Lois and Kip have *any*thing in common? They *do. Both* my parents have great but *ve*ry *dif*ferent senses of *hu*mor. My dad's more often the ... silly, pull-my-*fin*ger, take-it-too-*far* kind of *yuk*ster. *He* dishes out what we call in our family *"mem*orized *wit,"* often telling jokes he has heard from someone *else* and taking *full* (if too *fre*quent) ad*van*tage of the *"For*ward*"* button on his com*put*er.

My *mom's* humor, on the *oth*er hand, tends to be more in*ci*sive, less *ob*vious, more so*phis*ticated. She manufactures her *own* mirth ... in the *mo*ment. ... She's a *big* fan of Raymond *Burr* and the old *Perry Mason TV* series. Perry provides an ex*am*ple of her subtle *hu*mor. She and my dad watch an episode to*geth*er one night.

"Is he still aLIVE?" my dad *won*ders.

"Oh, NO, he died YEARS ago," my mom answers.

My dad points to the TV image of Raymond Burr and asks, *"When was THIS made?"*

My mom smirks and says ... *"BeFORE he DIED,"* chuckling at her own *wit.* They *both* laugh at their own *jokes. Neith*er finds the *oth*er very funny, and *that* makes for good comedy for the *rest* of us.

Opposites? No. My parents share i*den*tical politics (let's not *go* there) and *ad*mirable, even excep*tion*al, *char*acter. They *both* have ex*treme*ly high IQs. I recall they took an IQ test in the mid-'70s as a silly kind of *con*test, each thinking they'd score *high*er than the *other*. It's probably a *good* thing for marital *harmony* that they ... *tied* ... at 146! Be*yond* in*tellect*, they *both* have what I consider ex*treme*ly high standards for their own *con*duct, which translated into what *I* per-ceived as a *child* and *teen*-ager as ex*treme*ly high ex-pec*tat*ions of their *progeny*.

My sister, the *first*born, über-successful CEO, says *I* felt the weight of our parents' expectations more than *she* did. I'm not sure I felt those expectations *more*, but I sure re*act*ed to them *differ*-ently. That may explain why *I'm* the sister running a*mok*, wearing workout duds from *Tar*get and writing a *book*, and *she's* the sister running a *com*pany, wearing St. *John* suits and winning *big* ac*counts* in the world of public re*lat*ions.

Cathy Standing Dunkin.

... At least from the perspective of their *daugh*ters, Lois and Kip Standing, the hockey skate and the *feath*er duster, have what *should* go down in *his*tory as one of the all-time *great* ro*mances. [PAUSE] Given all the romance and fun we witnessed between our parents and the high expectations those qualities ignited in us, one might say, *"Pity the fools who marry those DAUGHters!"* [PAUSE]

CHAPTER 7

STANDING at Pat O'Brien's in New Orleans ...

The *last* thing you must know ... in order to feel the full weight of my parents' *love* story: my mom *loves* pianos and piano *music—play*ing it, *lis*tening to it, lu*xur*iating in it. Cathy and I feel very blessed that, es*sen*tially, our mother set our entire *child*hoods to *mus*ic ... pi*an*o music. Every *week*, every *sea*son, every occasion in the Standing household had 88 little black-and-white *ham*mers beating like a heart in the *cen*ter of our *fam*ily—*soft*, *sil*ly, *sa*cred, *sen*timental *heart*beats. [PAUSE]

There's almost *no* better place on the *plan*et to in*dulge* a passion for pi*an*o music than at Pat O'Brien's in New Orleans, where they have 2, *count* 'em, *2* big, beautiful Steinway grand pi*an*os side-by-*side* ... *and* ... where they have a roster of ac*com*plished pianists *wor*thy of those renowned *in*struments ... ready, willing and *able* to play almost *any* composition patrons can *think* to re*quest* ... at any *mom*ent. The skilled musicians play *song* after *song*. They per-form everything from simple *everybody-knows-THIS-one* tunes ... to complicated chords and rhythms. They *even* throw in familiar *ad*vertising jingles when the mood *strikes*. They complement each other in perfect sync, *us*ually from *mem*ory—with*out* sheet music—although, just in case someone throws them a musical *curve*ball, they have HUGE *books* of sheet music to tackle the never-ending stream of requests patrons scrawl on *cock*tail napkins.

Now ... fast-forward from my parents' *first* date in 1954 to 1970. Lois and Kip are sitting at a table in that famous piano bar at Pat O'Brien's. They feel mellow, thanks, per*haps*, to a couple of the bar's *sig*nature Hurricane *drinks*, concocted at that famous *copper-topped bar* ... AND ... feeling mellow thanks, per*haps*, to the comfort that comes from almost 13 *years* of *mar*riage, a marriage with only a *few* [DEEP VOICE] *"Whatzamatter-Bay-bee?"* moments.

A familiar 1970s *fog* of ciga*rette* smoke hangs over the dimly lit *bar* and gives it a *hip*, romantic *vibe*—kind of Bogey and Bacall meet Harry Connick *Jr*. My parents arrive be*fore* the crowd swells to its typical standing-room-*only*, so there's *room* for the *Stand*ings.

My mom remembers that they snag a *perfect* table, not *every*one's first choice, *not* up *front* in the coveted *first* row of *ta*bles but perfect from *her* perspective ... as a connois*seur*. As a life-long admirer of pianos and a studier of classical *music*, *she* knows Steinway's repu-tation as *"the world's FINest pianos ... the piano by which all OTHer pianos are JUDGED."* She knows each *one* takes nearly a *year* ... to *make*. My mom knows that most of the world's *top* pro*fes*sional pi*a*nists choose to perform *only* on a *Stein*way.

Lois and Kip sit toward the *back* of the *bar*, in the *mid*dle, with an ideal view of *both* magnificent instruments. From that *dis*tance, with the piano lids hoisted open and musicians' fingers *fly*ing, my parents can almost *feel* the vibrations of the music wash *over* them.

My mom gets mellower by the *mo*ment, a condition *not* lost on my *dad*. She's in her *el*ement, doesn't get much happier than *this*. *Still*, he thinks of something he can do and say that will put her ... *over* the *top*. He takes out a pen and slides the soggy cocktail napkin out from under his *curvy*, colorful *cock*tail glass. He begins to write and playfully cups his hand around his scribbles so *she* can't *see*. ...

Mind you, I have heard this story *so* often and in such *detail* I feel as if I *wit*nessed it with my own *eyes* ... felt it with my own *skin* ... *breathed* the ciga*rette* smoke into my own *lungs*, but, a*las*, they didn't *take*, nor would Pat O'Brien's have wel*comed*, their *then-10-*year-old daughter along for the *ride*. *Still*, I remember it vividly from the re-*tell*ing. [PAUSE]

At *first*, Lois assumes Kip has thought of a romantic re*quest*. As she watches him scribble, several ad*di*tional thoughts go through her *head*:

"He's STILL very cute, even after ALL these YEARS." ...

"Even in this LIGHT, I STILL can see the twinkle in those brown EYES." ...

"I wonder what he'll reQUEST ... OUR song MAYbe ... 'My Funny VALentine'?"

She chuckles to her*self*, *"With Kip's apPALling PENmanship and dyslexic SPELLing, they may not be able to READ his request at ALL, much less PLAY it ... but, STILL ... how SWEET!"*

Based on past be*hav*ior, my mom makes a silent *bet* with herself: either he'll request something *silly* ... *or* ... he'll use the napkin to jot down something suggestive for *later* (Ick! *NOT* something a daughter likes to con*template*). He takes *neither* tack. In*stead*, he writes both a *hope* ... and a *prom*ise, *not* to either of the pianists across the *room* but to his *wife* across the *table*.

My dad *loves* it when he can do something *truly* unexpected for my mom. She's so quick and *clev*er it's almost im*possible to throw her a curve, even under the *in*fluence at Pat O'Bri*en's. He knows what she ex*pects* him to *do*, but he has just had a *brain*storm. He's *certain* she won't see *this* coming because *he* hadn't thought of it him*self* until a *min*ute ago. He draws out the su*spense*.

He looks her right in the *eye*, leans *in* ... *this* time *all* suave and *no* smarm. He smirks, doesn't say a *word* and makes a *big* show of folding the mysterious *nap*kin so she can't *see* what he has *writ*ten on it. He *sloo*owly returns his pen to his pocket with his *right* hand, all the while holding his *left* hand over the napkin so *she* can't *peek*.

He can *tell* she's *just* about to lose her *pa*tience with his drawn-out pro*duc*tion. That's my mom's *one* recur*ring com*plaint about my *dad*; he tends to take his comedic or romantic antics *too far*. Not *this* time. He turns as if to summon a *server* to deliver his re*quest* but then, abruptly, turns toward my *mom* in*stead* and slides the napkin across the table toward *her*.

Rolling her eyes a bit at all the pomp and circumstance, and *certain* now that he has written something *sex*ual, she finally *peels* open his *mes*sage. She reads his cocktail-napkin *promise*: [PAUSE] *"SOME-day you'll play on a Steinway of your OWN."* [PAUSE]

He succe*eds* in surprising her. She thinks, [DREAMILY] *"How SWEET! ... How THOUGHTful! ... How PERfect THAT would be! ...* [SPELL BROKEN] *How enTIREly UNlikely."*

Lois spends the rest of the evening at Pat O'Brien's indulging the *fan*tasy and imagining her *own* fingers gliding across her *own* Steinway *iv*ories. She knows my dad would like nothing *more* than to make that dream come *true*, but she dismisses it as little more than a *charm*ing, romantic, financially unrea*list*ic, *more-than-likely-ALcohol-induced im*pulse.

CHAPTER 8

STANDING around a Piano ...

Once back at *home* in St. *Lou*is, the New Orleans spell broken by work, laundry, household *bills* and *bur*dens, Lois for*gets* about ... *a Steinway of her own*. In*stead*, she re*signs* herself to the lovely but not at *all* luxurious *hand*-me-*down Chick*ering *up*right piano she has played *so* often and well in our *living room, tr*uly the center-piece of *every* family celebration of my *child*hood ... and *even* the centerpiece of many *ord*inary days, *then* and *still*.

Even if it *did*n't qualify as one of the *"world's finest pianos,"* that Chickering had a happy history of its *own*. My grandfather gave it to my grandmother for Christmas in 1941, when my mom was 7 years *old*. *That* year, she starts what turns out to be 9 *years* of piano lessons. My mother remembers her stern, German, *music*-loving *fath*er firing her *first* piano teacher after only a few *les*sons. He'd lis-ten to my mother practice and bellow from the next *room*, [GRUFF] *"TEMpo! TEMpo! That child doesn't know a QUARter note from a WHOLE note!"*

Lois learns to play on a Chickering piano.

Enter Mr. *Walk*er, *"a dear man"* who came to my mom's house *every* week for an *hour* and charged ... *one dol*lar. That grand sum included *all* her *sheet* music. My mom still *has* some of that vintage music with Mr. Walker's *scrib*bles on it. ...

While Lois may for*get* the promise Kip makes on that sog-gy *cock*tail napkin, Kip *never* does. The Universe conspires to help him *keep* that promise in 1984, 14 years *after* that trip to Pat O'Brien's.

As an industrial chemical *sales*man in the 1970s and '80s, my dad calls on *rest*aurants, *nurs*ing homes and *hos*pitals attempting to sell *gi*ant drums of *floor* wax, *solv*ents, commercial *dish* soap and *toilet*-bowl cleaner. His customers just *happ*en to include a restaurant chain with 3 outlets in a suburban *shopp*ing mall—*Pope's* Cafe*teria*, Seven *Kitch*ens and the *Round*table *Rest*aurant. The mall just *hap*pens to have a pi*ano* store *right* across from those *rest*aurants.

When he has time between *sales* calls, my dad darts into the store to see whether it has any Steinways *"on sale."* Between 1970 and 1984, he learns that a *new* Steinway of the size and style he *want*s would cost more than $29,000—*alm*ost as much as the *home* on which he and my mom are still making *pay*ments! Un*daunt*ed, he asks about *used* Steinways. He learns even *those* don't come to market very often, and they hold their value so *well* he will have to sell a LOT of dish soap even to afford a *used* Steinway. When he calls on Pope's, he *al*ways checks, but the piano store never has any in the store when he *happ*ens to *v*isit.

That routine plays out for 14 *years*! [DEJECTED] *Ho, hum!* Almost *noth*ing makes my dad *sad*der or more *frust*rated than a good i*dea* he can't *ex*ecute, *e*specially one that would set my mom's toes to tappin' the way *this* one would. Fourteen years seems a *long* time to pur*sue* something he can't *find* and probably can't af*ford* even if he *does* find it. He leaves the store that day in 1984 on the brink of giving *up*, fearing he might *nev*er perform this *mir*acle.

As things *of*ten happen in my family—just in the nick of *time* ... just when Kip's about to give *up*, the woman from the piano store tracks him *down*. She says she knows of someone who has a spec*tac*ular Steinway *baby grand* piano she hopes to *sell* ... *"to a good HOME."* However, be*cause* this Steinway owner doesn't plan to *sell* her Steinway through the *store* at the *mall*, the piano clerk didn't feel she should *say* anything *ear*lier, while *he* was in the *store* and *she* was ..."ON the CLOCK." My dad *loves* a salesperson with company *loy*alty, in *part* because he *is* one him*self*. Even before he *sees* the *Stein*way, *his* timing and *her* in*teg*rity make my dad wonder whether *this sale* is ... *meant to be*—the sale he has waited 14 *years* to *close*. [PAUSE]

Re*mem*ber ... my parents have an ar*rang*ement ... my *dad* makes all the really im*port*ant decisions in their *mar*riage, except they never

HAVE any really important decisions to *make. This* one falls into a *new gray* area. My dad *knows bet*ter than to buy something *that* big, *that* expensive and *that per*sonal with*out* involving my *mom ... but* ... true to his mission and sentimental *nat*ure, he wants to sur*prise* her.

That means he must a*bandon* Boy Scout virtue *#1:"A Scout is TRUST*worthy." He will have to *lie ...* just this *once.* Once he makes *that* decision, not *only* does he *lie* but also, it seems, for this *worthy* cause, Kip morphs from straight-arrow *Scout* into dia*bol*ical *genius* in the space of a single *week,* and he recruits lying *min*ions—Cathy and *me,* and even perfect *strangers*—to help him pull off his *caper.*

He can't *sleep* that night because he's thinking about how he'll nudge my mom toward that *new, old Stein*way una*wares.* He *knows* he'll have to craft his lies *care*fully, say just e*nough* without say-ing too *much—*admittedly *not ...* his best *skill.* He'll have to behave contrary to his *char*acter ... keeping something from our *moth*er, something the Boy Scout in him *never* would do under *nor*mal cir-cumstances.

When my dad has what he *thinks* is a good id*ea ...* when he's about to make someone *really happy,* he practically *quiv*ers. I'm *not kid*-ding. He can't con*tain* himself. Like a little *kid,* the electricity of a good idea practically crackles from every *pore.* I'm *really not* exag-gerating. *Once,* to capture that *quality,* one of my dad's *colleagues* affectionately (or *not*-so-affectionately) *nick*named him *"N.L.B.,"* for *"Nervous Little Bastard."* It fit *so well ...* we even adopted and adapted the nickname at *home,* too, calling him *"N.L.B."* for the same *reason* but *trans*lated *"Nervous Little BuckaROO."* (I believe one should re*sist* calling one's *fath*er a *"bastard" ...* unless the slur *fits,* of course—and *may*be not even *then.*)

This time, Kip, a.k.a. *"N.L.B.,"* knows he can't let his excitement *show.* He can't carry his antics too *far.* He can't *quiv*er. If he *does,* my mom will catch *on.* He decides, *first,* he'll re*mind* my mom of the prom-ise he made 14 years *ear*lier at Pat O'Brien's—a *risky move.* She's a sharp *cook*ie. *A*ny *men*tion of his distant New Orleans pledge might tip her *off,* but he *has* to set the wheels of this deal in *motion,* so he settles on this daring *strategy.*

He comes home from work the afternoon *after* his sleepless night and *cas*ually says, *"Remember when I said, 'Someday you'll play* *on a Steinway of your OWN?' ... Well, I guess we both knew that wouldn't HAPpen ... and ...* [DEJECTED/ASHAMED] *with Kelly's WEDding coming up, it's even LESS likely NOW.* [HOPEFUL] *But I came across something today that WOULD give you a chance to play someone ELSE'S Steinway."* My mom *frowns*, all set to issue a knee-jerk re*fu*sal.

Unde*te*rred and with*out* quivering, Kip *lies*. He says the piano be-longs to one of his *cus*tomers. He *doesn't* say this *"customer"* has a Steinway for *SALE*, just that she shares my mom's love of pianos. He says ... when he told this ... *"customer"* ... about the promise he made at Pat O'Brien's, she in*si*sted he bring my mom by to *play* her *Stein*way.

"She invited us to come Friday after WORK. She'll let you play as long as you LIKE."

Kip *knows* his offer sounds *odd*. He *knows* she won't *like* the idea. He anticipates a reluctant re*ac*tion from his *wife* ... and *gets* one. Lois feels both grateful for and an*noy*ed by the opportunity he has pre-*sent*ed. She can *see* he's very pleased with himself for remembering his *pro*mise ... for resurrecting those good New Orleans *mem*ories ... and for *orche*strating this *very* thoughtful *plan* ... but ... she fears an *aw*kward *in*terlude. She as*sumes* the customer will greet them *warm*ly and treat them *kind*ly and *cor*dially, but she *doesn't* wish to feel like a pauper, sniffing for crumbs at some ex*clu*sive musical *ban*quet ... a banquet to which she suspects he may have *grace*-lessly *beg*ged an invitation. Not normally shy *or* lacking in con-fidence, under *these* circum-stances, Lois fears she won't play to Steinway *stand*ards. She doesn't want to *try*. She feels no com*pul*sion to *say* why *not* ... no need to *jus*tify her de*ci*sion; she just issues a guilt-free *"No."* [PAUSE] (*God, how I wish she had in-stilled that aBILity in ME!*) [PAUSE]

Would you buy industrial chemicals from this man?

No longer that *ti*mid *tender*-foot in the Coronado Club

*park*ing *lot,* Kip stands *his ground this* time, ready to over*come* ... *her* objec*tions.* He knows by *now* how to sweet-talk Lois *Hart*nagel. Marshaling his *best* sales skills, he appeals to her ... as his *part*ner. He ex*agger*ates the importance of this *"customer"* ... claims a *big* order hangs in the *bal*ance, so, *e*ven if Lois isn't *keen* on the idea, he asks her to take one for the *team,* so to speak. He says he doesn't want to decline the invi*ta*tion ... and risk the re*la*tionship. Liar, liar, pants on fire!

She de*clines.*

He *sweet*ens the deal by saying, *"I'll take you to dinner at Reuben's and Coco's AFterward,"* one of my parents' *favorite spots,* conveniently close to the *"customer's"* home.

[ASIDE ...] Throughout my *child*hood, my mom's favorite thing to make for *dinner* ... was ... reservations. ... My dad *knows* she will *nev*er, *never* turn down a dinner *out,* even with*out* a Steinway attached. He thereby *tricks* Lois into going to his *"customer's"* home for a test-*tick*le of those *cov*eted *i*vories ... with the promise of favorite food and wine to fol*low.* [PAUSE]

She agrees to *go,* but, in de*fi*ance, she doesn't even bring along any *sheet* music. She intends to stay and play *just* long enough to indulge my dad's *fant*asy, to help his *ca*reer, and then hurry off to *din*ner.

How quickly she changes her *mind*! My mom *viv*idly remembers the first time she saw (and *play*ed) the piano she *now* affectionately refers to as ... *"Victoria."* In my mother's world-*view,* pianos (particularly *Stein*way pianos) are *born,* not *made,* and one should give them *names* and *birth*rights like the precious family members they be*come.* Hence, my mom names *this* Steinway, *"born"* in 1889, for the era of Victoria's *"birth."*

In *con*trast, my *dad* considers it *very* clever when *Bud*weiser starts putting *"born on"* dates on its *beer. Still,* he has always indulged my mother's custom of naming their cars and other possessions as if they were *child*ren.

"Victoria" is an extraordinary, in*cred*ibly beautiful *ins*trument ... with a buttery black *fin*ish, stout-yet-striking *perf*ectly turned *legs,* an elegantly carved *music* rack and, *odd*ly, only 85 keys—3 fewer

than the standard 88 keys you find on to*day's* models. *Some*how, Victoria's in*tent*ionally missing *keys* make her even *more* appeal-ing to my *moth*er. My mom would say it gives her ... *charac*ter ... perso*nal*ity, like a birthmark on a *child*. Borrowing a PR spin from her eldest *daugh*ter, she *might* say, *"Only the COOLest pianos have 85 KEYS."* [PAUSE]

For *Lo*is, it's love at first ... *listen*. For far longer than she in*tends*, my mom can take neither her eyes ... nor her *fin*gers ... off Vic*tor*ia. [PAUSE]

My dad stands *by watch*ing, barely able to contain his *e*motions and the secret he shares with their *hos*tess, his *"customer,"* Victo-ria's soon-to-be *ex*-owner. [PAUSE]

Even if you *don't* pant over pianos the way my *moth*er does, you'd almost have to lack a *soul* not to respond to the sight of a glossy black Steinway grand piano on a concert-hall *stage*, polished and ready to per*form*. If you *let* it, that sight can take your *breath* away: its golden strings ... its propped-up *lid* ... its sheer size and com-*mand* of the *stage*. It always strikes me as such a *powerful im*age, so full of po*tent*ial, sitting there like a promising box full of *notes* just *wait*ing for some talented *some*one to string them together and set them *free*. ... Not *me*, of course, but *some*one.

Vic*tor*ia takes that breathtaking phe-nomenon to an even *high*er *level*. She's *stun*ning— was *then* and still is *now*, more than 25 years *lat*er, at more than 110 years *old*. She's softer and mellower and, in *her* way, even *more* elegant than the shiny, *show*-offy Steinways born generations *af*-ter her ... the ones designed to per-form in *pub*lic venues. *No*, Victoria's a *priv*ate, more *bash*ful, less *boast*ful member of the Steinway *fam*ily—*per*-fect for the *Stand*ing family.

"Victoria."

The *best* music to my *dad's* ears in all of this? ... Victoria doesn't have a stunning *price* tag to match her ster-ling qualities. Ap*par*ently, Victoria's owner cares *more* about finding the right *family* than she does about fetching the best *price*. It turns out my dad can keep his promise to my mom for a mere $4,500 plus *moving* costs—a *steal*!

Still, Kip *chokes*. He s*weats*. He quietly tugs at his co*llar*. *He* crunches the *numbers* while his *wife* falls deeper and deeper in love with this tall, dark and handsome *strang*er *right* before his *eyes*.

Does he *dare*? Given their *bud*get, even that re*mark*ably *reas*onable price qualifies as a stretch. He comforts himself with the knowledge that $4,500 falls considerably be*low* the out-of-the-*ques*tion $29,000 showroom *stick*er price of a *new* Steinway.

The visit turns out to be less *awk*ward and more ro*man*tic than my mom i*mag*ines. E*ventual*ly, she tears herself away from the keys but not until she plays my dad's *favorite* re*quest*, Victor Herbert's *"Thine Alone."* As she steps a*way*, she notices even the piano *bench* looks mag*nif*icent, as carefully crafted as the *rest* of Victoria's *fine feat*ures. She comments on how un*us*ual it is and how *perf*ectly it matches the design of the pi*ano*. She learns they didn't *come* together, but they *go* together—thoughtfully chosen, *now* ins*eparable*.

That *clinches* it! For *this*, my thrifty, feather-duster *dad* decides he can spend $4,500 without consu*lt*ing and a*lmost* without *fear* of my hockey-skate *mom* ... even *with* my *wed*ding on the *way*.

It *never* occurs to my mom that she has just taken what a*mounts* to ... a *test drive*. Victoria's owner plays *her* part *flaw*lessly. She pre*tends* she issued a purely *so*cial invitation. She pre*tends* she could *never* part with Victoria. She shows her *off* as a *per*manent family *fix*ture, *all* the while knowing she has a *done deal* with my *dad*—one that in*cludes* that magnificent *bench*.

My mom heads happily to dinner at Reuben's and Coco's, probably with the same dreamy, slightly in*tox*icated look on her face she had at Pat O'Brien's way back *when*, *this* time under the influence of a 95-year-old *Stein*way, *not* a rum drink in a curvy *glass*. Over *din*ner, my *dad* soaks up my mom's *gen*uine *acc*olades for his in*spired* idea. She ad*mits* she thoroughly en*joyed* herself and refers to the outing as *"a lark."* Lois *loves* larks.

With *that*, Kip's thoughts turn to Phase *Two*: sneaking Victoria's 750-pound immensity unscathed and undetected into their living room.

My mom unwittingly cooperates with the deception. The week Victoria joins our family, Lois's job as office manager and editor at McGraw-Hill keeps her especially busy, planning and presiding over the celebration of an important company milestone. She must entertain a *lot* of McGraw-Hill brass from New *York*. Normally more of a nine-to-fiver, she gets up early to plan the high-profile shindig and stays *out late* for *days*.

She *loves* her job. She *loves* her colleagues. She *loves* the mixing and mingling and the after-hours cocktails, but she HATES mornings—always *has*, always *will*. For business *and* pleasure, Lois reads constantly, often staying up past 1 or 2 a.m. *This* week's extra work and even longer hours make her a [HIGH-PITCHED] *little* cranky. She does *not* suffer in silence. She shares countless party plans and pains with my *dad*. He welcomes these details. Like a good military strategist, he knows they'll help him in his subterfuge.

All those early mornings and extra duties at *work* keep Lois too busy to notice all the measurements Kip takes, all the *phone* calls he makes, all the furniture he moves—too busy even to notice all the *checks* he writes to Victoria's owner and to the piano movers ... too busy to notice the bottle of champagne he puts in the fridge to chill ... too busy to notice how suddenly and how much her *"N.L.B."* hubby has started to ... quiver. With something approaching the complexity of D-Day logistics, Kip spells out the plan of attack to his *"troops"* —Cathy; Cathy's husband, Carter; my fiancé and *me*.

[CLIPPED MILITARY TONE ...] Shortly after she leaves for work on Friday morning, piano movers will sneak our mother's antique Chickering piano out and move an even older Victoria in. The McGraw-Hill celebration won't end until 2230 hours. (ASIDE: We don't really use military time in our family, but *this* day has an armed-forces feel to it.) Just in case the festivities wrap up early, we must all be in position by 2030 hours. We must take no chances, drop no hints, leave no clues. Loose lips sink ... surprises. After the last guest departs, Lois will head home, exhausted. We know this.

We're to park our cars out of sight. Cathy will position herself on the piano bench and stay there until instructed to begin playing

"For She's a Jolly Good Fellow" on Victoria's 85 *keys.* She'll play *soft*ly at *fir*st and then gradually *in*crease her speed and volume as my mom moves *clos*er to the *liv*ing room. [NORMAL VOICE ...] As the only other pianist in the *fam*ily, Cathy plays a key *role* (pun in*ten*ded). She must play *loud* enough so my mom will *hear* her in the *kit*chen but *not* so loud that my mom will detect the change in tone and touch *too soon.*

[RESUME MILITARY TONE ...] When the designated hour ar*rives* and when instructed to *do* so, *I* will fill 6 champagne *flutes.* I'll de-liver *one* to *Cathy,* but she is neither to set it *on* Victoria nor to *sip from* it until she moves safely a*way* from those precious Steinway *hamm*ers and *strings.* I'll arrange the *oth*er 5 flutes on a silver *tray* and position them *and* myself in the *break*fast room, near the ga-rage *door,* through which my mom will enter the *house.* My *dad* ... will watch for headlights through the *front window*—lights *off,* cur-tains *drawn.* Once he makes visual contact with our *"TARget,"* he'll *bolt* to the breakfast room at the *back* of the house to greet her at the *door* with the *rest* of us.

Carter and my fiancé will serve as *block*ers/*tack*lers/*sheep*-herders, making sure Lois heads into the *kit*chen and *through* the *fam*ily room, NOT into or through the *din*ing room, where she might *see* Victoria too *soon.*

[RESUME NORMAL SPEAKING VOICE ...] [ASIDE] My dad might blush to hear me *say* so, but I find it so ... *cute* ... a*dor*able, in fact ... to watch my Air Force veteran *fath*er put his military training to the test in this uncon*ven*tional *way.* [STERN/SERIOUS] Opera-tion: Standing *Stein*way! [MOCK SALUTE]

As if on *cue* and with*out* the benefit of a cell-phone *warn*ing (since we didn't *have* such helpful devices in *those* days), my dad sounds the a*larm. "She's pulling into the driveway! BATtle stations! BATtle stations! Assume the poSItion!"*

My mom comes in through the garage and is shocked ... (*not* ex-actly *happy*) ... to *see* us ... at *11* o'clock on a *Friday night.* She tries to shed her purse and boxes of *party-rel*ated efflu*vium* as a lock of hair falls across her *weary face,* as if to say, [DEFLATED] *"Party's O-ver!"* With her arms *full,* she juts out her lower lip like a little *kid* and attempts to puff the errant strands *back* into *place* with a big blast of *air.* It doesn't *work.* The hair falls back across her nose and one eye. She *wilts*. My dad helps her un*bur*den herself, lifts a champagne glass off the *tray,* hands it to my *mom,* takes one for him*self* and urges we 3 kitchen musk*eteers* to follow *suit.*

"She's HOME! She's HOME!" he cheers, raising his glass. He proposes a *toast* ... *"To the end of an AWful WORK week."*

Carter and my fiancé do their *part.* They clink glasses and block *all* paths to the *din*ing room. *Shell*-shocked and slumped over, my mom goes through the toasting motion ... *sort* of.

She's *not* loving this ... not loving the *crowd,* not loving the *fuss,* not loving the *noise* ... which my dad considers the *PERF*ECT re*a*ction.

She half-heartedly welcomes the cham*pagne* ... sips from her glass but seems dazed and con*fused,* almost on the edge of an*noy*ed. She just wants to *sit down.* She had *hoped* just to *come home,* shed her *work* duds and plop down on the *couch* ... or ... better *yet,* head straight to *bed.* In*stead,* here we *are,* ex*pect*ing her to feel *fes*tive, invading her *space,* disrupting her plans to *un*wind.

We usher her through the *break*fast room, into the kitchen toward the *family* room. As in*struct*ed, Cathy has been playing *"For She's a Jolly Good Fellow"* softly in the background the whole *time.*

Still dazed, my mom asks, *"Where's CATHy? ... Is SHE playing the piANo?"*

"YEP," my dad answers. With *that,* we all start *sing*ing, *"For SHE'S a jolly good FEL-low ... For SHE'S a jolly good FEL-low ..."* Cathy plays *loud*er. We have my mom trapped in a claustrophobic *clus*ter. She seems likely to spontaneously com*bust* if we don't give her some *space.*

We spread *out.* She makes her way to the *family* room. Taking a *deep,* cleansing *breath,* she gets more in the *spir*it. Even though this *isn't* the capper she had *plan*ned for her *even*ing, she can't knock a champagne toast and a loving *family.* She hopes, *"MAYbe Kip won't take these antics TOO far, and maybe the kids won't stay too LONG."*

As my mom cheers *up,* Cathy plays *loud*er and *fast*er. Lois starts to make the curve from the *family* room into the *liv*ing room. We all slide in a*head* of her so she can't see a*round* us or over our *heads.*

She looks utterly confused, cocks her head like an inquisitive puppy and says, *"Boy! I really MUST have had a HARD WEEK. That doesn't even SOUND like my piANo."* She cranes her neck to try to say hello to *Cathy*. We block her *view*, trying *not* to make it look intentional.

She becomes curious now, wondering why we're moving like synchronized swimmers minus the *pool*. She moves again trying to see *Cathy* and says again, *"That doesn't even SOUND like my piANo."* We step apart.

My mom shrieks, *"THAT'S NOT MY PIANO!! ... THAT'S NOT MY PIANO!!"*

My dad stands off to the side, past Victoria's upraised *lid*, watching exactly the reaction he *hoped* my mom would *have*, the reaction he has waited 14 *years* to enjoy. Tears *stream* down his face. He sobs, barely able to say, *"YES, it is! YES, it is! This is YOUR Steinway ... a Steinway of your OWN."*

Imagine an image *not* unlike Mary Tyler Moore as Laura *Petrie*, in the midst of one of her ... [IMITATE] *"Oh, Raaaaahhhhhb"* scenes. My mom's knees *buckle*, but she stays on her *feet*. In a *frenzy*, she flings both hands straight up in the *air*, brings her open palms down on her *head*, then *back* in the *air*, then onto both sides of her *face*, in a Macaulay *Culkin "Home Alone"* expression, and then back on her *head* while she shakes her head back and forth with her *mouth* hanging open. She looks into *each* of our *faces* with disbelief.

My mom throws her arms around my dad's *neck*. She's gasping, pushing him away, pulling him *back*. She looks at Victoria ... then back at *him*.

Tears *stream* down *all* of our cheeks. My mom is beside herself, hugging my dad, clutching each one of *us* on the *arm* before she practically hip-checks Cathy off that beautiful *bench*.

She sits down at that magnificent *key*board, fingers poised to play but *frozen* above the keys. She sits like that for a long *moment*. She seems to want to memorize the *scene* ... to mark the *moment*.

She's breathing *so hard*. With her *right* hand still poised above the *keys*, she pats her chest with her *left* hand close to the base of her *throat.* She wears a stunned ex*pres*sion, blinking *hard*, trying to take it all *in.*

*Every*one's hugging *every*one. It becomes a *blub*ber fest, *so* emotional, everyone *laugh*ing, *cry*ing and getting a kick out of my dad as he tries not to dis*solve* on the *spot.*

My mom finally regains a *bit* of her com*pos*ure. She looks up on that a*maz*ingly ornate Vic*tor*ian music *rack* and notices something she hasn't *seen* be*fore.* ... It's a *cock*tail napkin ... a cocktail napkin on which my dad has written, *sim*ply ... *"I TOLD you so."* [LONG PAUSE]

CHAPTER 9

STANDING around *Another* Piano ...

The piano story *could* end *there*, but it *doesn't*, not with Kip *Standing* running the show ... [PAUSE]

Deep into wedding plans at this point, my future *hus*band and I have *just* told our wedding musicians we *want* them to play *"Edelweiss"* as the backdrop for our *first* dance. Perhaps *that's* why my mom chooses to play *"Edelweiss"* as Victoria's welcome-to-your-new-home *melody*—a *sweet*, *simple* family *favorite*.

She plays. *We* sing a*long*. Then, out of the *blue*, Cathy asks, with her lower lip puckered into a *pout*, [CHILDLIKE] *"Where's the CHICKering? ... What happened to the CHICKering?"*

My dad says, *"I'm SORry, Cath, I had to trade her in to help pay for the STEINway."*

Cathy's face *falls*, her eyes wet with fresh *tears*. No*t* wanting to spoil the *moment*, she displays her un*fail*ing PR poise and recovers *quick*ly. She says she would have *liked* to keep the Chickering in the *family* but she unders*tands*.

The celebration breaks up shortly there*after*. It's *late*. We're all *tired*. Carter and Cathy leave *first*. The *rest* of us turn from the door and breathe *half* of a satisfied *sigh*. We can expel only *half* of a sigh because ... as *soon* as the door closes be*hind* them, my dad goes *back* into *mil*itary mode.

"QUICK! Come with ME! We're goin' to Cathy and CARter's."

"WHAT?!"

[SCOLDING, AS IF WE'RE DIM ...] *"I DIDN'T trade in the CHICKering; I had the movers take it to their apartment this MORNing."*

"WHAT?! ... You're KIDding!"

"No, I'm NOT kidding. And right about NOW, Carter's telling Cathy they need to stop for GAS, so we have just enough time to get over there and HIDE before they pull UP."

I can't be*lieve* he has held back part of his *plan*, even from his *troops*. I feel a little in*sul*ted, but I under*stand*. He wants to surprise everyone. He suc*ceeds*. How *crafty*! How creative! How excruciating my *Nervous-Little-Buckaroo/Boy Scout* dad must have *found* it ... to keep *all* those secrets and tell *all* those *well*-in*ten*tioned *lies*.

We drive the short distance between my parents' house and Cathy and Carter's a*part*ment with hearts *racing*. We hide our *cars* and sneak into their a*part*ment to *wait*. We needn't have *hurried*. Carter's a *very tho*rough *gas-get*ter. He records the *octane*, the *price*, the number of *gallons* ... *and* ... he calculates the miles per gallon on the *spot* after *every fill*-up.

We huddle there in the dark for a *long* time, reliving my *mom's* surprise and an*tic*ipating *Cathy's*. We giggle so hard we *all* nearly wet our *pants*. *F*inally, Cathy and Carter ar*rive*. Be*fore* they flip on the *lights*, my mom starts playing *"For She's a Jolly Good Fellow"* on our grandmother's be*loved hand*-me-*down Chick*ering *up*right piano.

The *rest* of us burst into song. *Cathy* bursts into *tears*. My dad's *heart* nearly bursts out of his *chest*. ... [PAUSE]

And *so* ends the most memorable night in Standing *history* ... *and*, I would submit, not a bad night for *Steinway*, *eithe*r. [LONG PAUSE]

CHAPTER 10

STANDING on Ceremony ...

Even though, *technically*, the piano story isn't about *me* ... I couldn't leave ... our *all-time best* family *story* ... *out* of my autobiography ... because it *tells* you a lot a*bout* me. It tells you where I get my sense of ceremony and cele*bra*tion.

Sure, my dad *could* have made good on his Pat O'Brien's promise more *simply*. He *could* have purchased and presented Victoria in a less e*la*borate *way*, but why *would* he? Why settle for a mere trans*ac*tion when, with a little planning, a little pizzazz and a *lot* of pas*sion*, you can a*ston*ish and de*light* everyone you love *most* in the *world*? In *my* family, anything we consider worth *cele*brating, we celebrate *BIG* ... out on a *limb* ... over the *top* ... off the *charts*! I *like* that about us.

Be*yond that*, watching my *parents*, I learned that Standings keep their *word*. We don't take vows we don't intend to *keep*, whether we *say* them in our wedding ceremonies or *write* them on cocktail napkins in smoky *piano* bars. We find the failure ex*cru*ciating if we discover or decide we can't keep a *promise*—even a promise we *should*n't *keep*.

Right or *wrong*, good or *bad*, for *bet*ter or *worse*, this story illustrates how we *lived*. Watching my parents' marriage, *hear*ing their *stories*, told me how love should look and *feel* ... or at least how it *could* look and feel. As you might i*mag*ine, I emerged from childhood with some fairly *un*realistic expec*ta*tions about *love*. In *your* childhood home, love probably didn't look and feel the way it looked and felt in *mine*, but I didn't *know* that growing up. As most kids *do*, I as*sumed *every*body had parents like mine. I assumed *all* marriages worked like theirs did. I assumed *all* couples laughed and loved the way *they* laughed and loved.

I was *wrong*. *Some*day, perhaps I'll write *another* book about *how* wrong, titled something like *"Miss UnderSTANDING."* Fear *not*, I feel *bet*ter, not *bit*ter, and that mythical future book would include some hearty *laughs*. In *spite* of that *om*inous *ti*tle and the married life that *prompt*ed it, I have had a *great*, often hi*lari*ous, *life*.

Long before I got married, life forced me to ad*just* my knee-jerk *opti*mistic outlook to fit the *less* positive reality that existed *out*side my childhood *home*. That adjustment took a *long* time and inflicted a fair amount of pain along the *way*. I *hope*, over *time* (and even *at* the time), I mas*saged* that pain into a kind of *wis*dom. Where I *haven*'t, I hope, at *least*, my story stands as an entertaining *caution*ary tale for others whose lives *veer* off into *unforeseen snags*—be they *self*-inflicted or imposed by *oth*ers.

Bottom *line*: over time I adopted the quixotic philosophy that has served me *well*. *Simply*, *"If you don't get what you want, find a way to love what you get anyway."* [PAUSE]

I tend to agree with the conventional wisdom among psychologists that says people often look *up* their family trees and either *sub*consciously be*come* one of their parents ... or ... *quite con*sciously choose *NOT* to become *either* of them. [PAUSE]

Our parents' 50th Anniversary party in 2007.

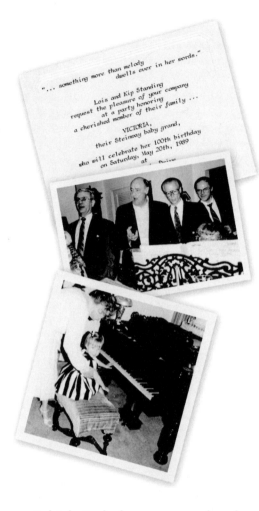

"... something more than melody
dwells ever in her words."

Lois and Kip Standing
request the pleasure of your company
at a party honoring ...
a cherished member of their family ...

VICTORIA,
their Steinway baby grand,
who will celebrate her 100th birthday
on Saturday, May 20th, 1989
at _____

If that's *true*, I must have looked up *my* family tree and decided to become a combo platter of *my parents*. I realized I didn't have it *in* me to become my *mother* en*tire*ly. Oh, I followed in her footsteps pro*fess*ionally—writing, editing, debating, *story*-telling. We're peas in a pod in *many* re*spects*, but, in re*lations*hips, I followed in my *father*'s footsteps. I became ... a *feather* duster ... to a *fault*. Like my *dad*, I tend to give *great*, unexpected *gifts*. Like *both* of my parents, I've been known to throw some pretty memorable *parties*. I'm better at brainstorming *ideas* and fixing things in the *moment*—great in a *crisis*—but you wouldn't want me running the show day to *day*. You'd want my mom and my sister, *Cathy*, for *that*.

I think *Cathy* became a *combo* platter of our parents, *too*—full of mirth and clear-headed in a crisis like our *father* but smart in many of the ways our *mom* is smart—executive smart, *visionary* smart. ... Cathy inherited our *mother*'s ability to direct the show day to *day* ... and to say *no* when she *should*. [PAUSE] My dad and I don't *have* that.

I love a line credited to Confucius: "Seek not all qualities in one individual." [PAUSE] During my teen years, I should have applied that wisdom to the Standings, but I was too young to grasp it. Each of us brings certain "gifts." Maybe I run into trouble later because I "seek all qualities" in my individual family members. I expect the wrong things from the wrong people, even myself. We work so well as a unit that I miss the subtleties in our personalities.

There's nothing subtle about our celebrations, however. Cathy and I laugh about Victoria's "STANDING" in our family. When Victoria turns 100 in 1989, our parents call a caterer, roll up their rugs, hire the St. Louis Ragtimers to play, put up party tents in the back-yard, order a multi-tiered cake and throw her a party bigger than either of our weddings. People bring amazing gifts—an antique metronome, sheet music from the year she was born, a Victorian-era doll—all gifts ... for a piano!

The fun begins at 6:30 p.m! Please join us for

Cocktails and dinner

Music, dancing, and entertainment
with THE ST. LOUIS RAGTIMERS

A songbook sing-along and "afterglow"

We don't mind. We think of Victoria as our sedentary, dark-complexioned, much older, musically gifted sister ... one who deserves her place at the center of our family. [PAUSE]

For the record, if you ask our hockey-skate mom how to care for one of "the world's finest pianos," she'll tell you ... "With a feather duster, of COURSE." SHE oughta KNOW.

PIANO-STORY EPILOGUE:

Years *later*, *long* after Victoria's ar*ri*val and *e*ven after her 100th-*birth*day cele*bra*tion ... at my Uncle Earl's funeral *lunch*eon ... to lighten the *mood*, my dad decides to send my mom a*noth*er cocktail-napkin *mes*sage, *this* time rolled up and stuck in a *gi*ant green *o*live.

As he passes it down the *ta*ble to her, my mom gets all ex*cited* and says, *"Ooooh! Good THINGS usually come from messages like THIS."*

She *unrolls* it expectantly and reads my dad's *"LOVE note"* for all to *hear*: [PAUSE]

"Someday ... I'll SELL your Steinway." [LONG PAUSE]

When he sees the *horrified* look on her face, he says, *"Whatzamatter, Bay-bee?"* [PAUSE]

CHAPTER 11

WithSTANDING Idle Gossip ...

[HIGH-PITCHED, CHILDISH TAUNT] *"Sticks and stones may break my bones, but WORDS ... will never HURT me."* [PAUSE]

[RESUME ADULT VOICE] What a *crock*!

Anyone who be*lieves* that *"sticks-and-stones"* line ... doesn't live in the same world *I* do ... doesn't live among the *hu*man population, anyway. In *my* world, *words* ... are just about the *ONLY* things that *can* hurt me.

As long as they don't *kill* me, I can withstand *rope* burns and light-ning strikes and out-of-control cars and speeding *bul*lets, but ... I will carry *some words* ... some entire conversations ... to my *grave* ... even if words *can't* put me *in* one.

Oh, no *doubt*, I have delivered *my* share of *hurt*ful *words*. If and where I have *done* that, I am *truly sorry*. I cringe at the thought that someone may go to his or *her* grave bearing a verbal bruise *I put* there.

Under*stand*, I do *not* apologize for *"telling the truth in love,"* as the Bible and many of the world's religions say we *must*—holding each other ac*count*able, serving as witnesses to each other's lives in a way that builds us *both* up and builds up the human community as a *whole*—but ... where I have told the *"truth"* ... *not* in love ... but out of my own *ego*, my own *hurt* or hostility, I *do* apol*o*gize. [PAUSE]

On the *flip* side, if I could go back and erase *one* person's unkind words said *to* or a*bout me* ... the person whose words unleashed—unwittingly perhaps—3 of my life's *worst* nightmares, one on *top* of another ... *I* would *erase* the words of ... Jeff *Hub*bard (*not* his real name).

I change his name here as a sign of for*give*ness. He was young and behaved *stupidly* ... re*peat*edly ... but I have *no* wish to *"out"* his stu-pidity *here*, more than 35 years *after* the *fact*.

Still ... "MAN, JEFF, that's ONE do-over I wish I could grant ... to YOU ... FOR me."

William Shakespeare, as usual, said it better than I *ever could*:

> *"... he that filches from me my good NAME*
> *Robs me of that which ... not enriches HIM*
> *And makes ME ... POOR inDEED."*
> —*Othello*, Act III, Scene 3
> [emphasis added]

Jeff Hubbard robbed me of my good name. Beginning in 7th grade and pretty much all the way through 9th grade—2 solid years (an eternity in the cruel confines of junior high), Jeff spread rumors about me that, simply, were ... NOT ... true. He told anyone who would listen, *"Kelly Standing is a whore."*

That almost makes me laugh now, given how far-fetched it was. I don't doubt there are 7th-grade "whores" in some neighborhoods now, and, maybe some even existed in some neighborhoods then, but in our buttoned-up St. Louis burb ... back then? NO WAY.

7th Grade.

If Jeff meant I was a girl who took *money* for *sex*, he was just com-*pletely* in*sane*. Even if I had *wanted* to, I couldn't have made that work. [RUSHED] I had a be*fore*-school *babysitting job, an after-school *babysitting job ... *field* hockey practice ... *plus* home*work*. [MOCK ENTHUSIASM] Hey, *wait* a *minute*! I probably could have made a *lot* more money *his* way. [EXASPERATED] *Ugh! Jeff, you doofus!*

If he *merely* meant I was a girl who *"... would have sex with anything that MOVED ..."* ... or that I ... *"slept aROUND,"* as I heard Jeff frequently worded it, he missed the *accuracy* mark *there, too.*

I'll ad*mit* I got started *early sex*-wise—but not *that* early—and when I *did* get around to it, I explored the subject dis*creetly* and monoga-mously, *under* my parents' *radar* and between 2 ine*xperienced but consenting *teens*, if not a*dults*. Hey, it was the '70s, the era of *"If it FEELS good, DO it!"* I didn't have to hold my *nose* to drink *that* Kool-Aid.

My parents qualify as *truly stel*lar *parents*—BOTH of them. They didn't overlook *much* in terms of raising responsible, law-abiding *citizens, *but* if my *not* having sex *mat*tered to them, they *both* forgot to *men*tion it.

Years *later*, when I ask my mom why they never brought *up* the sub-ject, she says, *"I was always waiting for you to ASK."* [GAME-SHOW BUZZER SOUND!!!]

[DEEP ANNOUNCER VOICE] *"I'm sorry ... WRONG answer, but thanks for playing."*

They told me not to *steal*. I didn't *steal*. They told me not to *cheat*. I didn't *cheat*. If *not* having sex *mat*tered to them, I think they should have told me not to *do* it. ... I *get* it. The world was morphing be-fore their very eyes in *those* days—from the merely *flirty '50s* to the downright *sexy '60s*. *Their* parents hadn't prepared *them* (except for my English grandmother's ob*scure* observation to my *dad* ... about a*voiding "nasty girls"* ...), so *my* parents didn't prepare *me*. A*gain* ... [GAME-SHOW BUZZER SOUND!!!] [PAUSE]

For the *record*, I went about it *differently* with my *own* child. ... I felt *so* strongly about the lack of preparedness *I* felt ... and saw among my *peers* ... about that oddly intimidating but en*tirely natural topic

... I ended up *researching, writing* and de*livering* a program for *par*ents *titled "Where Do PARENTS Come From? ... How and When to Talk to Your Kids about S-E-X."* It drew the school's highest attendance *EV-ER* at a PTA meeting—standing room *only*—not because of *me* but because *so many* parents struggle with the *topic ... fear* it, in *fact* ... but want to approach it *bett*er and more *com*fortably with their *own* kids than their *parents* approached it with *them*. I began the session by inviting audience members to *share* what turned *out* to be hi*larious* recol*lections* about the *various* ways parents had gone about sex education ... *or* ... the elaborate ways they *avoided* it. [PAUSE]

A few months into 7th *grade*, classmates, many of whom I don't even *know*, start telling me, [YOUTHFUL] *"Jeff Hubbard is spreading RUmors about you."* Mind you, I *barely know* Jeff at *this* point. We had hung out with a bunch of other kids over the summer between 6th and 7th *grade* at a neighborhood *park*, where we *rode* bikes, hung on playground equipment we had out*grown* and didn't do much of *anything, really* ... just *laughed, talk*ed, kicked the dirt a*round* under our *feet*, the way awkward middle schoolers *some*times *do*—only *mem*orable for how *un*-memorable it all seems.

As 7th grade wears *on*, things get *ugly* ... then *hid*eous. I almost never *see* Jeff. We don't have *any class*es together, and we rarely pass each other in the halls of our big s*ub*urban *school. Still*, I keep hearing what he's *saying* about me, and I can't wrap my *head* around it.

At *first*, I try the family *formu*la: *"PerseVERE!"* [THRUSTING SWORD GESTURE]

I try just to let it roll *off*, attempting to channel Winston Churchill with a*noth*er English chestnut my family holds dear: [DEEP] *"If you're going through hell, KEEP GOing."*

Jeff wears me *down*. It seems he tells *every*one a never-ending series of sa*lacious lies* about me.

"She's a whore." ... "She's a whore." ..."She's a whore."

Boys start showing me stupid, suggestive cartoons and talking to me in *un*welcome, *too*-fami*li*ar *ways. One* kid I *barely* know even clips a *"REGular"* comic from his Sunday funny papers (one I had en*joyed* my*self* up until that *point*). He brings it to *school* on

*Mon*day and waves it in my *face* in the cafe*teria*, not caring *who* sees or *hears* him, saying, [TAUNTING]*"Look at THIS, Kelly ... 'Boner's ARK' ... I bet you know a lot about THAT ... BOH-ners ... BOH-ners."* [GRIMACE]

Occasionally, Jeff spreads his venom to people he doesn't *realize* are my friends or *team*mates, and they helpfully (*and hurt*fully) tell me what he has *said*. I don't think they set him *straight*; they don't *dare*, for fear of becoming a *tar*get and/or being identified with *me* ... but ... *help*ful or *hurt*ful, they fill me *in*.

"He told you WHAT?!" ... "And he based this on WHAT?! ... I barely KNOW him." ... "Why would he DO that?!" ... "I don't GET it." ... "Why would he SAY that?" ...

I never get *any* answers. Ap*par*ently, he never sticks around to de*fend* or ex*pand* upon the character-assassinating gre*nades* he lobs ... *about* me ... but never ... *to* me. He doesn't vary his *theme* ... *"whore, slut, sleeps with ANYthing"* ... *"whore, slut, sleeps with ANYone"* ... *"whore, slut ..."* [TRAIL OFF ... PAUSE]

In terms of de*fend*ing myself, I don't know *how* ... don't have a *clue*. How do you prove a *neg*ative? How do you prove you're *not* do-ing something? I figured ... *maaay*be ... by not *doing* it, but I was al*ready "not doing"* it. It's not like you can pass around a picture of yourself NOT having sex ... as *proof* you're NOT having *sex*. [EX-ASPERATED SIGH] I figure de*mand*ing evidence or challenging him *pub*licly would *not* be the way to go ... 'cause ... if *HE* would lie about me ... who's to say he doesn't have *oth*er guy friends willing to do the same *thing*? I feel stuck ... with no good way to dig myself *out*. ...

Given my early childhood ad*ven*tures and my sup*por*tive-but-*strict* up*bringing, I'm a *strong* little *miss*, able to endure a *lot*, but, eventu-ally, Jeff *gets* to me. I go from *mad* ... to *sad* ... to pa*thetic*.

Kids often beg for spare change at the end of our *lunch* line so they can buy the *Twink*ies, Hostess *fruit* pies and Lay's po*tato* chips that don't *come* with our plate *lunch*es. I *fool*ishly hand over *fist*fuls of my *hard*-earned *ba*bysitting money ... and *des*perately hope *that* might help turn the *tide* ... *des*perately hope it might *"buy BACK"* the *good name* Jeff has *sto*len from me.

That strategy *back*fires. Kids I *don't want* to like me start seeking me *out*. Kids I *do* hope will like me, under*stand*ably, find my *new* form of *pub*lic generosity *strange* (or, perhaps they see it for the cloying effort it *is*), and *they* keep their *dis*tance.

I feel inex*pli*cably a*shamed*, even though I haven't *done* anything. I want *so* much to be *liked* ... to be for*gi*ven for whatever it is I *did* to ignite this *mad*ness. I want people to see in *me* ...the good I find it *so easy* to see in *them*. I go about it the wrong *way*. I make costly mis*takes*. I don't want my *par*ents to *know*.

I experience my solo flight through this troubling storm as a hefty *down*side of my parents' über-high *stand*ards and ... *usu*ally stellar *par*enting. Over the years, as I grow *up*, they tell me I'm *smart*. They tell me to ... *trust* my *in*stincts. *Ear*ly and *of*ten, they *tell* me I can be *any*thing I want to *be*. I can clear *any hurdle*. *All* good *mess*ages ... to a *point* (like *"Battle Hymn of the Tiger Mother"* with German and British *ac*cents). *Some*how, I guess I mis*take*nly believe that ... all their *con*fidence in me ... means I should have *all* my *own* ... answers. I think it means I'm not al*lowed* to have any flaws or to make any mis*takes*, and I *guess* I fear they will see this mess with Jeff as a weakness in *me some*how, as if I de*served* it or pro*voked* it or should have handled it *bet*ter or *soon*er. [PAUSE]

When I *fin*ally have had e*nough*—when someone shares whatever Jeff's *"last-straw"* statement *is*, I break down in my *math* class, *sob*bing. I confide in my teacher, and he sends me to see one of our *sev*eral *prin*cipals. I tell *him* my story but *beg* him not to *do* or say *any*thing to *Jeff*. I fear *that* would only make matters *worse*.

And, *"Please, oh, please, oh, please, DON'T tell my parents. I don't want them to know the things he SAID about me. It's too emBARrassing."*

Why don't I want them to *know*? Why do I *beg* the principal *not* to *tell*? It's *not* that I don't *trust* my parents. I *do*. I know they love me and probably, on *some* level, I even know they could *help* me, but *what* little girl wants her *par*ents to hear such *aw*ful *things* about her?

Still, my reluctance to tell them goes be*yond* embarrassment ... be*yond* shame. At *that* age, I want to make my own *way*. I had often heard my mom recite a poem about *par*enting, *"As parents we give* *our children 2 things: one is roots, the other wings."* They had given me such *great* roots. I guess I figured, by 7th *grade*, I should have sturdy enough *wings* ... to fly *solo.*

Be*fore* Jeff starts spreading his *lies*, I *love* wearing fairly feminine *clothes—cute, cur*rent and *co*lorful. Within a few *months*, I a*ban*don my *style* and try to become ... in*visible*. I start wearing flannel shirts and the *same* pair of jeans to school *every day—*jeans with a shredded *rip all* the way up to my *knee* on one *leg*.

"Look at ME."   *"Look AWAY."*

The early '70s brought a ridiculously lax *dress* code to my public *school*. We could wear almost *anything*—except for *one* kid who gets suspended for wearing an American *flag* on the seat of his *pants*. The leg of my jeans gets caught in my *bicycle* chain one morning as I pedal to my be*fore*-school *babysitting job*. I re*fuse* to *fix* it. I don't take any heat from the *school* about it, but my "*wardrobe mal-function*" prompts *many* heated arguments with my *mother*. She thinks I'm being re*bell*ious (and maybe I *am*), but, unbeknownst to *her*, I'm also being *bull*ied, and I see my an*drog*ynous *wardr*obe as a kind of *arm*or against Jeff's at*tacks*.

When you're 12, 13 and 14 years *old*, you can't always *see* possibilities beyond your *pain*. You *ov*erestimate how much other people *think* about you. Things seem ... black and *white*. At *that* age, *I* feel like the "*WHOLE WORLD*" thinks *ter*rible *things* about me ... every *day*. Jeff's pretty *tho*rough ... pretty re*lent*less. Hardly a day goes *by* that *some*one doesn't say *some*thing. I begin to think terrible things about my*self*. I don't want my parents to *know* because, from my limited, junior-high per*spec*tive, I think they're the only 2 people left on the *plan*et who still think *high*ly of me. I don't *want* them to know because I'm *not* willing to make it ... *100%*.

I don't think I fear *pun*ishment if they find *out*. Aside from wearing clothes my parents don't *like*, I haven't done anything *wrong* ... yet. In*stead*, I *think* I fear pol*lut*ing that *am*azing, *cel*ebratory atmosphere we Standings have en*joy*ed. We have a *very* close *family* with a lot of cherished tra*dit*ions, *in*side jokes and colorful *stor*ies ... lovingly pre*served* and *fre*quently, hil*ar*iously re-told by my *mom*. I don't want to add *this* story to our family *al*bum. I can't *imag*ine a happy *end*ing. *No*, I don't withhold this part of my life because I don't *trust* my parents; I withhold it because I *do* trust them and because I value the *idyll*ic childhood they gave *Cathy* and me. I don't want it to *end*. [PAUSE]

*Sad*ly—irre*spons*ibly, I believe—the principal honors *both* of my re*quests*. He doesn't confront *Jeff*, and he doesn't contact my *par*ents. I don't think *he* wants to deal with this any more than *I* do. In *ret*rospect, I *firm*ly believe ... he *made* ... the *wrong choice*. It was his JOB ... his *DUTY* to *deal* with it ... or to find someone ... *high*er up the *lad*der ... who *would*.

Later, when my *own* daughter reaches *middle school* and encounters an unrelenting bully of her *own*—ironically, just before *Columbine*—I speak *up*. Based on *my own* experience from junior *high* and observations as a parent volun*teer* ... and based on my *daugh*ter's experience, our school district hires me to write and launch a program I title *"Civility Becomes Reality in America's Middle Schools."*

It shouldn't sur*prise* me that *her* school encounters in the '90s what *my* school failed to address in the '70s. Bullies keep doing what they *do* because they get a*way* with it ... because no one *stops* them and everyone *fears* them, *e*ven the people in *charge*. This makes me think of Danny *Beck*ett, the bully from 1966, with a penchant for *noos*es. I didn't think of Danny *then*, in the midst of Jeff's junior-*high* harassment or even during my daughter's trials, but, as I tell this part of my story *now*, it reminds me of *Danny*.

As great as my dad's reaction *was* to the Baby Pattaburp incident ... and it *was* great ... phen*om*enal ... extraordinary ... the fact re*mains* ... Danny Beckett *"got a WAY with it."* Not a good *prec*edent. I a*gree* Danny shouldn't have been the *main* focus that day, but he probably should have gotten *some* attention. Something tells me he's getting a *lot* of it *now* ... probably behind *bars*. [PAUSE] I believe bullying *can* stop; we just have to take it *seriously*. Con*front* it ... in*tell*igently.

That *day*, at my junior *high*, on the way *from* my *prin*cipal's office *to* my *Span*ish class ... already in *prog*ress ... after 2 very *diffi*cult *years*, the Universe finally *puts* me *face-to-face* with *Jeff*, *just* the 2 of us, in a wide, *emp*ty hall lined with metal *lock*ers. *He* comes from *one* direction; *I* come from an*oth*er, like a scene from *High Noon* and a scene from *Glee* morphed into *one*. When he *sees* me, he turns as if he's about to *run*.

I say, [FIERCE] *"DON'T YOU RUN ... AWAY FROM ME."*

He stops mid-*piv*ot and turns back to *face* me. I think he *knows* I will hunt him down like a *dog* if he runs. I'm *furious*, suddenly breathing *hard*, with hot, *an*gry tears spilling down my *cheeks*, but I'm in con*trol*, white-hot ... laser-sharp con*trol*. The tears come with*out* sobs; I'm *not* boo-hoo*ing*. They're not that kind of *tears*. It feels *al*most like I am *lit*erally boiling *over* and the *tears* are just *steam* ... finding an *exit*.

"WHY?!" I de*mand* to know from 20 feet a*way*. Slowly, moving closer and closer *to* him, I ask a*gain*. His eyes look like those of a stricken *deer*.

"WHY?" I in*sist* he answer me, now with maybe *10* feet between us. *"WHY?! ... WHY have you spent the past 2 YEARS saying AWful things about me?"* I stop about 5 feet a*way*, *not* wanting to get *any* closer to someone I consider *so vile* ... someone who has *hurt* me *so* much for *so* long.

At *first*, he takes a kind of *half*-hearted de*fens*ive posture, *"YOU know WHY."*

That sur*prises* me. It throws me off my *game* for a moment. [STAR-TLED] *"I do NOT know why. How would I know WHY? ... What did I EVer DO to you ... to deserve THIS?"*

"YOU ... KNOW."

[ALMOST QUIVERING W/ ANGER] *"I do NOT know."*

I can *tell* by the look on his *face* that he realizes for the *first* time I *really* ... DON'T know. Then he goes from de*fens*ive to this *odd* kind of ... *hurt-little-boy* posture and *tone*. A*gain*, it throws me off *balance*.

"I LIKED you," he says, his lip starting to quiver.

[INCREDULOUS] *"What?!"*

"I LIKED you. ... When we hung out at Whispering Hills Park, I LIKED you."

"AND ..."

"And ..." He looks down at his feet and *sniffles, "And ...* [HURT] *YOU didn't like me BACK."*

"What?!" I can't be*lieve* what I'm *hearing*.

"I didn't even KNOW. That was 2 SUMmers ago. Are you KIDding?! You have made my life a living hell EVery day ... from THEN to NOW ... because you LIKED me? This is how you LIKE someone?!"

He doesn't *speak*. He doesn't *dare*; I'm on a *roll*, asking my questions *only* rhetorically now. His *juvenile* explanation hangs out there be*tween* us like a piece of *used den*tal *floss* ... of *NO* use to *any*one.

[AS IF SORTING IT OUT] *"You didn't TELL me you liked me ... but you LIKED me, and ... I didn't like you BACK."*

When I *sum*marize it for him like that ... I can *tell* he realizes how *stu*pid it sounds.

"That's what ALL this has been aBOUT. ..." [SHAKE HEAD IN DISBELIEF] [PAUSE]

After *that,* I'm *spent* ... and *speech*less. I head down the hall to *Span*ish class ... suddenly sorry for *him,* suddenly aware that *I'm* not the *only* one who feels *ill*-equipped to handle *junior high.* I realize I have more of *my* poop together than *he* does. All a*long,* I thought *he* had all the *pow*er, when, in *fact,* all he *real*ly had was ... *fear* ... and *hurt* ... and *cow*ardice ... [SOFTER] *and* ... a *crush.* [LONG PAUSE]

Jeff Hubbard didn't *cause* the nightmares on my immediate ho*ri*zon; his words merely lit a *fuse,* and then my *own* ... *ill*-advised *choices* ... doused that spark with *gas*oline. We go *on* to make a le*thal *tag* team, Jeff and *I,* and he never even *knows* it, *his* role mostly *fin*ished at *this* point.

Good or bad, that's the *power* of *words*; once we *speak* them, we walk a*way* and may *nev*er realize the *harm* we've *done* or the *help* we've *been* ... to the people we leave in their *wake.*

Sticks and stones, in*deed*!

CHAPTER 12

STANDING and Forgiving ...
or *Not* ...

Briefly, things cool down a bit *after* my junior-high hallway show-down with *Jeff.* In *fact,* he even calls me that evening as my family's heading out the door for dinner at Rinaldi's, our *favorite pizza* place.

"I'm REALly sorry," he says earnestly. *"I hope you can forGIVE and forGET."*

Too easily ... *too* automatically, I say, *"I can forGIVE you, Jeff."*

"CAN I?" I wonder, with the words already out of my *mouth.* Knowing what I know about sticks and *stones,* I add, *"... but the forGET-ting part will be a LOT HARDer. It'll take a lot LONGer."*

"Yeah," he admits. *"I guess SO."*

We *both* know that's not *his* problem. Forgetting will be *my* job. Clearly, 35 years *later,* I'm still *work*ing on that ... but ... actually, I have come to *realize,* as long as I *truly* forgive, I don't *need* to forget. I couldn't if I *wanted* to. Relative to Jeff and the angst that *followed* ... I have attempted, in*stead,* to reframe those memories. I have applied the *"Baby Pattaburp Forgiveness Formula"*: Look for the *good. Find* the good. Celebrate the *good.*

On the phone with *Jeff,* I suggest he could *help* the forgiveness process along by going back to everyone he has *lied* to about me ... and *tell*ing them he *lied. Not* sur*pris*ingly, *that* prompts a *long silence* from *his* end of the *line.* He says he can *see* how *that* would *help.*

It *never happens.* Even during that *phone* call, we *both* know it won't. We *both* know by then ... *I'm* the stronger person. *I* will have to repair the damage with*out* his help. [PERKY] On the *plus* side, he *does* stop lying, so *that* helps ... a *little.*

80

Un*bur*dened, Jeff gets off the *phone*. My mom hears just a *snip*pet of *my* side of the conversation.

"What was THAT about?" she asks, grabbing her purse and heading for the *door*.

Very casually, trying *not* to display even *one drop* of the day's emotion, I say, *"Oh, that was just a guy from SCHOOL. He said something MEAN about me and just called to say he was ... SORry and hoped I would ... [LIGHT] forgive and forget. I told him I can for-GIVE, but I'm not sure I can forGET."*

"Well, you know, Kell ... if you DON'T forGET, you'll never really for-GIVE." ...

Hmmm ...

What does she *mean*? I don't want to *ask*. Back *then*, I don't want to *press* my mom about it for fear of launching a conversation I don't care to *have* ... for fear of revealing this *"flawed"* part of myself I don't want my parents to *see*.

Still, back then I think, *"SHE tells stories from HER past about people who hurt HER—playmates, co-workers, even her PARents. She laughs when she tells HER stories. ... Will I EVer get to the point where I feel comfortable telling 'The JEFF HUBBARD Story'? ... Is THAT what forgiveness LOOKS like? Is THAT what forgiveness MEANS ... being able to tell a story for OTHers' enterTAINment or eduCAtion ... withOUT hurtful emotions atTACHED? ... Hmmm."*

In *any* event, in that *moment*, I'm not sure *how* my mom's *"if-you-DON'T-forGET-you'll-never-REALLY-forGIVE"* com*ment* should inform my *own* horizon.

I pre*fer* to focus on the thin-crust sausage and onion on my more im*med*iate horizon at Ri*nal*di's. ...

Uh, oh! Looking *back*, perhaps my decision not to tell provides the quiet *kick*off for a *life*time of emotional *eat*ing. ... Stuff your *face*; stuff your *feel*ings.

CHAPTER 13

STANDING with My Back against a Wall ...

It ap*pears* I may not have been the *only* one who can't for*get* Jeff's un*for*tunate trashing of my character and theft of my *"good name."* Shortly *after* our confron*tation* and *his* con*tri*tion, we head from *ju*nior high to *high* school. One Saturday *night*, I attend a *party*, a hot, sweaty, parent-sanctioned *party packed* with kids, *most* of whom I vaguely *know* but hope to be*friend*, somewhat *less* desperately *now*, thanks to the passage of the *crisis* and *clearing* of the *air*.

We're all jammed into the *basement*, rockin' and rollin' to the blaring beat of Bachman-Turner Overdrive ... with the lights *off*, of course! *Pic*ture it ... one big roiling mass of 14-*year*-old hor*m*onal hu*m*anity.

*Apparently, Cathy didn't **always** have better taste and better clothes than I did.*

It gets *so* hot several of us spill out onto the concrete slab of patio off the *back* of the *house*. I know *one* of the *boys* ... from classes we've had together. I neither particularly like *nor dis*like him. He asks whether I'd like to take a walk to cool *off* ... maybe walk around the *block* to our *high* school—just around the *corner*—and *back*.

"Sure!" ... [PAUSE]

We interrupt this story ... to bring you ... a few observations about the fashions of the day (the mid-1970s). ...

A girl who's trying to enhance her social prospects can't wear just *anything* to a gathering like *this*. I want to look *really* cute ... *casual* ... *current* ... but ... *not* look like I'm *try*ing too hard. Nothing in *my* closet fits that de*scrip*tion. But, just down the *hall* ... lies the [AWE-STRUCK] ... Holy *Grail* of *gar*ments ... my *sis*ter's *clos*et. ...

*U*sually, re*mark*ably, Cathy *willingly and *gen*erously shares her clothes with me. She HATES it, however, if I borrow them without *ask*ing ... if I even enter her *room* without *ask*ing. She sets 2 very reasonable *bound*aries:

First, "If you want to borrow something for SCHOOL, ask me the night beFORE; DON'T wake me up in the morning begging 'cause the answer will be NO." My early-morning babysitting job gets me up and out the door before *her* alarm goes *off*, hence *that* stipula-tion.

... and ...

"Don't go into my room if I'M not THERE."

[BUSINESS-LIKE TONE] *Very* rea*sona*ble *bound*aries, in*deed*. [PAUSE ... SMIRK] I ig*nore* them re*peat*edly. ... I don't *do* it to make her mad. Typical of *first*borns, Cathy is more of a *plan*ner when it comes to wardrobe (and almost everything *else*). As the *baby* of the family, *I* approach fashion (and almost everything *else*) with more of a ... *down-to-the-WIRE, see-what-FEELS-good/LOOKS-good/SMELLS-good-in-the-MOment* attitude.

*Clear*ly, Cathy and I find ourselves at cross-*pur*poses over that ... a LOT ... en*tirely my fault*. Eventually, occasionally, I *do* start ignor-ing Cathy's boundaries ... *just* to make her *mad*. The more *"sphinc-tery"* she *gets* about it, the more I push that *but*ton. We can't be the *only* siblings to display *THAT* dynamic. ...

This par*tic*ular Saturday *night*, I hope to borrow something that fits my *needs*. Cathy has *THE* perfect shirt to go with my *bell*-bottom *jeans*—a *silky* 100% poly*ester (of *course*!) *long*-sleeved *"Saturday Night FEver"*-style *shirt* ... with a *muted pas*tel blue and purple *land*-scape printed *all* the way around the blouse, *front and back*—even across the *but*tons—and a *big* collar and *cuffs*. My sister has *great* taste! She always knows what's *"on trend"*—did *then*, does *now*.

By the time I *realize* I want to *borrow* this ... [GUSHING, EXCITED] exquisite shirt ... one that makes *just* the statement I want to *make*, [GLUM] I *also* realize, [ALARMED] *"Noooo! Cathy's not HOOOOOOME!"*

We don't *have cell* phones. I can't *call* her. ... I decide it's worth whatever penalty she might exact *later* ... or ... [EXAGGERATED SINISTER EXPRESSION] maaaybe I can ...[FAST] take it *out*, put it *on*, wear it *out*, bring it *back*, air it *out*, hang it *up* ... and she'll *never know*. [WIDE EYES, SMILING]

"As long as I don't 'PIT it out' too much, THAT could WORK. If she's BAbysitting, she PRObably won't get HOME until after MY curfew, ANYway." This strikes me as *a brill*iant though abs*olut*ely *forbid*den *plan*. [PONDERING ...]

[ABRUPT] *"This is an eMERgency,"* I *tell* myself. Rules are made to be *broken* ... in *e*mergencies. [PAUSE]

To this *day*, perhaps because of some *deep-seated guilt* from my *teens*, I don't *like* breaking *rules*. I *really* don't. I suffer ex*treme* self-re*proach* and even *phys*ical dis*com*fort when I *do*. If a sign says *"No Parking,"* I don't *park* there. If a *coup*on expires *Tues*day, I don't try to *use* it on *Wednes*day. If I come upon a sign that says *"Private Property,"* I wouldn't *dream* of jumping the *fence*.

Under*stand* ... I don't re*sist* for fear of getting *caught*. I re*sist* because my parents (the *Eagle* Scout and the *editor*) made that idea part of who I *AM*. They raised me to believe, [PARENTAL] *"Character is what you do when you THINK no one is WATCHing."*

I figure I'm *always* watching ... always watching *me*. I don't want to chip away at my *own char*acter. My parents tell me (*or* ... I interpret what they *say* to mean ...), *"You can't CLAIM to have good character if you do things—even LITTLE things—you know you shouldn't DO."* That's why I've *never* understood the al*lure* of ... *shop*lifting. Why would you want to *tell* yourself, *"I'm a THIEF!"*? Why would *any*one want to compromise his or her own *char*acter—over a *candy* bar or a 6-pack ... a bottle of *nail* polish or even a sweater or a *neck*lace? If *I* did that, when I con*sumed* those things or every time I *wore* them, I would be announcing ... to my*self*, if not to the *world*, *"I'm a THIEF."*

I once practically *ruined* a concert for myself and my *date* because he found some *better, unoccupied* seats *much* closer to the stage than *ours* ... and moved us *into* them. [GASP ... BITE NAILS] I *practically* broke out in *hives*. I sat there *mortified* ... *sure* the *rightful ticket* holders would ar*rive* ... *sure* the people who had had an *unobstructed* view until *we* came along were *angry* ... feeling like I was ... *"breaking the RULES,"* taking something for which I hadn't *paid* ... something that didn't be*long* to me. I tend to be a *stickler* about such things. [PAUSE]

Now, having said *all* of that in my highly *sanctimonious tone*, in *this* case, in 1974, I de*cide* ... *"A girl's gotta DO what a girl's gotta DO. ... Hand over that HANGer!"* [PAUSE] Breaking the *rules* doesn't *feel* like breaking the *rules* when standing (ahem, *Standing*) in front of your sister's *open*, unat*tended closet*.

So here I *am* ... walking in the *dark* ... toward my *high* school on a Saturday *night*, absol*utely cert*ain I have made the *perfect choice*, *clothing*-wise if *not char*acter-wise. The *moon*light, my *dance*-in*duced* perspiration and the silky sheen of my *sister's* pilfered ... polyester ... com*bine* to give me what I i*magine* is a ... *romantic glow*. It seems to have the desired ef*fect*. This guy is *talk*ing to me ... seems to *like* me even ... *may*be ... a *litt*le. It doesn't oc*cur* to me to *ask* myself whether *I* like *him*.

It turns out he's a *smok*er and wants to have a *cig*arette.

"Uh, oh! Will that SMELL linger on Cathy's SHIRT?"

I decide to stay *up*wind. He suggests we go to the smoking lounge at school. Yes, for those who *don't know* ... in the '70s, we *actually had* smoking lounges ... at our *high schools*—usually 2 of them, in *fact*: one for *staff* and *one* ... *FOR STUDENTS!!* This guy, this sup-posedly promising new *friend*, wants to visit *ours* ... in the *dark* ... on a Saturday *night*. [PAUSE]

What part of *that* did I not detect as a *bad* idea? I missed *all* of it, I'm afraid.

In*stead*, I focus on *his* comfort ... on the *distance* ... on our inconve-nience ... and ... *last* on the list ... I focus on my *own* comfort and my not-en*tire*ly-comfortable platform *sandals*, which al*ready* hurt my feet from so much dancing and, *now, walk*ing.

I say, *"If you want to have a CIGarette, have a CIGarette.* [CELE-BRATORY] *It's Saturday NIGHT, you don't have to go to the SMOKing lounge."* ... Clearly, I *TOTALLY* miss his intention.

He tries *one* more *time* to steer me toward the *back* of the school, all the while walking toward the *front* of the school ... *through* the *park*-ing lot, a*cross* a strip of *grass* to a concrete area surrounding one of the school's *massive curved,* exposed-aggregate *stair*wells—well lit, *thank*fully.

*A*rchit*ect*urally, it's a striking *build*ing ... brand new, *very* modern with an award-winning design that includes *soft* colors, *smooth* contours with *rough tex*tures—an interesting *mix.* Too *bad* I can't say the *same* for what goes on in*side. A*cademically, *so*cially and *func*tionally, this trendy, open-space *school* never *works* ... and *not* just for *me.* They start erecting walls and *"UN-doing"* the design *al*most before we *grad*uate.

We walk *slow*ly, *grad*ually, talking about nothing in par*tic*ular, as I re*call,* flirting a little, *may*be, but nothing even re*mote*ly *vul*gar or suggestive *at all.* We end up next to the exterior wall of the stairwell—a really rough, rocky *wall.* The exposed *aggregate* features walnut-size stones with *ir*regular, *nat*ural *edges* that give it a *chunk*y texture you can see *even* from the *street.*

He finishes his *cig*arette ... the cigarette he re*luc*tantly chooses to smoke *this* side of the *smok*ing lounge. He tosses the butt a*way* with a *kind of* exci*ting* ... but *bun*gled version of a bad-boy, too-cool-for-school, James Dean/Charlie Sheen move. [FLICK IMAGINARY BUTT] He tilts his head and blows the *last* of the smoke *up* and *out* ... a*way* from me. [BLOW SMOKE]

"How poLITE!" I think.

Remembering it *now,* at 51, I hear how pa*thet*ic that sounds. At 14, I'm *so* used to mis*treat*ment I consider it *polite* when someone *doesn't* blow smoke in my face, not *rude* if he *does*—a subtle *differ*-ence but a *powerful* statement about my self-e*steem,* my state of *mind* and the psychological resources I had at the time (or *didn't* have) to pro*tect* myself. [PAUSE]

With the smoke *out* of his *lungs,* he turns to what he *has* ... *on* his *mind* (or *low*er, in his *pants,* I realize *now* but didn't see *then*).

He moves in *awk*wardly for what I be*late*dly realize is a kind of [FROWN] ... *kiss.* I say *"kind of"* kiss because I'm aware the energy between us has *shift*ed. I *mis*read it as at*trac*tion ... or af*fec*tion even ... romance, *may*be? In *truth,* it's *none* of the a*bove.*

We're *both* laughing ... kidding around, *I* think—engaging in that *slap*py, *tick*ly boy-girl stuff from ele*men*tary school you *even*tually out*grow.* It shows up occasionally even between *teen*agers, as they try to master the art of a*dult*hood. Based on my *re*cent experience with *Jeff* and his [POUT] *"You-didn't-LIKE-me"* tantrum, I didn't need *more* evidence that *boys* can remain *really* immature long after *girls* grow *up.*

I think *this* boy is just being *"THAT kind"* ... of *sil*ly.

With *both* hands, he grabs both of my arms just below my *shoul*ders. If this is supposed to be *"ROmance,"* as *I* understand it, he grips me a *bit* too firmly and squeezes me a *bit* too *force*fully ... with his thumbs digging *in* ... just above my *bi*ceps. At *this* point, I *still* think we're just 2 classmates taking a friendly, mildly flirty break from a *near*by *par*ty. If *he* has a*noth*er idea ... *I* have *NO* IDEA.

He steps *toward* me and pushes me against the *wall*—that *crag*gy, *rag*ged, oh-so-at*trac*tively *tex*tured *wall.*

"Stop!" I shriek. Listen to what I say *next.* ... Listen to where my mind goes *in*stantly, auto*mat*ically, *sad*ly, sub*con*sciously ...

"Stop! You're gonna snag my SHIRT!" Still *laugh*ing, I confess to him that I have borrowed my *sis*ter's *shirt* ... with*out* per*mis*sion, and she will *kill* me just for *wear*ing it.

I laugh, *"She'll kill me TWICE if I RUin it."*

I'm protecting Cathy's *shirt,* com*plete*ly oblivious to my *own* vul*nera*bil*ity.

He pushes a*gain,* and, *this* time, *kiss*es me ... *hard.* My 2 priorities— Cathy's *shirt* ... *and* ... being *liked*—clash. I can't concentrate on the *"kiss"* (such as it *was*) because I can't take my *mind* off ... the *shirt* ... which, as it turns out, is a *good* thing.

I say, *"SERiously, stop! You're gonna snag my SISter's SHIRT!"* I start to get *seriously* a*larmed* ... [PAUSE] ... about the *shirt.*

He's laughing. The more *I* struggle, the more *he* laughs. We engage in what I *think* is an affectionate *wrestling* match, now a few inches *away* from the wall because I *have* stood my ground *that* much. He's still laughing. I'm laughing a little *less* but still completely blind to any bad intentions ... *if* he *has* them.

Just as he moves in for another *kiss*, I see headlights over his *shoulder* ... a car pulling into the *parking* lot ... the security guard making his rounds of the *campus*.

With *that*, my *"suitor"* quickly releases his grip on my *arms* and shuts down his *engines*, and we *both* decide it's time to return to the party—me, my *bell* bottoms, my platform *sandals and* my sister's silky *"Saturday Night Fever"* shirt, *thankfully, intact*.

I think I manage to return the shirt to her closet without *out* arousing her suspicions. *This* time, on *both* counts, it appears I'll be ... *"Stayin' Alive"* to dance another *day*. [IMITATE TRAVOLTA'S ICONIC DANCE MOVE + BEE GEES' LYRIC] *"Ah, ah, ah, ah ..."*

CHAPTER 14

STANDING in High School ... and ... at the STANDINGs' Dinner Table ...

Over the next *year*, I don't recall breaking many *rules*. I keep my head *down*, get *better-than-good grades* ... ([MOCK FORMALITY] ... a rule one did *NOT* break ... if one knew ... what was good for one ... in *my* house).

I grew up in the *early* days of Title IX. The courts had *just* decreed schools must offer equal ath*letic* opportunities to girls *and* boys. Schools didn't have to offer the *same* sports to both *genders*, but, as I under*stand* it, they had to offer the same *num*ber of *options*. That meant I had a *wide* array of sports *open* to me. I lettered in *several*; field hockey ranked as my *favorite*. You gotta love a sport that lets you wear what they call a hockey *"frock" and* a *mouth* guard simul-*taneously*. At the *time*, I have mild *asth*ma. A few *less*-than-mild at*tacks* set me *back* on long *runs*, but, for the *most* part, I feel strong and *healthy*.

In the year following my brush with that James *Dean*/Charlie *Sheen* character ... against the stairwell *wall*, it seems I spend every *non*-studying, *non*-sweating, *non-snooz*ing hour ... *babysitting*. Our parents *reasonably* expect Cathy and me to make our own *spend*-ing money ... and to save for our own college tu*ition*. They instill an un*stint*ing work ethic and ... [DEEP FATHERLY VOICE] *"the value of a dollar."* Early *on*, we know they expect us to bring home a little *bacon* ... a*long* with As on our re*port* cards.

During that *year*, I *also* endure some *more fall*out from the lingering effects of Jeff Hubbard's *lies*. Someone I consider a close *friend—* my *best* friend, in *fact—*abrupt*ly* moves out of our *shared* locker and says, as a *cheer*leader, she *"can't afford to be associated with"* me anymore. She *does* it in a way that feels *cowardly* and insensi-tive, without *warn*ing, in a *note* left inside our al*ready-empty* lock*er*. After *that*, she a*voids* me. I have *casual* friends in *every* clique, *one* friend I *really* like but don't *see* very often and almost *no* one *else*.

My parents tend *not* to *ask* about the mundane details of my day. It's not that they don't *care*; they *do, very much,* but, from early childhood *on,* they encourage us ... even ex*pect* us ... to talk about things be*yond* our own *table* at *din*ner. When I say we *"talked,"* I re*ally* mean we *"held forth."* ... We debate *any*thing and *every*thing ... from *all* sides—except, of course, S-E-*X*. I know how my parents feel about practically *every*thing—re*li*gion, po*lit*ics and issues that fall in be*tween,* like a*bor*tion and capital *pun*ishment.

They don't insist Cathy and I a*gree* with them, but, if we *don't,* we *bet*ter come to the table ready to de*fend* our positions ... with ar*ticu*late *arguments* ... with *facts, not* with *fluff.* I think that prepared my sister and me for suc*cess*ful careers in public re*la*tions ... because we could talk our way *in*to or *out* of *al*most *any*thing.

Because our dad covers a *lot* of territory as a *sales*man and our *mom* works for a BIG *com*pany and reads *lots* of *books,* we always have better things to *talk* about than the daily drama of *high* school. They tell stories about the *in*teresting people they en*coun*ter at their *in*teresting *jobs.* All their *sto*ries make *work* seem like *fun* ... like an es*cape* rather than a *chore.* It makes me look *for*ward to the day when I will be *out* of high school, *out* of college and able to work full *time.* I consider that a*noth*er *great* gift of my *up*bringing; my parents taught us to LOVE and look *for*ward to ... *work.*

My parents made sure we knew what they did for a *liv*ing. It gave us a much better sense of who they *were* and why they be*haved* the way they *did*—why they expected certain things from us. My *mom* expected us to think, speak and write *clear*ly ... because that's what she *did* all day. My *dad* expected us to measure *care*fully and to clean stra*te*gically ... not slopping a dirty mop over an already-clean *floor,* for example, because *he* sold industrial floor-cleaning chemicals and knew a better *way.* I might stand there rolling my *eyes,* wondering, *"Who CARES if I push the broom THIS way or THAT way?"* but, you *know,* when I did it *his* way, more often than *not,* it worked *bet*ter and took *half* the time, *darn* it!

My parents tell us how their jobs fit into the rest of the world's ac*ti*vities. When they *like* their work, they *say* so, and they say *why.* When they *don't* like a current job or as*sign*ment, they talk about where they'll go from *there* and why they're willing to *do* something they don't *like*—saying, for example, *"Other things are more imPORtant right now. We're saving for THIS ... or planning for THAT. ..."*

When my best friend stops coming a*round*, my parents *n*otice, but they don't *pry*. I don't let them *see* what a big *deal* it is. I don't want them to *know*.

"How IS she? We haven't SEEN her in a while."

I don't re*mem*ber whether I even tell them she moved out of our *lock*er. They like her a *lot*; she laughs at my dad's jokes and holds her own in conversation, so she fits right *in*. I fear ... talking about what she had *done* ... might make them think *I* have driven away a good friend, never considering the possibility they *might* think *she* has de*sert*ed an even *bett*er one.

I gloss over her a*bs*ence, *"Yeah ... we're both really BUSY."*

I begin to *r*ealize, high school, particularly *my* high school, isn't exactly over-populated with brave or com*pass*ionate *class*mates. I don't expect *oth*erwise. Even *then*, as part of the *"herd,"* when I thought of *teen*agers ... *"unselfish"* wasn't the *first* adjective that sprang to *mind* (no offense if you *are* one; it's just the *n*ature of that *phase*, but, *I* be*lieve*, the teen years don't *have* to and *should*n't *sanc*tion *cow*ardice or *un*varnished *cru*elty).

My friend's departure from our locker (and my *life*) hurts me *ter*ribly, *but*, at the *sam*e time, I under*stand*. She's only doing pre-emp-tively what *I'*m trying to do retro*ac*tively—protect her good *name*.

Again, I chalk it up to differing levels of *cour*age. I say to my*self*, *"I'M the stronger PERson."* Jeff isn't strong enough to correct his *lies*. *She* isn't strong enough to stand up for the person she *used* to say was her *best* friend. I chalk it up to what I see as our differing degrees of com*pass*ion, different *up*bringing, incompatible priorities. *That* makes me feel more and more *diff*erent, even less and less like I fit *in*. I become an *is*land—a friendly little *mis*understood *is*land *no* one wants to *vis*it.

I feel torn between pride and hu*mil*ity—I'm still STANDING, and that's a *great* thing, but I'm *Kelly* Standing, and, *some*times, *that's* awful.

It's *funny* ... people tell me *all* the time they think I have a *"great name."* Yes, I *do*. I think so, *too*. They say I'm lucky because I was *born* with it. I would say *"blessed"* versus *"lucky,"* but, yes, I *am*. My *"great name"* —Standing—*is* wonderful. In junior high and *high* school, however, at *times* I find maintaining a ... *"good name"* to go *with* my *"great name"* ... excruciating.

In one class I *really like*—business *law*—we work on projects in *groups*. I notice people *like* to have me in their groups. Whatever *else* they may think I am—*"whore, slut ... pariah"* —they know I *also* happen to be *smart* and hard-*work*ing and even a *little* bit *funny*. I start to feel a *little* bit *better*.

I get to know a boy on one project. We hit it *off*, laugh like *crazy*, get a lot *done*. I develop a crush, soooo, when the Sadie *Hawkins dance* rolls around, I take a *deep* breath, summon *all* my baby *girl* balls, probably borrow something from *Cathy's clos*et, head to *school* ... and ... ask him to *go* with me.

He says, in the sweetest way *possible*, bravely looking me right in the *eye*, *"I think you're REALLY nice ... and I REALLY LIKE you ... but my mom ... wouldn't want me ... to go OUT with a girl LIKE YOU."* [LONG PAUSE]

I blush ... close my *eyes* ... bite my *lip* ... drop my *head* ... take a *deep* breath, then I look *back up* and say, *"I underSTAND,"* ... because I *do*.

CHAPTER 15

STANDING between a Mama Bear and Her Cub ...

"Jeff Hubbard, what have you DONE??! Now people's MOMS are talking about me??! ... Barring their sons from DATing me ... sight un-SEEN? I wonder whether you have ANy iDEa the agony YOU have unleashed."

That thought had never occurred to me, but, of *course*, the tarnishing of my ... *"GOOD name"* made me a ... *"BAD girl"* ... in the eyes of people's *parents* ... or *would* ... and this guy said *no* because he knew and respected his family's *stand*ards. I didn't *meet* them.

Parents think I am pre*cisely* the kind of *"nasty girl"* my *grand*mother tried to warn my *fath*er about. I *don't* mean this boy's mom ever *men*tioned me to him or even *knew* I existed (although she *might* have, given my 2 YEARS of *"advance publicity,"* courtesy of Jeff Hubbard Reputation *Man*agement, LLC). I *hope* not, but, I'm *sure* ... if she *did*n't ... when I asked him to the *dance,* his imag*in*ation took *off.* Perhaps he fast-forwarded to the moment he would stroll in from *school* ... and tell his *mom* Kelly *Stan*ding had invited him ... to the *Sadie Hawkins dance.*

Then the *"SPY network"* that functions *so* well within the ranks of PT*As, sports* boosters, *march*ing-band parents, parental *stage*-hands and *school* boards ... would kick into *high gear* and dish out the ... 4-1-1. Who *is* this ... [COMICALLY PRISSY, LIPS PURSED] *"... brazen little tart, Kelly STANding, who has the auDAcity to think she's good enough for MY PREcious SON?"*

This boy's mom would wobble if I had a *spot*less reputation. It's just the nature of Mother Nature ... and *Mama Bears.* But, if she found out *all* there was to know about *me* ... *well* ... she might lock him up until he turned ... *30.*

I understand com*pletely* why he declines. He knows it *hurts* me, but he does it with *class* and *kind*ness, a *rare* commodity in our high school com*mun*ity ... and about to get *rare*r *still.*

CHAPTER 16

STANDING beside a Rapist ...
Every Day ...

Along the *way*, I start making some co*lo*ssally bad decisions. A*mong* them, I begin to feel but don't en*tirely act* upon the idea that *"if I'm going to have the PAIN of this repuTAtion ANYway, maybe I should explore the PLEAsure that goes WITH it."*

*For*tunately, and I consider this a HUGE saving *grace*, I lost my vir*gin*ity to a boy I really *cared* about ... a boy who, on *some* level, I re*ally loved* ... who cared about and perhaps even loved *me*. We stayed together a *long* time by high school standards, and the relation-ship worked remarkably *well*, in *spite* of what Jeff's comments did to rock my *world*. I think my boyfriend *knew* what Jeff said, knew it wasn't *true* (because *he* was with me) ... *or* ... maybe he *hadn't* heard Jeff's as*sess*ment of *me*. He was *old*er ... at another *school*. If he *knew*, he recognized it for what it *was* ... *id*le *gos*sip ... and chose to be grown-up enough to ig*nore* it. God *bless* him!

I'm not a girl (now a *woman*) who necessarily *wants* to be *"taken CARE of." "Taking care"* of me would be a tall order for *any* man, but this high school boyfriend took care of me in a way I needed at the *time*, and I remain pro*found*ly *grate*ful.

I remember I wore a *red sweat*er on our first *date*. I think we went to a *movie*. While we sat in the *thea*ter, he put his *arm* around me in a *most* gentlemanly *way*. He put his arm around me in the *car* on the way *home*—*very* sweet and re*spect*ful. When I got *home*, I could *still* smell his Old Spice deodorant on the shoulder of my *sweat*er. I didn't wash that sweater for *weeks* ... sniffed it several times a *day*, in fact. ... Ah, puppy love! [PAUSE]

*Much la*ter, I take a *sexual miss*tep, *too* ... develop a deep crush on a guy. I think *he* feels the same *way* ... I go where I shouldn't *go* ... do what I shouldn't *do* ... and re*gret* it *in*stantly. A few days *la*ter at *school*, one of his creepy little friends comes up to me and says, *"I was wondering if you would do with ME what you did with HIM."*

"What?! ... NO! ... I don't even KNOW you. Get aWAY from me."

At least I wasn't *that* much of a *people-please*r. *Still*, thanks to *that* vivid, *m*ortifying *wa*k*e*-up *call*, I realize I have plunged myself *deep* in the *very* pile of man*ure* Jeff had de*li*vered and *from* which I so *des*perately hoped to ex*tract* myself.

"What were you THINKing?! Maybe you ARE what everybody seems to THINK you are."

Dark days, in*deed*, and about to get *dark*er. And to *think*, I helped ex*tin*guish the *light*. [PAUSE]

Through much of the earlier stuff with *Jeff*, I had a good, *good* friend who had my back ... or *tried* to ... as much as *one* really quiet, *very* shy, very sweet, privacy-seeking high schooler can have the back of another not-at-*all*-shy, seemingly-*al*ways-at-the-center-of-controversy high schooler.

As I re*call*, we have a bunch of classes together, get to be friends and end up double-dating a *lot*, often going to a funky little res-taurant across town that allows us to sit there sipping *s*oda, eating French-fried *mush*rooms and all the free *pop*corn we can *hold*, all while soaking up the soothing sounds of *"House at Pooh Corner,"* among other *favo*rites. Sometimes *4* of us would go, sometimes *6*, but we tended to be a fairly se*date* little all*i*ance, in *spite* of *my* in-clusion in the *group*.

I'll call this friend ... *Penny. Why Pen*ny? Because she de*serves* a name for the quiet but powerful role she played ... I think of her as my ... *Luc*ky Penny. I could *not* have endured parts of my high school years with*out* her. I'll hold her—my *"Lucky Penny"* —in my *heart*, if not my *hand*, as I attempt to capture this difficult *next* leg of my *jour*ney in *print*. Here *goes* ...

I break a boatload of rules on this particular night in 1975. *Penny* does, *too*. *Ummmm!* ... I make *more* unfortunate choices, and they *were* choices. I *"own"* what happens next.

Penny invites me to sleep *o*ver. All our parents are *o*ccupied for the *e*vening. For some *dumb reason—REALLY* dumb—we decide it would be a good idea to remove (OK, *steal*) some vodka from my parents' *cabinet*, then go to a *McDonald's restaurant* about *6 blocks* from Penny's *house*. We mix that vodka with *orange soda* to make *THE* WORST screwdrivers *ever conco*cte*d*; then we sit at McDonald's first getting *giggly*; and, then, unaccustomed as we *were* to *al*cohol (and we WERE unac*cus*tomed), pro*ceed* to get *utt*erly *smash*ed. Bad decisions in *so many* directions they're almost incalculable.

A group of our *friends—*my now-ex-boyfriend (on *OK-to-slightly-rocky terms*) and several guys from the *neighb*orhood who *al*so attend our *high* school ... just *happ*en to walk into McDonald's and *join* us at our little ... *"party."*

My boyfriend and I broke up for a *lot* of *re*asons. In *r*etrospect, it began to look like *he* liked/loved *me* more than I liked/loved *him*, and I thought it would be cruel to lead him *on. Al*so, our families were very *diff*erent. *Un*fairly, I thought at times, my parents didn't ap*prove* of him. They didn't really get to *know* him. Maybe he didn't *let* them get to know *him.*

He treated me more kindly than almost anyone I ever *dat*ed. My parents chose not to *see* that. They didn't approve of his *friends ...* a*gain,* I felt, *un*fairly, because it seemed they made *little eff*ort to see past the *surf*ace with *any* of them. They had chains attached to their *wall*ets (*What's inherently wrong with THAT?!*) and *dirt* under their *nails* occasionally, but *that's* because they *loved* working on *cars ...* just like my *dad* did. I thought they *could* have connected over what they *did* have in common but ... *nope.*

I remember at *one* point my mom expressing *very* articulate doubts about my taste in friends ... and *boy*friends. We held *opp*osite views about friends, *she* and *I.* My *mom* considered some of my friends *"unworthy"* of me. My opposite *view*? ... Given the *circ*umstances, *I* considered it miraculous I *HAD ANY.*

Already disappointing my parents on SO many levels (about which they *didn't* know), I decided *not* to disappoint them on the *one* level they *DID* know about—this *kind,* caring but, *ul*timately, incompat*ible boy*friend. *I* thought my boyfriend and I broke up *am*icably, as much as *any* 2 people (*young* people) with *so* many happy memories and *so* many dashed hopes ... *can.*

Among the revelers at this *"party"* ... the James *Dean*/Charlie *Sheen* wanna-be ... the guy from the party a year *ea*rlier. I'll give this *crazy-cru*el character a name of his *own* now. ... *Let's* call him ...*"Pill,"* short for *"PILLager."* [PAUSE]

As I re*call*, we don't *all* drink. ... In *fact*, I think maybe *only* Penny and *I* do. The boys arrive to find us al*ready* at least one patty shy of a double *burg*er, thanks to our *own* brand of *"Special Sauce."* I don't know *how* much we *drink*, not a *lot*, but enough to *"toast our buns,"* I'm afraid.

We're *not* being *row*dy, dis*rup*tive or *loud*. *No*body asks us to *leave*. The evening wears *on*. The alcohol runs *out*, and the fun dies *down*. Maybe it's *clos*ing time at McDo*nald's*; I don't re*member*. Everyone decides we'll con*tinu*e the party at *Penny's* house. I seem to re*call* ... we *think* her mom will likely be *home* by then, so we're *not* plotting an *un*sanctioned *bash* ... just a few *friends*. We hope to slide in *un*der the radar to sleep off what's left of the vodka in our *systems*— and *not* try this again *any*time *soon*. With the arrival of Mr. *Pill*ager, I'm already beginning to *realize* ... *this* was a mis*take*.

Several of the boys have *cars*, but *no* one has room for extra *pas*sengers. That's *fine*. Penny and I *walked* to McDonald's *any*way. We don't have cars or driver's *li*censes; we're only *15*. My parents had dropped me off at her *house*. We decide it will do us *good* to walk *home*. ... It'll give us a chance to get some *air*. Penny's *broth*er will let the boys *in* since they'll get to her house before *we* will. We're all *set*. All the boys take off in their cars (one, I be*lieve*, in his *parents'* *sta*tion wagon).

It strikes me as kind of an *ug*ly but *ad*mirable *motor*cade—holey mufflers *rum*bling, hubcaps *miss*ing, mis-matched *fend*ers, the kind of cars you sometimes see touched up with primer instead of *paint*—with a com*bined* value of about ... [TILT HEAD AS IF CALCULATING] $750, I sup*pose*. I ad*mire* these guys ... for the *mo*ment, anyway. Like my *dad*, they buy their cars *cheap* and fix them *up*, and these cars have the *one* quality *every* teenage *boy* (*and* my *dad*) desires *most*—they *run!*

They have to travel only *6 blocks*. That shouldn't be a *prob*lem, but the short trip runs *up*hill the *whole way*, so they all cross their fingers and take *off*, hoping they have enough *gas* and enough *horse*power to make it up the *hill*.

Penny and I feel clear-*head*ed enough to make it across the shop-ping-center *park*ing lot next to McDonald's ... clear-*head*ed enough to cross a busy *int*ersection ... clear-*head*ed enough to remember to walk/wobble on the *left* side of the street, finally observing ONE rule for our own *saf*ety: *"Drive on the RIGHT; WALK ... on the LEFT."*

The houses are mostly modest 3-bedroom *split*-levels, fairly close to*geth*er. A few have fences, but *more* have *fol*iage to establish boundaries between *prop*erties. It must be *late*, but I don't know *how* late. Most of the lights are off in the *neigh*borhood. I don't remember many T*V*s flickering through the picture *wind*ows. We don't encounter *any* traffic on the *street*.

Under *norm*al circumstances, it should take us about 10 or 15 *min*-utes to cover the *dist*ance. It might take us a [HIGH-PITCHED] *litt*le longer to*night*, considering our intoxicated con*dit*ion, but Penny and I seem to be making good *time*. We run out of steam now and then but giggle, link arms and hang *onto* each other the way a couple of *tank*ed-up teen*age* girls *would*.

At *one* point, I seem to re*call*, we try to *im*itate the synchronized walk we've seen on the TV show *The Monkees*. [DEMONSTRATE W/ HANDS WHAT MONKEES DO W/ THEIR FEET]. We fail *mis*erably and end up laughing *ri*otously, getting all tangled *up* and then shushing each other *loud*ly, fearing we might bring an-gry *neigh*bors out onto their *porches*. We turn *quiet*, running out of *steam* again. We just walk for several *yards*. We put on *ser*ious faces, almost *march*ing, which we can maintain *only* until we *look* at each other again. We laugh *hard*, double over to catch our *breath* ... then we trudge *on*. [PAUSE]

You know how when you're laughing *really* ... *really* hard, uncontrol-lably for a while, and then you wind down and there's that final hard exhale that signals the *end* of the *out*burst? [DEMONSTRATE] Penny and I have one of those *moments*. We hit that wall ... the *end* of our convulsive *laugh*ter ... and heave that satisfying sigh almost simul*tan*eously. ... That would be the *last* time I would laugh for *some time*.

The fun ends *there* for Penny and me. *Now*, Pill takes *his* turn break-ing the rules ... *all* the rules. Before I can take a*noth*er breath, he bursts *out* from be*hind* some *shrub*bery and shocks us *both*. He grabs *each* of us by *one* arm and yanks us several paces from the *street* and deeper into the *bush*es. He has *seen* us at McDonald's and *knows* we're *drunk*.

... At *first* I'm not even *sure* it's *him*. He comes *at* us *so fast*. It's *so dark*, even darker *off* the street. Then I see his *face*. He makes *no* effort to con*ceal* it.

"Oh, my GOD!" —half swear, half *prayer*.

My mind flashes to that rocky wall at my *high* school, but *now* I see it in an en*tirely* di*ffer*ent *light*. My brain sobers up *in*stantly. My *body* ... lags be*hind*. I can *see* what's happening, under*stand* what's happening, re*act ment*ally and *ver*bally to what's happening, but I can*not* physically *stop* ... what's *happening*. My *still-into*xicated *body* can't keep up with the signals it gets from my *frantic*, suddenly *sober brain*.

It becomes *ob*vious he's not after *Penny*; he's after *me* ... here to finish what he started a *year* ago. I pick up on the signals a lot *quick*er *this* time. *"Fool me ONCE..."* as they say.

As I relate the *rest* of this chapter in my *life*, I won't relate *every* detail. I make that decision, in *part*, to spare *you*, the reader ... in *part*, to spare my *parents* and others who *love* me ... and, in *part*, *frank*ly, to spare *me* ... from having to *re*-live the trauma I believe it would serve *none* of us to be*labor*. For *some*, what I *do* share *still* may be too *much*. For *some*, what I *do* share won't be *enough*. I'm *sorry*. I wish I had a different story to tell or a better *way* to *tell* it, but *then*, if I *did*, I wouldn't be *me* ... and I *like* me ... *now*. With *that said*, I continue ...

"What are you DOing?!... Let GO of me!... STOP it!"

His features look *freaky*, his eyes seemingly not even *focused*, but, at the *same time*, he moves *al*most me*chan*ically, as if he has thought all this out a*head* of time, which, I suppose, he *has*.

He's not saying *any*thing, just moving *fast*, throwing both of us to the *ground*, im*mob*ilizing Penny with one *el*bow, me with one *knee*, and *some*how pulling us across the *grass*. We must be under or near some *pine* trees because I can feel the needles shifting *und*er us and there's a *heavy*, *earthy*, slightly *piney smell*.

First, Pill pins us *down*, lining us *up side* by *side*. He yanks at *my* clothes, *unzips* his *pants*. He tries to get *my* pants *off* and *his* pants open and down to his *knees*. Then he yanks the 2 of us a*part*—Penny and me—forming a kind of *"V"* with Penny's body and *my* body so he can con*trol her* while he ... does what he *wants* to do ... to *me*. We've had *too* much to *drink* to muster much re*sis*tance ... *physi*cally, anyway.

"Get off!" ... *"Get ... off!"* ... *"Stop!"*

Still, he doesn't *say any*thing. Never re*sponds*. Never tries to ex*plain* or *jus*tify what he's *doing*. Doesn't tell us to be *quiet*. Doesn't tell us what to *do*. He just uses *brute force*.

He has really *strong hands*. I re*mem*ber that from a *year* ago. He has sur*prising* upper-*body* strength for a guy who seems almost *weak* and *wiry* otherwise.

Away from *here*, when I see him at *school* and *else*where, it seems to *me*, he *u*sually stands on the *outs*kirts, with a *dull look* on his face—not tuned *in*, it seems—displaying what *I* would call slouchy, *in*secure *pos*ture ... kind of like my *yester*year *bully* Danny Beck*ett*—dark and *brood*ing ... but with*out* Danny's *energy*.

Now, in the *dark*, Pill appears to *find* the confidence I haven't *seen* in him at *school* (except for that *one* time a *year* ago, when we were at *school* ... *al*so in the dark).

At *one* point, he gathers the fabric in my *sleeves* and pulls it tight around my *arms*; he uses my sleeves, almost like handles on a *suit*case, to lift me *up* and *re*-position me.

It may sound like a lot of ac*tiv*ity, but it all unfolds in this surreal combin*a*tion of *fast* action on the *out*side, *slow* motion in my *head*. *Again*, he moves *fast*, biting his lower *lip* at *one* point, concentrat*ing* ... trying to tug someone or something *into* or *out* of his *way*. I can't *see* everything he's *doing*; it's so *dark*, and he keeps *shift*ing. It seems like he may have dragged us under a tree with low-hanging *branch*es. There's not as much grass under us anymore.

He expels little grunts as he shifts his weight and attempts to keep us where he *wants* us. Penny and I thrash as much as the *alcohol* al*lows* ... not able to take measured or ef*fect*ive *swings* ... but making him work *hard*er to pin us *down*.

Always the *optimist*, even in *this* suddenly in*sane* *u*niverse, I think if I can make *eye* contact with him, *may*be he'll snap *out* of this ... or ... I'll under*stand* it somehow. It's *so dark* he can a*void* my *eyes* ... or ... he doesn't *care* to *be "understood."* He never looks me in the *eye*, but his *sneer* is more *blank* than sinister. It's in*tent*, *not ang*ry, kind of de*tached* but in*tent*ional, if that makes *any* sense at *all*.

"STOP it! Get OFF of me! ... GET ... OFF ... OF ... ME!" I yank and twist and thrash as best I *can*, but it doesn't *help*. *Noth*ing helps.

■ ■ ■

Pill disap*pears*. Penny and I pull ourselves to*gether* and walk *back* toward the *street*, not as worse for the wear clothing-wise as I imag-ine. Almost as soon as we *get* to the *street*, the kid who had driven his parents' *stat*ion wagon pulls up offering us a *ride*.

"Where have you BEEN? I came back to GET you. I've been driving back and forth LOOKing for you."

I don't re*mem*ber what we say in res*ponse*. We get to *Penny's*, and I try to pull my *ex*-boyfriend aside to tell him what *happen*ed and to ask for his *help*—what *kind* of help, I don't *know*. Ap*parent*ly, Pill either *is* there or has already *been* there and *left*, and my *ex* seems *host*ile for some *rea*son. I don't know *why*. I can't make *sense* of it. I don't know if he's less *OK* than I imagined about our *break*-up ... or if Pill has *said* something. ... I don't *know*. Either *way*, he doesn't seem willing to hear *any*thing I have to say about *any*thing.

I wonder *now* whether Pill went to Penny's house be*fore* we *got* there and *told* my ex I had *sex* with him that night ... volun*tar*ily ... so soon after our *break*-up and *that's* what made him *ang*ry. I don't *know*, and I'm be*yond guess*ing or trying to make *sense* of it.

Word spreads among the *boys*. *No* one asks any questions. *No* one does ... *any*thing. No one *says* anything, including *me*. I'm *shell-*

shocked ... and probably *still* a little *drunk*. Penny and I end up going to *bed*.

She has a really cool fabric *treat*ment on the ceiling in her *bed*room that she designed and installed her*self*. I wake up under its splash of friendly colors feeling de*ci*dedly *un*friendly ... feeling *vul*nerable, *stu*pid and con*fused*. I hear Penny *shift*. That tells me she's a*wake*.

"Did what I THINK happened last night ... happen last night? Did HE ..."

"Yeah. He DID."

I wasn't sure what to *do* with this new ... this new ... infor*mat*ion.

Instantly, I blame myself. I had put myself in harm's way. I broke the rules ... stole alcohol from my parents ... and this was the price I had to pay for my utter stupidity ... a steep price that was about to get even steeper.

I had already made myself feel (and been made to feel by others) like ... *"damaged goods"* ... not just by Jeff's lies but by the other boys' reactions to them—the taunt from the funny papers in the cafeteria, requests for sexual favors from total strangers. At one point, maybe in 8th grade, someone, maybe Jeff, actually spray-paints a vulgar invitation ... with my name and phone number attached ... on a concrete wall near the park where, in Jeff's imagi*nat*ion, he and I had had our "15 minutes of ... FLAME." ... Awful! I did get my dad to take care of *that*. I couldn't leave it there. As I recall, he didn't ask a lot of questions. I couldn't tell him who did it because I honestly didn't *know*. Given my reputation (still undeserved at that point), it could have been *any*one.

I absolutely do NOT blame Jeff for the worst outcomes of his behavior. I put my*self* in harm's way, but, if boys (and girls) knew what lasting, far-reaching, devastating impact their gossip can *have* ... I'd like to believe ... they might think twice before spreading it. [PAUSE] In some small way, I hope my book helps illustrate that point ... so my pain might morph into ... possibility ... into progress ... for other targets in other times. [PAUSE]

If I hadn't felt like damaged goods al*ready*, this latest attack by Pill and my self-inflicted, drunken inability to fight him off, made it *pain*fully official.

．．．

About a month or so *after* the incident, Penny moves out of *state*. We send a couple of letters back and *forth* and *then* lose touch com*plete*ly. We didn't talk much about that night, even be*fore* she moved, but, just having her at *school* with me, *near* me, gave me *strength*. She displayed what I *now* recognize as the *"ministry of presence."* She just ... *was*. [PAUSE] Penny sat with me when no one else *would*. She talked about *"normal"* things when *noth*ing felt *nor*-mal. She seemed to see the *good* in me that no one else *saw* ... or at *least* she overlooked the *bad* in me that blinded everyone *else*. Penny had perhaps the purest heart and the sweetest disposition of anyone I had *ever* known—one *very* val*u*able *penny*.

With Penny *gone*, I felt more alone than *ever*. I honestly don't know how I made it through most *days* ... other than some *tiny*, almost imper*cep*tible voice *deep* in*side* of me saying, *"Perse*VERE*!"*

Even *clos*er to the *sur*face, I give myself very loud, clear and con-sistent *mes*sages, probably prompted by and *plant*ed there by my *par*ents and *wat*ered by ... *God* ... the *Uni*verse:

"Fear NOT. THIS WILL NOT LAST FOREVER. You will rise aBOVE this and beYOND this. This is not ALL the world has in STORE for you. This isn't the REAL you. You are a GOOD person. They don't KNOW you. They don't underSTAND you. They don't beLIEVE you, but someone WILL, SOME day."

I be*lieved* those statements and attempted just to hold my *breath* and hold my head *high* until that day *came*, which I as*sum*ed wouldn't *happ*en until I went away to *college*. *Thank*fully, it hap-pened *soon*er but not without several more en*or*mous *set*backs.

*Some*how, Pill gets to the boys who had *been* there that night. I don't know whether he *tells* them we *had* consensual sex ... *or* ...

whether he tells them we didn't have sex at *all*, but they side with *him* and gang up on *me* in ways *almost too* painful to *bear*.

Our high school has an art wing off the back of the *buildi*ng, separated from the *rest* of the school by *big* sets of double *doors*. On more than one occasion, when one of Pill's *buddi*es sees me coming from the other side of the *doors*, he hides be*hind* them and, when I'm *just* about to walk *through*, he *jumps* into my *path* ... with his arms out like an en*raged* gori*lla*. He roars, *"Arrrrrggh!"* Then, as I try to get *past* him ... to get a*way*, he runs along be*side* me. In a sinister *whis*per, he says, *"I'm gonna RAPE you! ... I'm gonna RAPE you."*

I never know what awaits me at *school*. I keep my eyes open and my guard *up* ... and ... mi*rac*ulously, I keep my *grades* up, *too*.

To this *day*, I can't really *say* which part of that whole ordeal hurt me *more*.

With Penny *gone*, I hope I might have *one* re*main*ing a*lly* in the boy who had come *look*ing for us in the *sta*tion wagon that night. He saw us not far from the spot where Pill jumped out of *hidi*ng. He knows Pill's time line for that night is *off*. He knows Pill slipped out and showed up *later* with time *una*ccounted for in be*tween*.

Using my best dinner-table de*bati*ng skills to plead my *case*, privately, I say to him, *"You said you drove up and down and didn't SEE us between McDONald's and PENny's house. There's only ONE way to her house ... ONE route we would have TAken. We weren't ON it because he dragged us OFF of it. YOU, of ALL people, HAVE to know this happened the way I SAID it did. I'm not asking you to DO anything to him or to say anything to anyone who wasn't there. I'm not going to get anyone in TROUBle. Just, PLEASE ... tell your friends to stop TORturing me."*

He seems *almost* sympathetic. *Actually*, the boy who inflicts the *most* pain, after the *fact*, is the station-wagon driver's *broth*er. Surely, I think, he can persuade *him* to leave me a*lone*.

He *doesn't* ... or *can't*. I don't blame *him*. Things spin *so* out of control it seems there is nothing *any*one can do.

I find it almost unendurable to go to school every day *knowing* my rapist is under the same *roof*. To have all the other boys look at me the way boys *do* if they think you're *dam*aged *goods* ... well, that just *amp*lifies my outrage ... *and* my sadness ... *and* my *shame*.

I find it almost easier to understand *Pill's* actions in this scenario; *he* was a *ra*pist. He did what rapists *do*. I find it *more* difficult to comprehend the *oth*er boys. *They* were just *"normal"* American teenagers, but their treatment of me bears *no* resemblance to any-thing ... *"NORmal."*

I wonder whether those boys re*mem*ber how they be*hav*ed. I won-der whether they have daughters of their *own* by now. I *won*der how they would react if someone treated *their* daughters the way *they* treated *me*. [PAUSE]

I never go to au*thor*ities. I don't recall telling *any*one what hap-pened, beyond my *ex*-boyfriend and the immediate circle that *night*, not even my *par*ents. Who would be*lieve* me? With my repu*ta*tion, who would believe *me*? E*ven*tually, I tell my *sis*ter. *She* believes me.

It didn't occur to me until fairly *re*cently that Jeff Hubbard's lies may have pushed my rapist *toward* me ... may have put me on his *ra*dar screen, so to speak, prompting him to choose *me* as a *vic*tim. ... A *"whore"* or *"slut"* who *"sleeps with ANYone"* makes a *per*fect *tar*get.

Once my mom finds out, more than a year *lat*er, *some* of what I have endured in the *un*friendly confines of *high* school, she describes my classmates as *"savages."* On some counts, at least, I cannot dis*agree*.

CHAPTER 17

STANDING between Two Life-Altering Choices ...

I *try* to have a *"normal"* life ... to find new friends, even *boy*friends, the way *"normal"* girls do. During a summer driver's *ed* class, I meet and start dating a cute *boy* (über-cute, *I* think, *"hubba-hubba"* cute). During the regular school year, he attends a nearby (but not *too* nearby) *all-boys* Catholic *high* school. Even though he has a few friends at my *high* school, it seems he hasn't heard anything a*bout* me—a welcome *clean slate!*

I fall. *He* falls ... in *love*, that is, or so we *think.* We date happily for several months and then somewhat *less* happily for several *more* months. I *still* haven't shed my making-unfortunate-*choices* phase, and I wind up ... *preg*nant. By the time I *real*ize it, my boyfriend al*ready* has moved *on.*

At *this* point, it appears, to *me*, anyway, I have only 2 choices: com-mit *sui*cide ... or ... have an a*bor*tion (with*out* tel*ling anyone, in-cluding and especially not ... my parents). The more conservative among you might balk and say I overlook an obvious 3rd (and even 4th) possibility: *have* the baby and raise it my*self ... or ... have* the baby and put it up for a*doption.*

One would think the latter 2 options constitute options *only* if he or she were NOT raised in *my* household.

Remember ... thanks to our dinner-table conversations, I know ... or *think* I know ... how my parents feel about everything ... ironically, everything except S-E-X. Despite their profoundly *right*-leaning politics when it comes to *fiscal* matters, when it comes to certain social issues, they lean the *other way.* They were what came to be known as that rare breed called *"Pro-CHOICE RePUBlicans"* ... staunch believers that the world is over-*pop*ulated ... staunch be-lievers that children deserve better *parenting* and better home en-vironments than many children re*ceive* ... staunch believers in *birth* control … staunch believers, *I* thought, that smart, ca*reer*-minded young *w*omen should *not* de-rail their entire lives and upheave their entire *fami*lies with an unanticipated *preg*nancy.

I felt *certain* that if I *had* an abortion, I would be proceeding according to my parents' unspoken but ad*mi*ttedly *unsought wis*dom. I felt *certain* that of the admittedly wrenching array of *op*tions, they would choose *that* one, too. No *question.* [PAUSE]

Speaking of *questions* … growing up, on *several* occasions, I recall my mom reprimanding me for my various misbehaviors by asking me a par*ti*cularly *bur*densome *question.*

She would ask: *"Do you THINK … the way you just beHAVED … suggests you're … destined for GREATness?"*

[SHELL-SHOCKED] *"Wow! … Destined for greatness? …* [MULLING] *Destined for GREATness?! Is THAT the bar we've established here … GREATness? …* [UNEASY] *That's a VERY HIGH BAR. … That's a LOT of PRESsure. …* [ADOLESCENT] *That's, like, just THIS side of perFECtion, right?"*

My mom claims she expected of us only what she knew we could accomplish. In *her* book, that meant … *"greatness."* In *my* book, *this* book, you're discovering there can be a bit of a *down*side to such high expe*ct*ations. And I'm willing to ad*mit* … the downside *may* have arrived *more* because of *my interpretation* or *mis*interpretation of the standards in our home than it *did* because of the standards them*selves*—what I *thought* my parents wanted and expected versus what they *real*ly wanted and expected. At the same time, I think it's *also possi*ble that the standards in our home were *impos*sibly *high* … or so they felt at times.

"I can't believe I ever SAID that. It sounds inconCEIVably POMpous," my mom says *now*. Two *phon*ographic memories col*li*de in this case.

It's *possi*ble I imposed that standard on my*self.* In the *end*, it doesn't *mat*ter what she … *meant* … or even *if* or how *of*ten she *said* it. Right or wrong, joking or *not*, I thought *ev*erything I *did*—every choice I *made*—had to propel me toward some sort of … *imagined great*ness.

I had a very clear sense that the greatness to which my parents *hoped* I would a*spire* would take the form of a ca*reer*. Yes, a happy *home* life—a *hus*band, *child*ren for *me*, *grand*children for *them*—played *into* that imaginary greatness, *too*, I sup*pose*, but, first and *fore*most, I thought they expected me to make my mark pro*fession*ally—in a BIG *way*. After *all*, we Standings do EVERYthing in a big way.

At *this* stage in my life, *I* seem *only* able to ... mess *up* in BIG ways. I know having a baby at 16 would *NOT* meet my parents' standard of *"GREATness."* Ob*vious*ly, having an a*bort*ion doesn't, *either*, but, I interpret all they told me about my po*tent*ial ... to mean I can't let *any*thing stand between me and the great things I will *one day* do for ... my fellow man (and *wo*man).

I had just enough self-esteem to hope and be*lieve* they would prefer a*bort*ion to my own *sui*cide. I wasn't sure *I* did. [PAUSE]

I take a few days to sort that *out*. I choose an a*bort*ion. I pursue it on my *own*, pay for it my*self* (with $60 pitched in by my *now-for*mer *boy*friend) and, a*gain*, breaking *all* the rules, drive myself to the clinic and back *un*escorted.

The night be*fore* my ap*point*ment, I call Cathy, who's away at *col*lege by then. I tell her I *don't* want her to come *home*. I *don't* want her to tell Mom and *Dad*. I don't *need* any-thing; *I'm* taking *care* of it, but, I figure, in the interest of *safety* and good *sense*, (admittedly *not* quali-ties I have displayed up until *then*) *some*one should *know*, and I want it to be *her*. For a long *time*, I tell *no* one *else*. I *don't* tell Cathy that I con-sidered *sui*cide. I know *that* would bring her home in a *hur*ry.

Looking *back*, Cathy says she de-cided *not* to tell our *par*ents because she thought I would never for*give* her if she *did*. She's probably *right* about that; it wasn't *her* story to *tell*

Cathy at 18, my confidant.

... *and* ... if and when our parents found *out*, she knew *they* would understand why she didn't *tell* them. (They *do*.)

I'm not asking *anyone* to approve or *dis*approve. I don't think *any*-one can fully understand a woman's *com*plicated approach to this *very* personal matter—not *even* if they have *"been there"* and *"done that."* By definition, it's *personal*, *private* and indi*vid*ual. At the risk of angering or offending some people (even some people quite *close* to me), I will *say* ... and I *don't* mean to be flip ... just *clear* ... when it comes to a*bor*tion, I boil my opinion down to *one* line: *"Against abortion? Don't HAVE one."* [PAUSE]

Having experienced this my*self*, I would never *dare* invade some-one *else*'s personal space *so* intrusively as to suggest I know what is right for her ... and *certainly* wouldn't claim to speak for *God* if I *did*. Each person has his or her *own* u*nique* re*lationship with *God* ... with the *Universe*. We all have *choices. In choosing our *actions*, I be*lieve*, each of us chooses our *con*sequences, as well.

I certainly go *through* hell at this stage of my life, but *will* I, as *some* believe, go *TO hell* for my *choice*? Wait and *see*. ... Wait and *see*. ...

CHAPTER 18

STANDING in the Cafeteria Line ...

The rest of my school year unfolds fairly uneventfully. For *me*, that's sayin' a *LOT*.

By *then*, I have abandoned the low wages and irregular hours of *baby*sitting for the *high* wages and heady rewards to be found as a ... cook and server in a cafeteria ... for $1.35 an hour.

Destined for *great*ness, in*deed*! As Dr. Phil might say, *"How's that workin' for ya, Kell?"* To which *I* would say, *"Don't scoff, Dr. Phil. ... I've gotten at LEAST 3 nickel-an-hour MERit raises since I GOT here."*

During the *school* year, I work 3 afternoons a week and both weekend days at Pope's Cafeteria at West County Shopping Center in suburban St. Louis, the *same* res*taurant* and the same *mall* with the *piano* store that led my dad to ... "Vic*toria*." The name Pope's Cafe*teria* may ring a bell be*yond* my *book*; I'll remind you *why* shortly. ...

During the *sum*mer, I work practically non-stop at Pope's. One of the managers tells me he's never seen *any*one who can slice a turkey or peel a 40-pound bag of *carrots* faster than *I* can. Hey, I'll take my *"greatness"* where I can *get* it.

I *love* my job at Pope's. I love my *co*-workers, and they seem to ap*preciate me*. The line cook doesn't show *up* one day, so the manager plucks me off the veggie-serving line and puts me to *work* ... preparing *hun*dreds of servings ... of *count*less different *foods* ... from lengthy *recipes I've never *seen* ... in *quan*tities and units of *mea*sure that boggle my limited *math* abilities. *Still*, we make it through the *shift*, and I have earned myself a raise and a new *job*, one with *bet*ter and *more* summer *hours*—6:30 a.m. to 3 p.m. For a busy *teen*ager who loves softball leagues and cycling, that beats the heck out of having to close at 8 p.m.

I par*tic*ularly enjoy the wit and wisdom of several older women on my shift: Ruth, our hard-working sour *pick*le in *Sal*ads; Maddie, our delightfully laid-back matron of *Pastries*; and *Edna* (*oh*, *Ed*na!), a cantankerous old bird who has worked at Pope's for *decades*. She presides over the whole shebang—the line, the prep, the walk-in fridge and freezers, dry *storage*. She even keeps some lazy, mouthy *dish* boys in line when the need a*rises*.

Edna greets me *skep*tically, *cer*tain they have sent her yet a*noth*er teenage twink to do a battle-ax's *job*. I prove her wrong with my *work* ethic. I *show* up, *shut* up and *keep up*. She *likes* that about me, and we get *so* close I end up nicknaming her *"Grandma."* When I head to college 2 years *later*, I keep in *touch*, writing letters home to ... *"Grandma EDna"* and returning to *work* with her over my Christmas and summer *breaks*.

I love one of Pope's female *man*agers, Lee *Woods*. She and her husband, Jimmy, have *both* worked for Pope's for *years*. Eventually, I feel safe enough with Lee to share bits of my *story*. She gives off a kind of cool, not-exactly-hippie/motherly/edgy vibe I *like*.

I tell her about the *"repuTAtion"* I first have foist *up*on me and then, *sad*ly, live *up* to. I tell her about the *rape* ... and the *af*termath. I think I even tell her about my pregnancy and a*bor*tion. She listens

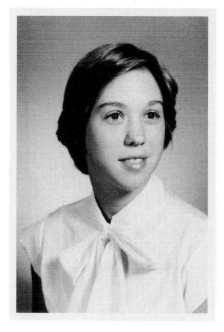

A "nice girl" at 17.

*thought*fully, *qui*etly, not at *all* judg*ment*ally. When I finish telling her all I have endured over the past several *years*, she says the most a*maz*ing *thing* ... the most unex*pect*ed thing. On the heels of my *story*, with*out* hesi*ta*tion, she says, *"I'd like you to meet my SON. I think you two might REALLY hit it OFF. He NEEDS a nice girl like YOU in his life."* [PAUSE]

"A NICE girl" like ME. ... Hmmm. [SMILE]

Lee's reaction provides a *rare* and *welcome* re-defining *mo*ment. Here I fear she might think *less* of me after hearing my tale of woe. In*stead*, she tells me she thinks highly enough of me to fix me up with her *son*. She *does* fix us up. We have one *fun date* ... *very* fun. He plans a lot of interesting things to *do*. We live too far apart to make it a regular *thing*, but I think we *both* consider it an evening well *spent*. *I* consider it a Godsend. [PAUSE]

I still attend school with Pill and the rest of his devoted *gang*sters, but I'm starting not to *care* anymore. I still play field hockey and softball and spend *so* much time earning nickel-an-hour merit raises at Pope's ... my universe has expanded. I have room to *breathe* ... room to consider the *"greatness"* on my horizon.

I *tell* myself, *"If I can just keep my head DOWN and my grades UP, I'll graduate in less than 2 years. I can start fresh in COLlege, where NObody KNOWS me. I won't have to see ANY of these people aGAIN."*

Then, without *warn*ing, my universe shrinks *back* in a profoundly disturbing *way* and takes my breath away once *more*. The former boyfriend with whom I had gotten *preg*nant gets expelled from his *pri*vate *all-boys* Catholic *high* school for doing I don't *know* ... and I don't *care* ... *what*. They send him to *slum* among the public *school* kids, so, *now*, I encounter *daily life*-size evidence of the 2 greatest *heart*aches of my young *life* ... well, *tech*nically, *3*. Jeff *Hub*bard still goes there, *too*.

This pile of manure is drawin' so many flies I almost can't see my *hand* in front of my *face*! [PAUSE]

CHAPTER 19

STANDING on a Therapist's Couch ...

I recently saw an office-cubicle sign that read:

"Everyone brightens up this space; some when they arRIVE, some when they dePART."

Let's just say my ex-boyfriend's arrival did NOT ... *"brighten up my space."* While he doesn't behave *bad*ly toward me, I want to move *on.* His presence makes that more *dif*ficult. He seems like the *bad* penny to off-set Penny's *good* one.

I'm a tough little nut, but even *I* start to crack under the weight of my assorted ca*lam*ities (admittedly, some of them *self*-inflicted). I start having stomach problems. E*ven*tually, they get *bad* enough I see my pedia*trician* about them. Yes, all these grown-up *problems* and I *still* see a *pedi*atrician.

"So, what's been going ON in your life?"

"Well, it's kind of a long STORy. ..."

"I'M not GOing anywhere. You're my last patient of the DAY. What's UP?"

I think I've gone in to talk about my *stomach; he* gets me to talk about my *heart,* too. I summarize the previous almost-4 years more clinically and less e*motion*ally than I imagine I *could.* My doctor listens *thought*fully. He's kind and clinical in re*sponse.*

"You have what we call 'a pre-ulcer condition,'" he says. *"You've been in a lot of emotional pain for a LONG time. That pain has to go SOMEwhere. You need to get it OUT ... or it will EAT its way out ... through your STOmach. We DON'T ... WANT ... THAT."*

This doctor has *known* me since 1960. He made *house* calls to ad-dress life-threatening *fevers* I had as an *infant.* My *"brushes with death"* start *early;* this man brings me back from the brink *more* than *once.* My parents LOVE him. He likes *them, too,* but he says he under*stands* why I might not *want* to ... or be *rea*dy to ... *talk* to them about *all* of this.

"I think it might HELP if you went to see a counselor, someone with expertise in rape crisis and post-aBORtion issues."

"OK."

I'm inclined to do what he *says*. After *all, he's* the one with the di-*plo*mas on his *wall*. Down the *road*, once almost im*med*iately and once many years *la*ter, that blind faith in diplomas and doctors will come back to bite me on the bum ... *lit*erally, but I can trust *this* doc-tor ... I *think*.

"I could give you all the medicine in the WORLD," he says, *"but I don't think your STOmach will get better until you TALK to some-one. It doesn't HAVE TO BE your PARents, but I think you should talk to SOMEone."*

He gives me the name of an organization to contact but not the name of an indi*vid*ual *coun*selor. *Uh, oh! Now* my doc gets an A for com*pa*ssion and an *F* for *fol*low-through. [PAUSE]

The *rest* of *this* chapter and *all* of the *next* ... shed some harsh light on some harsh re*al*ities. By the end of this and the next chapter, you may not feel all warm and fuzzy about ... *me*, my *boy*friend, my *doc*-tor, my one-shot *ther*apist, my mother or even my father, but don't miss the *point*. We're *still STANDING*.

As far as my family is concerned, we don't *let one* episode or one conver*sa*tion shatter the good we have built be*tween* us. *Af*ter this, we choose to get *bet*ter, *not bit*ter. Bitter is a *choice*. *Bet*ter is a *choice—al*ways. We may not always be able to *dodge* adversity, but *I* believe we *al*ways have a choice about how we re*spond* to adver-sity—*al*ways.

■ ■ ■

When I call to make the counseling appointment, they hand me off to a young woman who appears to have been out of school for ... maaaaybe ... 10 *min*utes.

... or ...

Maybe ... I see her by mis*take*. Maybe she was just ... hanging around the office that day ... chewing gum, emptying waste baskets and re-filling staplers ... and she decided to take a whack at this *"therapy thing."* She finds an empty office, I walk in and *"Voila!"*

... or ...

Maaaaybe ... she's the daughter of a *"real"* therapist who works there, and she's only visiting for some freakish field trip like, *"Take Your Short-Sighted-Daughter-Who-Shouldn't-Pursue-this-Line-of-Work ... to Work Day"* ... or *some*thing.

Can you *tell* I don't think much of her *skills*?

In our one and *only* 50-minute session, she has me relate my en*tire* story by working *back*ward from most *re*cent to most *dis*tant—an odd re*verse* chron*ology*, it seems to *me*. I find it *diffi*cult. I did a better job delivering this summary to my *doc*tor ... in *or*der. I don't *know* her. I don't *trust* her, sitting there in her well-worn jeans and wrinkled T-shirt.

I get the *feel*ing this place has made the environment in*ten*tionally *cas*ual. I can ap*pre*ciate their pursuit of re*laxed* hospi*tal*ity over starched pro*fes*sionalism, e*spe*cially since they treat rape victims and women who find themselves contemplating their reproductive *choices*—past or *pre*sent—women who may *need* a *"comfy"* place to sort things *out*. *This* therapist misin*ter*prets that memo, I *think*, and takes the dress code *too far*—from casual to *care*less. That takes a *toll* on her rap*port* with *me* ... not that she catches even a *whiff* of it.

She seems more *fasc*inated than *edu*cated, more sopho*moric* than thera*peu*tic, asking *ju*venile, tan*gen*tial *ques*tions ... and ... shoving *tiss*ues at me when I'm *not* even *close* ... to *tears*. I think my story makes *her* sad. Perhaps *she* needs the tissues.

It seems she *knows* she's sup*posed* to maintain a degree of profes-sional de*tach*ment and ob*jec*tivity ... but she can't *quite* pull that *off*. She seems to want me to share *her* feelings ... in*stead* of listening objectively while *I* share *mine*. She appears barely older than *I* am. When my story in*ev*itably hits the *low notes*, it seems *she* needs *me* to take care of *her*—to throw her a *line*. I had never *had* a counseling session be*fore*, but I felt certain *this* one qualified as an *un*qualified disaster. If there's an industry standard for *"worst practices,"* she deserves the *c*enterfold.

Harsh? I don't *think* so. Looking *back,* her irresponsible handling of my case could have shattered my relationship with my *parents, if* we *let* it, which we *didn't ... and ...* her methods didn't diminish my stomach pains, *either.*

With less than 5 minutes remaining on the *clock ...* in my *first* session ... *this* child psychologist (meaning, her*self* a *child)* announces ... with great au*th*ority, *"Well, I think it's OBvious what you need to DO here."*

"It IS?"

[SELF-SATISFIED] *"Mmmm hmmm."*

Part of me thinks, *"That's funny, because I've been living in my skin for almost 17 YEARS ... and in this NIGHTmare for almost 4 ... and up until NOW ... NOTHing about this has seemed obvious to ME. If you HAVE ... the ... OBvious ... answer, let's HEAR it."*

[DIRECTIVE] *"You need to tell your PARents. THAT'S what's making you sick ... the fact that you haven't told your PARents."*

She says it with such fin*ality ...* such *c*ertainty, I'm a *little* surprised she doesn't brush off her *hands,* put her feet up on the *desk,* lean back in her *chair ...* with her *head* resting against her interlaced fingers ... and smugly de*clare,* [SATISFIED] *"Case CLOSED. ... Glad I could HELP."* [WINK]

She reminds me of a *c*ontestant on a *game* show, one of those over-eager types who, *half-*way through the *q*uestion, blurts out, [EXCITED] *"Oh, I KNOW this ONE!"* ... and then ... like *this* inexperienced *ther*apist ... proceeds to *give ...* the *WRONG* answer. [PAUSE] [GAME-SHOW BUZZER!]

I'm *not* suggesting that telling my parents was the *"wrong answer"* for *all* time, but it *was* the wrong answer for *that* time. The therapist neglects to ask me one very, *very* impo*rt*ant follow-up *q*uestion. To her *half-*baked, *knee-*jerk ad*v*ice, she should *add ... "How are your parents likely to REACT to this news?" ...* [PAUSE]

We could have and *should* have devoted *SEVERAL* sessions to that question before she released me to my amazing-in-MANY-ways-but-not-*always*-great-in-a-*crisis* *"TIger Mother" ... and ...* my *great*-in-a-*crisis*-but-sentimental-and-likely-to-struggle-with-a-daughter's-sexual-con*fessions father.* The therapist *could* have asked a*noth*er question: *"Why haven't you TOLD your parents AL-READY?"* Despite the authentic-looking diploma on her *wall*, she doesn't *ask* those questions.

The therapist doesn't know the ... *back* story ... because she doesn't *ask.* At *17,* I don't know to volun*teer* it. I probably can't even articulate *most* of it. ... I don't know I'm allowed to *ask* for another *session* ... or *2* ... or *10.* It appears the motto *here* is ... *"One and DONE."*

The therapist emerges from her office into the waiting room announcing to my mom in a very judgmental way, *"Kelly has a lot of important things to talk about with YOU and her FATHer."*

I leave the therapist's office feeling like I have *"marching orders"* of sorts. ... I leave there on a *mis*sion ... to share my story (as painful as that will *be*) and, then, FINALLY, I *think*, to get the support and understanding I have de*nied* myself.

I decide I simply *cannot bring myself* to deliver this news di*rect*ly to my *dad.* I know this doesn't hold true in *all* households, but in *my* household, daddies and daughters have a sacred ... *something* ... a sacred *bond.* As a teenager in my teenage world, I *guess* I think girls should be able to go to their *moth*ers with things they would *never* tell their *dads.* Then, *moms* figure out the best way to bring dads *in.* I realize it's unfair for my *mom,* but I hope she'll under*stand; she* had that *"sacred SOMEthing"* with *her* dad, too. [PAUSE]

I tell this next, pro*found*ly *diffi*cult part of my story with*out* sugar-coating because ... it's *real.* It's *true.* Kids screw up—*ALL* kids, even smart kids full of i*deas, energy* and good in*ten*tions ... like *me. Par*ents screw up—*ALL* parents, even brilliant, loving, supportive, well-*mean*ing, ar*ticu*late parents ... like *mine.*

With *that*, we head into some rough but, *ul*timately, for*giving wa*ters ... [PAUSE ... DEEP BREATH ...]

My dad tends to go to bed *early.* I decide I'll talk to my mom in our *liv*ing room, as *far* away from their bedroom as I can *get, after he* goes to bed. I decide I'll just tell my story in chronological *order* ... *stolen vod*ka, *rape*, then *pregn*ancy, and then a*bort*ion, but leaving *out* the Jeff Hubbard stuff as imp*ort*ant but *an*cillary ... for the time *being*. I figure I'll have opp*ort*unities to fill in the *back* story another *time* ... or in response to what I anticipate *may* be a bar*rage* of *ques*tions.

Leading up to this night, my parents were not *blind* to my *mis*ery. They would ask periodically what was *wrong*, and I would craft my answers *very* carefully. All those dinner-table de*bates* had made me into a fairly cunning com*mu*nicator. I become *very* good at con*cea*ling what I do not *want* them to *know*. After *all*, I had *lots* of practice because I had *lots* of *secrets*.

At *one* point, my parents *even* send me to *Dall*as for several days to visit my aunt and *un*cle because they hope ... *they* might have better luck prying my troubles out of me. ... *Nope.*

Before my ill-fated *ther*apy session ... before our *talk* ... during second se*mester* of my *junior year*, out of the *blue* one day, my mom asks, *"Do you THINK you would be HAPpier ... going to a different SCHOOL?"* I can't be*lieve* she sug*gests* it. She could tell I was hurting; she just didn't know why. I didn't *tell* her why.

Still, she proposed what struck me as a life-saving *cure*. I thought I had to make it *all* the way through my horrific *high* school.

I assumed people who were *"destined for GREATness"* wouldn't *quit*. ... I as*sumed* they wouldn't *leave* just because things got *dif*ficult. *Some*how, I thought people who were *"destined for GREATness"* might *find* their greatness through ad*versity*. They would ... perse*vere!* [PAUSE]

That implied I had to *stay. You mean there's another OPtion?! I don't HAVE to STAY?!* She *floored* me with the suggestion.

"Would I be HAPpier at another SCHOOL? Yes! Yes! Yes! ... Can I go toDAY? ... NOW?"

My *mom* had been part of the ... *"in"* crowd at her own *high* school. It a*mazes* me that someone who had such a *good* experience in high school could even con*ceive* of a plan that includes a transfer between *junior* and *senior year*, and, *yet*, she comes up with this ...

wonderful ... radical idea. I consider it a gift from my mom and from God ... timely, Divine deliverance.

We take steps right away to effect a transfer, one that will take place after my junior year. We say the open-space environment at my modern school, along with some profoundly difficult social situations, make my "special assignment," as they called it, imperative. The arrival of my expelled ex-boyfriend helps make our case, even before my mom knows the full extent of our previous relationship.

Without too much grumbling from the principal, he signs off.

"I'm outta here!" ... a year ahead of schedule ... and, given my deteriorating health, not a moment too soon.

The only catch? I will lose my sports eligibility. The district must bar me from playing field hockey or any other sport at my new school ... because (and I find this ... HILL-LAR-EE-US ...), God forbid ... someone might try to stack the field-hockey team by moving "key" players in our district all to one school. Thanks to Title IX, what applies to the boys (and football) also must apply to the girls (and field hockey).

Lose my sports eligibility? ... Done! NO problem.

Perhaps, in light of my imminent departure from my high school, anyway ... and the brighter prospects it promises, I could and should wait to have "the talk" with my mom ... to see how things play out at my new school. I wonder whether my gastro symptoms would cool down on their own if I just wait a few months longer ... until my junior year comes to a close.

I think my mom suggests the transfer and we complete the paperwork between my call to make the doctor's appointment and the appointment itself. Looking back, I should have recalibrated. I should have postponed "the talk" once we arranged my transfer, but now I have the appointments. I feel too deep in to see a way out.

The therapist didn't have me imagine how I might break the news ... what I might say or ... in what order. It may not seem like that matters, but it does. Context matters. If you don't know about Jeff Hubbard ... waaaay back in 7th grade, you can't really understand Kelly Standing in 11th grade.

Back *then*, I needed help to craft a good *"speech."* Later, for *years*, people paid me to do that *for* them. Maybe I owe my ca*reer* as a *speech*writer to the conversation I'm a*bout* to have with my *mothe*r ... and how *wild*ly it goes *off script*.

CHAPTER 20

A Total Lack of UnderSTANDING ...

The stakes are *high*. This occasion and the *content* deserve a prepared *man*uscript ... or at *least notes*. I don't *have eith*er. ... I don't think to pre*pare* them. In *truth*, in this *mom*ent, I am a little *girl* ... seeking sup*port*, for*giv*eness and *love* from her *par*ents ... on the heels of an e*nor*mously trying or*deal* ... a *ser*ies of ordeals, *act*ually.

A *good* therapist would schedule a few more *sess*ions, would get to *know* me better ... wouldn't rush to *judg*ment. A *bet*ter therapist would offer to col*lab*orate with me as a sort of *"speechwriter"* ... to make sure my messages *hit* their marks instead of *leav*ing them. A *comp*etent therapist would ask, *"Why did you choose to HANdle all this on your OWN? ... Tell me about your PARents ..."* In 50 *min*utes, we could barely scratch the *surf*ace of *what* happened, much less *why* and who else *knew* or *did*n't know. My *one*-day-and-*out* therapist doesn't do *any* of those *things*. [PAUSE]

We get *home*. We have *din*ner. My dad heads to *bed*. It's time to *talk*. I *hon*estly think, as difficult as this next hour ... or *coup*le of hours ... might *be* ... on the *oth*er side of it, I will feel im*mea*surably *bet*ter. The therapist isn't *wrong* that I need to get this off my *chest*, but her *tim*ing ... well ... her *tim*ing *stinks*!

My mom sits on the couch in our living room. We *face* each other. I intentionally don't mention Jeff *Hub*bard. Without a *script*, I for*get* to *men*tion Pill's *FIRST* attack in 1974. In*stead*, I start by ad*mit*ting that, waaay back in 1975 (it's now '77), on a night when I slept over at *Pen*ny's, I stole some *vod*ka from the cabinet above our *stove*, snuck it *out* of the *house*, then Penny and I took it to McDonald's ... and *drank* it. We got *drunk*, and on the way *back* to *Pen*ny's, one of my *class*mates (I won't say *who*) *raped* me. I say, other than the people who were *there* that night, I never *told* anyone. [PAUSE]

My mom con*ceals* whatever emotions she feels, which leaves me utterly *un*prepared for her next *words*. ...

"Do you consider any of your OTHer relationships to have been ... proMIScuous?"

[BAFFLED] *"I don't think of THAT as a ... 'reLAtionship.' ... ProMIScuous?!"*

I think to myself but do not *say, "What does RAPE have to do with promisCUity?!"*

Uh, oh! Already this train has run completely off the *rails*, and I haven't even gotten *started* yet.

I decide to answer the question I *think* my mom is asking, meaning, *"Have you had sex with anyone ELSE?"* but I'm *so* confused by her *non-*reaction to what I've just *told* her ... *so* confused that she glosses over the *rape.* ... [TRAIL OFF ...]

With a puzzled expression, I tell her that I *did*, in *fact*, have sex with the boyfriend of whom she and my dad didn't ap*prove* ... and ...

She freaks *out* ... (over *that!*) ... as if having *lost* my virginity to a *nice* guy who meant me *no harm* and *treat*ed me *kin*dly is the *worst* part of this tale *so far.*

I think I manage to say, *"The night with Penny, I didn't have SEX with the guy. ... I was RAPED."*

It *still* doesn't register. *Very* dismissively and disapprovingly, she says, *"Well, you SAID you were DRINKing,"* as if I got what I deserved for making such a profoundly stupid *choice*. I assume, *"Even my MOTHer agrees I am the IRreDEEMable 'whore-slut-sleeps-with-ANYone/nasty-girl' Jeff Hubbard SAID I am."* I assumed wrong. She loved me, but I didn't FEEL lovable. She didn't SOUND loving, but, remember, this came as a HUGE shock.

I almost stop right *there*, deciding this is bad *enough* al*ready*. I'm *so* taken aback by her reaction to my *long-*with*held* confession ... my mind *spins*. If my stomach didn't hurt be*fore*, it hurts *now.* I feel *sick*. My mouth waters as if I'm about to throw *up.*

I *swallow, breathe* ... try to *pull* myself to*get*her.

There's a long moment between us. I'm not sure whether we're *both* silent or whether she's *saying* something ... almost *lecturing*

... about the importance of *chastity* ... a *very* be*lat*ed addition to the list of re*quired* Standing *vir*tues ... if she *is*.

"Well, I just had no iDEa. I mean ... to THINK ..." She sputters and then goes *si*lent. Her tone sounds to me as if she's casting off *blame* and trying to make sure I under*stand* ... *this* didn't *hap*pen because *she* wasn't paying at*ten*tion (which I never suggested it *did*); *this* *hap*pened because *I* was irre*spon*sible (which I admitted I *was*).

Still, she's *si*lent. *That's some*thing; I have rendered *my* mot*her* ... my *never-at-a-loss-for-words-mot*her ... *speech*less. She finds her voice *short*ly.

But I *wonder, "Should I go ON? ... Has she HEARD eNOUGH? ... Have I HAD enough?"*

*Un*wisely, I decide to perse*vere*. This will *not* get easier, I conclude, by putting it *off*. And the counselor *said* I should *tell* her—the *SO-in-competent-even-a-17-year-old-in-CRIsis-can-SPOT-it* coun*se*lor ... yet ... here I *am*, taking her *bone*-headed ad*vice*! Every siren in my head screams, *"ReTREAT! ReTREAT! Abandon SHIP! ABORT! ABORT!"*

Which brings me to the *next* leg of our *now*-treacherous *jour*ney ...

I say, ominously, *"There's MORE. ..."* I take a *deep breath*, preparing to dive *back in. ...*

I honestly be*lieve*, in *many ways*, the thwarted attack at *14* and the *rape* at *15* mi*tig*ates the pregnancy and abortion at *16*. Women who are raped may, and often *do*, come to *think* of themselves as ...*"dam-aged goods." Ob*viously, *I* felt that way about myself even be*fore* my rape but felt it even *more keen*ly *af*ter.

Rape victims *can*, *some*times do, emerge from their experiences making poor, *yes*, even *"proMIScuous,"* choices. I *did* that, not *just* because of the rape but because I went looking for someone who would *care* about me ... who would want me in a *real* way ... not the *vio*lent, *ar*tificial, de*tached* way a rapist *"wants"* a *vic*tim.

Heading into this conversation (and even still to*day*) I think my rape should not ex*cuse* but should *"conTEXTualize"* my pregnancy and abortion. The rape provides my state of *mind*. It's not *enough* to say I made bad *choices*. If *anybody's* gonna learn *any*thing from this, you gotta ask, *"WHY? ... WHY did I make those bad CHOICES?*

*How was I FEELing about myself? What made me FEEL that way?
... What ELSE was going on at the TIME? ... If you don't know THAT,
you don't know ME. And if you, my PARents, don't KNOW me ... don't
acCEPT me ... don't HELP me ... I fear I may NEVer get BETter."*

I feel a little defensive and think to myself ... *"Hey, let's FACE it ...
you and Dad never told me not to have sex ... not ONCE ... so this isn't
ALL on ME." Wise*ly, I choose *not* to express that *thought.*

Once it appears my mom dismisses the rape as having been, essentially, *"self-inFLICTed"* (a bizarre *twist*), I know the *next* news ...
the *bigger* bombshell ... will blow her *mind.* I cannot im*agine what
she will *say.* I don't dare *wonder.* And, *actually,* come to *think* of it,
why do I think of my *next* headline as a *"BIGger bombshell"*? On
the scale of things that can go *wrong* in a teenage girl's *life,* it seems
rape and unplanned pregnancy and abortion pretty much tie for
first. I *mean, oth*er than death or dismemberment [TRAIL OFF ...]
[PAUSE]

*Some*how, I must know *this* bit of news will hit my mom harder than
the *first* bit, but I *don't* really understand why it *would.*

I don't *know* this woman sitting in front of me. She's not the *mother*
I *know*; she's some out-of-touch *prude* talking about wishing I had
waited until *mar*riage.

My internal dialog [INCREDULOUS]: *"Seriously, Mom??! I should
have waited until marriage ... to get RAPED??!! ... RAPE AND PRO-
MISCUITY ARE UNRELATED! ... Even proMIScuous girls can be
RAPED. ... I didn't go to some PARty, have too much to DRINK, flop
into bed with any old BODy, and then wake up the next morning re-
GRETting it! Oh, my GOD, Mom! ... A predator waited in the DARK
for me ... plotted for a whole YEAR, apparently ... jumped out of some
BUSHES ... assaulted my FRIEND ... ripped off my PANTS! NONE
of that gets exCUSED because I happen NOT to have been a virgin
when it ocCURRED. NONE of that gets exCUSED by the fact that I
was DRUNK. NO means NO. STOP means STOP. 'GET ... OFF ... OF
... ME!' means ... JUST THAT."* [PAUSE]

My mom never *hears* those details. ... She doesn't ask me any *ques*-
tions. She hears me say there was *al*cohol involved and doesn't inquire any *fur*ther. *"You BOOZE; you LOSE,"* ap*par*ently. [PAUSE]

When I say, *"There's MORE …,"* I can *see* my mom isn't *ready* … never *will* be.

I don't recall sugar-coating it. *"This past NoVEMber, I got PREGnant. … On December 15th, I had an aBORtion. I thought it's what you and Dad would WANT me to DO."*

My mom doesn't really say *anything* at *first* … for a *long time*. It seems *may*be she *thinks* she's talking out *loud*, but she just *sits* there *staring*, not with a look that someone has when they're trying to sort out a complex *prob*lem but with a look of pure shock—stunned … *blank* almost.

I find her silence *scary*. I want to know what she's *think*ing … at least I *think* I want to know. *"SAY something …,"* I *push*.

She can *tell* I'm *puzzled*, even *hurt* by her response … or *lack* of one. Her expression says she feels like I'm at*tack*ing her. I can *tell* she doesn't *like* the way I'm *look*ing at her, but I can't *help* it; I don't know what she's *think*ing. I don't know how *else* to *look*.

I need something from her she isn't equipped in this *mo*ment to *give* me. I don't *know* she's not equipped. I've never *seen* her at a loss for words … never seen her so *"inside her HEAD"* for *so long*.

I think, *"Just SAY it. Whatever it IS … SAY it! Say that this is the worst thing anyone has ever done in the history of the WORLD … if you THINK it is. … Say that we'll get THROUGH this … if you THINK we WILL. … Say that you're SO angry … or 'very disappointed' in me. That's an old fave. HELL, ask me the 'destined-for-GREATness' question, and I'll tell you, 'NO, Mom, I DON'T think the way I have behaved over the past several years suggests I'm destined for GREATness … not by a LONG shot.' If THAT'S what you're thinking, just SAY it."*

Or … Ask me some *questions:* *"Are you all RIGHT? … Did you get medical care when you were RAPED? … Why didn't you report your atTACK? … Who WAS this boy … the boy who raped you? … Later, when you got PREGnant, what made you decide to have an aBORtion? … What other options did you conSIder? … Did you tell your BOYfriend you were pregnant? … How did he reACT? … Did he HELP you? … Was he THERE for you? … Was ANYone there for you? …*

Do his PARents know? ... What do you need NOW? ... How can we HELP you?"

Or ... How about *this ... "Oh, Kelly, HONey. This is AWful, CRUSH-ing, uniMAGinable. I am SO sorry you have gone through such ... BIG ... SCARY ... LIFE-threatening ... LIFE-altering ... emBARrassing ... GUT-wrenching things—one AFter aNOTHer—all by yourSELF. I'm SO sorry you felt you couldn't come to DADdy and me. Why did you FEEL that way? When you're FEELing better, we need to TALK about that. We LOVE you. There is nothing you could EVer do that would make us STOP LOVing you. Come HERE, Sweetie, and let me HUG you and HOLD you. Go ahead and CRY. You've been holding it in SO long. Cry as long as you NEED to, and I'll cry WITH you. This is SO sad, and I am SO sorry this has HAPpened. As long as you LEARN from this ... as long as we ALL learn from this, we'll be FINE. Everything will be OK."* [PAUSE]

Apparently, my *mom* could use a *speech*writer in this conversation, *too* ... but ... like *me*, she doesn't *have* one.

Instead, when my mom finally *does* regain her powers of *speech*, she *says*, in a profoundly defensive *tone*, *"I'm SORry if you think I'm not HANDling this the way I SHOULD, but I'M trying to come to GRIPS with the FACT ... that ... 10 days before CHRISTmas ... I lost ... a GRANDCHILD!"* [LONG PAUSE]

I cannot be*lieve*, of *all* the things she *could* have said, she settles on *that*.

She adds, *"I don't know HOW I will tell your FATHer about this."*

That's it. No *com*fort. No discernable com*pass*ion. No inquiry about my needs or state of *mind*. We don't talk about it again, really (until *decades later*). ... We certainly don't talk about it *then* ... not in any *sub*stantive *way* ... *fun*ny, since we had always talked *so* freely and ener*get*ically about everything *else*. As you might *im*agine, the memory makes my mom *very* uncomfortable. To*day*, as a mother my*self*, I feel considerable com*pass*ion for her. In *that* moment, *not* so *much*. What a punch to the *gut* ... for *both* of us.

I head to my room ... spent ... not feeling *"immeasurably BETter,"* as I had *hoped*. In *fact*, I feel immeasurably *worse*. I don't remember *cry*ing, although I'm sure I *must* have. I *do* recall lying in my bed feeling com*plete*ly a*drift*. I had sought a port in a storm and had found it ... *"closed for rePAIRS."*

I sleep that night ... *when* I sleep ...with my face and body pressed up against the wall of my *bed*room. I try to take up as little space on the bed as *possible*. I want to disap*pear*. I wake with my fists curled up on my *cheeks*, knuckles under my *nose*, covering my *mouth*, as if wishing I could push back *in* *ev*erything that came *out* of my mouth the night be*fore*. I want a *do*-over. ... I imagine ... I *hope* ... my mom would like one, *too*.

Back *then*, I conclude I should have listened to my *in*stincts—the ones that told me *not* to *tell*. Given my mom's in*spire*d suggestion that I change *schools*, I was almost home free, *any*way. That might have *sound*ed ap*peal*ing, but ... unhealthy *secr*ets breed unhealthy *peo*ple. I wanted to have an *hon*est relationship with my *par*ents. We needed to *talk. Now*, looking *back*, I think some productive sessions with a better therapist would have helped tre*men*dously, but we didn't get them ... before or after. [PAUSE]

CHAPTER 21

Still STANDING ...

The next *morn*ing, I hear what I recognize as my dad's knock on my bedroom *door*.

I wonder how *he* will re*act* to my *news*. I want to *see* him, and I *don't* want to *see* him. He comes in and sits on the edge of my *bed*. I turn a*way* from him and *sob*, *"I don't want to LOOK at YOU. ... I'm SO sorry. ... I'm so aSHAMED. ... Don't LOOK at me."*

He reaches over, takes my chin in his *hand* and *forces* me to turn and look him in the *eye*. With tears in his *own* eyes, he says, [FIERCELY] *"You can look ANYone you WANT to ... RIGHT in the EYE. I LOVE YOU!"* [LONG PAUSE]

Hear this. Be*lieve* this. ... This *one* episode is *not* the measure of my mother's parenting ... nor of my *fath*er's ... nor of *me*. For the *record*, as it turns *out*, it was my *moth*er who told my *fath*er what to *say* to me that morning. He says he had *no* idea what to say ... the man ... who had found the *words* ... to turn the 6-year-old victim of a near-*hang*ing into the *"luckiest little girl on the BLOCK"* ... didn't know what to *say*. This calamity was SO enormous even *he* found himself at a loss for words. *This* time, *I* was the *"ruiner."*

"What should I SAY?" he remembers asking my mom.

"Tell her you LOVE her," she advised. *"She probably needs to HEAR that."*

She was *right*; I *did*. I would have liked to have heard that from *her*, but I knew she loved me de*spite* how far off my desired script that evening *went*. It would have made a difference to be better pre-pared by a better therapist, but *that* conversation could *not* have gone *per*fectly, no matter *how* well prepared we *felt*. We *all* did the best we could with the information and emotional depth we had at the *time*. That's all any of us *can* do in *any* *moment*. I told my mom things she didn't want to *hear* ... things *no* mother wants to hear—

ever ... things she couldn't take *in*. She froze. Under*stand*able and for*giv*able. [PAUSE]

I kept my story to myself *all* that time for a *lot* of reasons—*shame*, *fear*, con*fus*ion, em*bar*rassment (maybe de*nial*). Perhaps more than *any* of those reasons, I kept my story to myself because I didn't want to ... pol*lute* ... the ... loving, sup*port*ive, *al*most idy*ll*ic domestic environment my parents had so carefully *cre*ated. I didn't want to inflict *my* pain on anyone *else*, e*spe*cially *not* my *won*derful *par*ents. [PAUSE]

Still, the night of that conversation, I should have re*mem*bered that practically from the womb *for*ward, I had felt like *I* was the kid whose *job* it was to make my *mom feel* better. Right or *wrong*, I forgot to factor that *in*.

I forgot that my parents aren't *like most* parents. *They* divvy up the household responsibilities in *non*traditional *ways*—our mom works *"outside the home"* from 1962 *on*. More often than our *dad, she* reads the *whole* newspaper and dishes out the *dis*cipline. I remember see-ing her cry only *once* ... after some par*tic*ularly painful *den*tal work. Our *dad*, on the *other hand*, gives us our *"tubbies"* and, more often than our *mom*, sheds sentimental tears over ... *ev*erything ... John *Den*ver lyrics ... patriotic *cer*emonies ... *Hall*mark com*mer*cials ... and special songs we sing around the pi*a*no.

As I head into that conversation, I for*get* ... my *mom* is the one who runs the *"Standing Show" day-to-day*. She runs it *bril*liantly, with style and good *hum*or. *She's* the one who pays the bills and plans the vacations and buys our *school* clothes ... *and* our *gro*ceries ... *and* our *Christ*mas presents ... the one who cuts out *pa*per dolls and leaves them lined up on the couch as a surprise for us to find the next *morn*ing. *She's* the one who plays the pi*a*no and tells all those entertaining *sto*ries to *our* friends and to *her* friends ... at *birth*day parties and *din*ner parties and on silly Saturday after*noons*. *She's* the parent who plays *ban*ker, organizer, editor, decorator, hostess ... and, *yes*, hard-ass ... in a way intended to bring out the best in her children.

I for*get* she's *al*so the parent who has the hardest time with ... hard *times*. When she and my dad end up snowed in and nearly *pover*-ty-stricken in Plattsburgh, New *York*, after Korea, she *cries* ... for a whole *year*. ... *She's* the one who freaks out when I wake her *up* one morning with a gash over my *eye*, dripping blood on her *pil*-lowcase, because Cathy and I get carried away playing catch on top of our *coffee* table. ... *She's* the one who goes into *shock* when she gets a call from a CB *radio* operator ... telling her I've *to*taled my Ford *Pinto* in the *snow* on the way home from *work* at *16*. (Oh, yes, I haven't mentioned *that* ... brush with *death*. Too many *other* crises to deal with.)

Heading into that conversation, I for*get* ... it's my *dad* who puts out *fires*, fixes flat *tires* and keeps his *head* in a *crisis*. *He's* the light sleeper who comes when we cry if we're *sick* at *night*. ... *He's* the one who runs me to the *emergency* room when I'm barely *2* burning up with a fever *so* high I have con*vulsions* ... *so* hot it burns the enamel off my not-yet-visible *permanent teeth*. He has to stop at a *gas* station to splash my face with cold *water* from the *drink*ing fountain to bring my *fever* down. ... *He's* the one who saves me from being hanged. ... *He's* the one who grabs a *shovel* and, with one precise *blow*, kills a copperhead *snake* ... *right* before it reaches 11-year-old *me* on my grandparents' *lawn*. ... *He's* the parent who plays *peace*-maker, *handyman*, mech*anic* ... and, *yes*, sentimental *softie*.

As I head into the evening's conversation I for*get* ... my mom has a *REALLY* hard time seeing or imagining *either* of her children in *peril* ... or ... considering the prospect of out*living* us. The news I share isn't easy for her to *hear* (even *after* the fact). It wouldn't be easy for *any* mother to hear. And, since *I'm* the one *bring*ing the news, it's unlikely *I* can be the one to make her feel *bett*er about it.

I knew it wasn't gonna be pretty. I take a hasty, poorly calculated risk telling my parents at *all*—with only *one* therapy session under my *belt*. I take an equally hasty, poorly calculated risk telling my mom with*out* my *dad* there ... to help *her* take it all *in* (and to help *me* sort it all *out*).

I bucked the wisdom handed *down* by Confucius about *not* seeking *all* qualities in *one* indiv*idu*al. I go in *un*reasonably expecting my mom to wear *all* the hats in the family. Looking back on it *now*, we all a*gree* we would say and do a *lot* of things *diff*erently, but we don't waste time lamenting the *past*. We learn from it. To paraphrase Gerald Jampolsky, *"The time to be happy is now ... and there will never be a time that it is not now."*

Did that night go the way *any* of us *hoped* it would? *No*.

Did we choose to let it define our relationship forever *after*? No!

Are we still Standing? Abso*lute*ly!

Did my transition to my new school go *smooth*ly? Yes ... yes ... *yes*!

CHAPTER 22

STANDING in "Prison"...
in a *Good* Way ...

Never underestimate the value of a fresh *start*. My senior year ar-*rives*. Unburdened of my emotional *bagg*age, I charge into my new school with new energy and a whole new, refreshingly *simple game* plan. Two words, four *letters: "Be me."*

If *"open-space"* schools are *in*, let me *out*! Rumor had it the same *ar-chi*tect who designed the Missouri State Peni*tenti*ary designed my *new* school, unlike the funky, dysfunctional *"open-space"* school I left be*hind*. That suits me *fine*. I feel like I have just gotten *out* of a prison, *any*way. At my *new* one, I have ... ma*xi*mum se*cu*rity.

My new school offers more *calm, less cha*os. It feels like *hea*ven to have walls and halls and desks in rows and a teacher at the front of the *class* again, instead of cavernous rooms that blend the ca*coph*onous sounds of ... squealing biology students dissecting frogs ... *typ*ing classes clacking away (in the days of *type*writers) ... Span-ish fiestas next to Russian-verb conjugators ... algebraic theorems and bouncing basketballs, not to mention lunch in the Commons for hundreds of teenagers at a *time*. I can't be*lieve* how much safer I feel just from the design of the school it*self*, not to *men*tion the blessedly *un*familiar student *body*.

At *first*, I am *"completely bummed"* that the system requires me to lose my sports eligibility ... but ... as it turns *out*, my *new* school has a phe*nom*enal—*nati*onally *recog*nized—speech and de*bate* team, so I swap my *hockey frock* for a de*bat*er's *stop*watch and start develop-ing the skills I will *use* throughout my c*ar*eer ... skills that take me *all* the way to the *World* Championship of Public *Speak*ing in 2001.

If it's nerdy to join the Speech and Debate Team, call me *nerdy*. I LOVE writing speeches, competing in tournaments, arguing both sides of every issue, bringing home trophies and earning lapel pins. I amass an impressive array of debater *bling*.

When the stopwatch starts ticking, I have 2 advantages: I have spent my *whole life* debating the issues of the day at my own *din*ner table ... *and* ... I am what they call a ..."*novice*" debater ... as a *sen*ior ... competing against freshmen and *soph*omores. It appears that, by for*bid*ding me from stacking the *field*-hockey team, they suc*ceed* in stacking ... the de*bate* team. My confidence restored and my stomach back in working order, I feel un*stop*pable.

Who becomes managing editor of the school's *lit*erary magazine? *Me.*

Who writes for the school *news*paper? *Me.*

Who *aces* her AP classes? *Me.*

Who goes to the football games happy as a clam that she doesn't know a soul? *Me.*

I rack up one glorious year of anonymity that bodes *well.* ... If I can start over successfully *here*, I can do it again *next* year at the University of Missouri. "*M-I-Z ... Z-O-U!*"

If it's *un*fashionable to wear a hairnet and work in a cafeteria, call me *un*fashionable. I'm doin' it. I LOVE working at Pope's. All the kids who work there form an after-hours softball team in the summer. We all camp, swim and go on float trips together. I meet a fun mix of new friends from all over the St. Louis burbs.

We have the coolest managers at Pope's. Jimmy Woods, husband to my *previous, precious* boss and *con*fidant, *Lee*, is a big, *little*-bit-shy, *bar*rel of a man with a se*vere speech* impediment. I never have a problem understanding *Jim*my. For *some* reason, I was born with this kind of *"Henrietta Higgins"* quality that *us*ually allows me to decipher accents (*and* impediments) *really well.* That skill helps me at Pope's long before I use it as a *speech*writer.

Jimmy and I click because I keep cranky old Edna happy. Everybody at Pope's knows ... in *that* kitchen, *"If Edna ain't happy, ain't nooobody happy."* Edna hates *waste* ... won't *stand* for it. Jimmy *loves* that about her, since *he* controls the *bud*get.

One never knows whether Edna's comin' atcha with a *com*pliment ... or a cri*tique*. One day I stand beside a trash can plucking every bit of meat I can *get* from a *bunch* of *tur*keys I had roasted earlier in the *day*, then tossing the *bones* away. *Near* me, *Ed*na presides over some trainees like a *drill* sergeant. She sees me at work, stops in mid-bark, *thrusts* her arm into the trash can ... *all* the way up to her *arm*pit ... and pulls out one of the greasy *tur*key carcasses. She holds it out in front of her ... rotates it on her *fin*gertips, in*spec*ting it like a jeweler assesses a *gem* ... and says, *"Now, THIS, ladies, is the way to clean a TURkey! There's not a scrap of meat on here worth eatin'."*

Shew! [WIPE BROW]

Seemingly *small* things make a *big* difference to *Ed*na. She notices people who do a good job ... and people who *don't*. I find her crusty exterior easy to *take* because, under*neath*, she's *pure su*gar. She has a good crew, and she keeps us hoppin' and *mo*tivated. I like a*no*ther Pope's staffer, a cutie patootie named Judy, always smiling. If we *real*ly want to bring out Edna's *sun*ny side, we ask to see photos of her grand*son*. She almost *al*ways carries one in her *pock*et.

I *do* make a happy transition the next year to college at MIZZOU, and it's full speed ahead toward journalism school. When I head back to campus in September of 1980, I say *big* good-byes to my Pope's pals because I *know* I have seen the *last* of my cafe*te*ria days. I'm ... *"destined for greatness"* else*where*—but I'll encounter my share of turkeys as I climb the *jour*nalism ladder, too. I plan to stay the next 2 summers on campus, so, *"Good-bye, Pope's!"*[LONG PAUSE]

CHAPTER 23

STANDING on the Outskirts
of a Mass Murder ...

[LOW, SOMBER] Early on the morning of October 23, 1980, less than 2 months after my departure from Pope's, one of my sorority sisters rushes up to me and says, [URGENTLY] *"Didn't you used to work at Pope's Cafeteria at West County?"*

"Yeah ... why?"

"Everyone there is ... [PAUSE] ... DEAD!" Not exactly the kindest, gentlest way to de*liv*er that headline—but ef*f*ective.

"What?!"

"I just saw it on the 'Today Show.' Somebody shot 4 people and emptied out the SAFE there."

My throat fills with bile just *think*ing about it *now*. At the *time*, I'm stunned ... heartsick. *"WHO? ... Do you know who DIED?"*

"I'm not sure of ALL the names, but I know they said the MANager. ... Is it WOODS? ... JAMES Woods."

"Oh, noooo! NOT Jimmy!" *Ins*tantly I think, *"Oh, MAN, I hope LEE wasn't there."* *Thank*fully, she *was*n't.

My sorority sister can't remember the rest, and, without *Int*ernet, I can't get instant updates. Still, I *am* in journalism school, so I call the city desk at the *Columbia Missourian* to see whether they're getting more details over the *news*wires. Sure e*n*ough, James Woods, sweet, sweet Jimmy; Edna Ince, the woman I affectionately called *"Grandma"*; and a woman whose name I didn't recognize, Carolyn Turner (maybe the Pope's staffer who replaced *me*) ... *all* had *died*. Reports said the gunman herded them into the office and gunned them down one by one, *all* for $4,000 from the office safe.

That cutie patootie Judy Cazaco came in as the robbery was unfolding. Maurice Oscar Byrd shot *her, too*, through *both eyes*. She hangs on, in a coma, for 10 days but dies of *her* injuries, too.

And there I was, just 6 weeks and 120 miles a*way* ... still Standing, the hugs and handshakes from my good-byes still fresh in my *memory*. What a *ho*rrifying, *s*obering *jolt*.

Byrd had worked for the pest-control service Pope's used, so I *guess* that gave him the lay of the *land*. There were security cameras all over the kitchen and in the *of*fice, but, I'm guessing, since Jimmy would have *re*cognized Byrd, he probably buzzed him right *in* ... the way he *al*ways buzzed *me* in.

Byrd fled to Savannah, Georgia, where he bragged to his *"wife"* that he had killed 3 people—actually *4* people—to be with her and their baby. She turned him *in*. Police discovered he actually had *2* wives—one he just never got around to divorcing before he *"married"* the second one. *"Wife"* #2 said she didn't want to be with someone who would kill 3 people to be with *her*. ..."*Ya think?!*"

He was found guilty of 4 counts of capital murder and sentenced to death on each count. After almost 9 years of appeals, the State of Missouri executed Byrd by lethal injection on August 23, 1991.

I started working at Pope's on my 16th birthday, *so* e*ager* to start making *"real"* money—$1.35 an hour. Pope's provided tiny doses of cash and huge helpings of friendship, acceptance and *love* ... plus opportunities to pursue my *"greatness"* in small ways. Pope's had a lot of good, good people on the *pay*roll. I'll always be grateful for the *"fresh start"* I found there—at a time in my life when I needed every ounce of what they dished out—*veggies and* vali*dat*ion.

It has taken some doing (and the passage of a *lot* of time) for me to come up with even the tiniest *up*-side to the Pope's Cafeteria tragedy. E*v*entually, I do come up with *2* glimmers of grace: the *first* one would be of *no* comfort to the victims' families, but, for *me*, someone *not* as close, ironically, *c*ruelly, the murders probably help me remember those fine people better than I might have ... had our lives just gone their separate ways more *n*aturally and pre*dic*tably.

I mean, how well and how often do *most* of us remember the people we worked with at our earliest *jobs*? I would *like* to think I never would have forgotten *Edna* ... and *Jimmy* ... and *Judy*. I *wouldn't* have forgotten com*plete*ly, but I *would* have forgotten the particulars, and, I believe, that's where we *really* get to *know* people ... to *love* them—in the particulars ... the way they smile, the way they *smell*, a word they pronounce in a funny way, a facial expression only *they* can make, a way they talk to you that no one *else* can get a*way* with. I will remember my co-workers ... in the particulars. Their unthinkable *deaths* ... burned their re*mark*able *lives* even more permanently into my *brain* ... in*del*ibly ... forever.

As for my second thought about this ... when you get to chapter 45, *"STANDING in the Bright Light ...,"* you'll read about the upside I imagine for *them* ... *and* their families. ... God bless them *all!* [LONG PAUSE]

CHAPTER 24

STANDING in College
at M-I-Z ... Z-O-U! ...

Speaking of *families*, *eventually*, I go on to have one of my *own*. I date happily in college – one guy I REALLY love and think might be *"the ONE,"* but [WISTFUL], alas, *I* want to put my journalism degree to the test in a big *city*, while *he* wants to stay true to his small town roots after *law* school. It breaks *both* our hearts to find out we are geo*graphi*cally incom*pati*ble when we seem so com*pletely* compatible in nearly every other *way* ... (ex*cept* for his love of Red Man *Chew*ing Tobacco). [REPULSED FACE]

Shortly after we break *up*, a*noth*er wonderful guy—an outdoorsy, Eagle-Scout type (yes, not unlike my *father*; *I* see it *too*)—makes me blush and swoon. He writes love songs just for *me* and plays them on his gui*tar*. He takes me on rustic and romantic dates – to look at constellations in the *sky* ... or to listen to The *Commodores*.

I didn't make a habit of this ... honest!

I feel flattered. My personality is so ... *loud*, but he never seems put off by my energy. In *fact*, he has a *calm*ing, *quiet*ing effect on me. We mesh well. More than almost anyone I have *ever* known, he seems to know the *real me*. He *likes* the real me. He says so with words and music and *kind*ness—a happy novelty. I don't scare *him*; he doesn't *hurt me*.

He could have swept me off my *feet* —nearly *did*—but I wasn't ready for someone so serious ... so *wonderful*—so soon after *"the one who got away"* and, truth be told, I had some lingering issues from my teens to work out ... about un*worth*iness.

I suspect those issues made me more than a little hard to take in *col*lege. I must have seemed pretty tightly wound most of the time – *not* under the *in*fluence of anything, just high energy – an *"N.L.B."* (*"Nervous Little ..."*) like my *dad*, but in female *form*. Between classes, I worked as many as 60 hours per week at a nearby *coun*try club (on the golf course by *day*, in the dining room or behind the bar at *night*) ... [AUDIBLE BREATH] *and* ... I often took 18 hours of classes per semester, including extracurricular speech and *ad*vertising competitions ... [BREATHLESS] *and* ... I served as house manager of my so*ror*ity, painting all the rooms in our house one sweltering summer ... by *myself* because our house corporation wanted it *done* but didn't trust a *"gaggle"* of girls to tackle the job.

We gave the "chicken & egg" debate its due at MIZZOU.

The University of Missouri American Advertising Federation Competition team with our Professor Russ Doerner and our cardboard mascot "Herman," who inspired us to place fourth in the nation.

After those two *"good"* guys in college, I tended to attract men who treated me *bad*ly—not abusive *phys*ically but *cruel*. I realize *now* that I must have *sub*consciously considered my*self* profoundly flawed and not deserving of *bet*ter treatment or healthier re*lation*ships.

Those issues I failed to address or even to recognize until *much* later led me into the arms of the man I would love *not wise*ly but with my *whole* heart for more than 2 *dec*ades. [PAUSE]

CHAPTER 25

STANDING in the Path of a Lightning Bolt ...

As a journalism major in *college*, I developed a good sense of how long it would take me to produce a certain amount of *writ*ing. I probably HAD that sense long be*fore "J-School,"* but it *really* takes hold from then *on*. I become *very* deadline-driven and apply that mentality to ALL projects, *not* just to *writ*ing projects. If I figure something might take me 5 hours to finish, I start *work*ing on it 5 hours and [PAUSE AND SQUINT AS IF FIGURING] ... 5 *min*utes before the *dead*line, adding those extra 5 minutes just for good *measure*— cocky and confident I won't *need* them, probably because I almost never *do* ... ex*cept* for the day the lightning struck.

To this *day*, I build in a *tiny* cushion in case something throws *off* my *es*timate. It rarely does, ex*cept*, as I *said*, for the day the lightning struck.

Oh, I've *tried* the seemingly more sensible, plan-ahead, do-a-little-work-on-a-project-each-day approach. Do *you* do that? If you *do*, I'd like to know what gene *you* have that I didn't *get*. Engineers and ac*count*ants may pull that off, but, in *my* work and with my personal*ity*, I find working ahead of a deadline *ag*onizing and un*nec*essary, even counterpro*duc*tive.

Supervising my homework growing *up*, my parents often observed that if I just started a little earlier: (1) I might produce better results and (2) I wouldn't have to *sweat* so much. Bulls*#%! ... I wouldn't have *dared* say that *THEN*, but I stand by it *now*.

I *tested* my parents' 2-pronged theory. After painstaking *research*, I can de*clare, "Bulls*#% on both counts."* Better re*sults*? No. Fewer beads of *sweat*? No. The papers and projects I produce working even a *lit*tle bit a*head* of deadlines lack energy and organi*zation*. With too much *time* on my hands, I gather too much informa*tion* I don't *need*. *Then* I can't *find* the *good* stuff when I *need* it.

My thoughts lack *clarity*. With *rare* exception, my professors dished out Bs and Cs on plan-a*head* papers but As and *"excellents"* on my last-minute *master*pieces.

How about *you*? Are you a plotter and a *plan*ner ... or a last-minute *slam*mer? I find I need the juice ... the a*dren*aline ... the elec*tric*ity ... that flows when I race against the clock. I *love* (and *hate*) that *feel*ing ... the feeling I get when I'm not sure the thoughts will flow freely enough ... not sure my mind will stay a*lert* enough ... not sure my fingers will fly *fast* enough over that keyboard to get an assignment in *und*er the *wire*. It can drive project partners or co-workers *crazy*, but they can't argue with the re*sults* ... *except* on a day when *light*ning strikes.

Now, if you're like me, the *down*side of our deadline-driven approach comes in the form of constant—and I mean unre*lent*ing—dissatisfaction with our *work*. The finished project *never* turns out *quite* as well as we think it *could* have. Another downside: my writing assignments almost *al*ways turn out *long*er than they need to *be*. At the end of this book, for example, you *might* dub me the *"Bach of Autobiography"* because I seem to follow the rule *"Why say or write ONE word when 12 will DO?"* not unlike Johann Sebastian's sometimes maligned over-use of *musical* notes. It reminds me of something George Bernard Shaw once wrote to a friend: *"I'm sorry this letter is so LONG; I didn't have TIME to write a SHORT one."*

Ironically, I think THAT'S what makes the practice of procrastination *work* for those of us who *cling* to it. Procrastination works ... *only* if you lace it with a liberal dose of per*fect*ionism. Procrastination plus perfectionism. People like *me* (procrastinating perfectionists), who work the way *I* do (right up to the bleeding edges of our deadlines), recognize that, per*vers*ely, by putting off our work to the last *min*ute, we rob ourselves of the very thing our perfectionism wants *most* ... the chance to do the *final* edit that might make our product ... *perfect*.

It ranks as a total *self*-inflicted mind screw. I *love* it! In *oth*er words, 2 wrongs make a right: procrastination + perfectionism = a near-great product *this* time and a drive to produce something even *clos*er to perfect *next* time ... a drive to fine-tune your estimating ability ... a drive *not* to drive the *oth*er people in your life crazy with *your* crazy work habits. I find I have to care *just* enough about the *qual*ity of the finished *product* and feel *just* cocky enough to think I can produce something great under *pressure* ... *but* ... remain *hum*ble enough to know ... that what I produce on the *fly* ... will, without a *doubt*, have flaws. *Some*how, for *me*, that *never* translates into *starting sooner*. I'm not even *sure* I wish it *had* ... the day the *light*ning struck.

That day, in August of 1988—now a mom, 6 years *out* of *"J-school"* and a free-lance writer living in Evanston, Illi*nois*—I sit on the end of a *bed* ... leaning over a desk in my friend Ginny's *guest* room ... frantically typing against a deadline on a monthly parenting newsletter she and I co-edit. As multi-tasking mothers of 2-year-olds, even if we *hadn't naturally* tended toward procrasti*nat*ion, we would have found ourselves scrambling the day before our humble little nonprofit 12-pager went to *press. So* many diapers, *play* dates and de*mands*, so little *time*.

I can't re*mem*ber what pressing parenting issue flowed from my fingers *into* Ginny's computer that night—thumb-sucking stoppers, babysitting co-op dos and don'ts or a bedtime *book* review. Who *knows*? That was 24 *years* ago, but I *do* remember the violent thunderstorm that raged outside Ginny's open *second-floor window*.

The weather that week felt uncharacter*is*tically sticky hot for an Evanston August—more like August in At*lan*ta. Without A/C in that *bed*room, even with a *storm* brewing, Ginny left the windows *wide* open. We couldn't have stood the heat with the windows *closed,* and the eaves on her house kept most of the rain *off* the *wind*owsill. We kept plugging a*way.*

Come to *think* of it ... *may*be Ginny and I propped that window open so the hot air *we* generated could get *out* ... *not* to let any relief from the scorching summer temperature *in*. When we procrastinating perfectionists get cranking on a last-minute project, it can *feel* (and maybe even *smell*) as powerful and pungent as a *physical workout*. *Some*times, we *lit*erally broke a sweat while trying to get that news-letter out. Of necessity, mothers of infants and toddlers sometimes have to bypass *bath*ing, too, so Ginny and I had what you might call a multi-sensory, triple-whammy *heat* wave going that night—steam rising off the *side*walks, friction flying off the *key*board and the fa-miliar fumes of peanut butter and *panic* wafting off our mommy *bod*ies. [PAUSE]

Because we worked that month at *Ginny's* house, *I* had computer duty, and *she* worked up a sweat running back and forth between our *"newsroom"* and her *family* room down*stairs*, where her two kids, Fritz and Jane, watched TV, bothered only occasionally by the increasing claps of *thun*der.

I don't remember *why* I sat on the end of the bed instead of in a *chair*. Maybe there wasn't *room* for a chair between the bed and the desk. That sounds *right*. Or *may*be Ginny didn't *have* a desk chair. I don't *know*. *May*be, since we took turns at the co*mpu*ter, *she* used a chair and *I* sat on the bed. I can't re*member*. *Eith*er *way*, I know I felt *really un*comfortable. I had to sit either tilted *for*ward, with the edge of Ginny's wooden footboard digging into my thighs and *bum* ... or ... tilted *back*, with my bum sinking into the mattress on the *bed* side of the footboard and my feet dangling over the end on the *other* side, not touching the floor and cutting off the circu*la*tion to my *feet*.

I must have looked ri*dic*ulous ... arching and releasing my back ... trying to balance on that narrow footboard with my *not*-so-narrow *bot*tom. *No* matter. Discomfort and indignity be damned; we had a *dead*line to meet! [PAUSE]

As a *kid*, I had always heard ... if you count the seconds between a clap of thunder and the bolt of lightning that *fol*lows it, you can tell how many miles away from the center of a *thun*derstorm you are. Obviously, the closer together the thunder and lightning *come*, the lower the *num*ber, so we knew when the storm was getting *clos*er. *"One-thousand-ONE ... one-thousand-TWO ..."* Two seconds meant the storm was *2* miles a*way*. *Eight* seconds, *8* miles away, or so *"they"* said. THAT kind of math I could *do*. I think someone told us that formula to help us know *when* to seek shelter ... and/or ... to help dis*tract* us from the fear factor of severe *weath*er.

If *you* grew up with that folk wisdom, don't you think you might apply it later in *life*? During a *thun*derstorm, for example, when you can't count past 1,001 between the *thun*der and the *light*ning, a *smart* person might close the *win*dow. A *smart* person might seek *shel*ter ... in a room with*out win*dows, perhaps. A *smart* person might put a little distance between her*self* ... and any elec*tron*ic devices.

Not *me*. Not a bath-deprived, deadline-driven perfectionist like *me*. No, like a *dum*my, I keep typing that night *right* up until the thunder and lightning arrive like synchronized *drum*beats right on *top* of each other ... right on top of Ginny's *house* ... right on top of the transformer on the *tel*ephone pole right outside her guest-room *win*dow ... her *still wide*-open guest-room *win*dow.

BAM! [PAUSE]

... A tre*men*dous lightning bolt strikes the transformer ... spewing sparks in every direction ... like an e*nor*mous, *one*-shot, *one*-color blast of *fire*works. It sends the transformer's high-watt contents looking for an immediate outlet. The charge *finds* that outlet just a few feet a*way* ... in *me*! I watch the fiery jolt (*lit*erally fast as lightning yet *seem*ing like slow motion) run along the short length of wet *pow*er lines between the telephone pole and Ginny's *house*. It blasts *right* through her com*put*er monitor and *key*board *in*to my face and *fin*gers and throws me off that al*read*y-out-of-balance *foot*board. I can *feel* the force *com*ing before it ar*rives*, and I hear a low, deep, *om*inous buzz rolling my *way*. I now know electricity makes a very distinct sound when it's on the loose looking for a new *home*. ZZZZZZZZZTTT! [PAUSE]

If you have ever rubbed your feet across carpeting in the winter and given someone a playful static *shock*, you have an *oh*-so-tiny sense of what that jolt *felt* like. My *dad* often played the *stat*ic game with us ... as *kids*. We'd sneak up and *shock* him [DEMONSTRATE W/ ONE FINGER AND ZZZT! NOISE], and then *he'd* retaliate. *His* touches always buzzed louder and stung more than *ours* did. We never understood *why* until we realized he had his *car key* ... *hid*den but pro*trud*ing from between his index and middle *fin*gers. Yikes! *He* employed ad*vanced weap*onry.

Es*sen*tially, the transformer outside Ginny's *win*dow becomes a *gi*ant *cos*mic *car key* ... playing a more intense *sum*mer version of that familiar *winter game. I'm* just grateful it didn't turn out to be a *"weapon of mass destruction"* for *me.*

First, sitting beside that open window, I feel goose bumps rise on my arms. All the hair stands up on the back of my *neck.* I *vaguely* remember an odd *smell*, like burnt hair, but I don't remember checking to see, then *or later*, whether the hair on my arms and legs suddenly seems crispy, discolored or ... *gone.*

The blast blows me clear off the *bed* ... lifts me up from under*neath* ... and sends me *fly*ing. I hit my head on the wall across the room, probably 8 or 10 feet away. I land on the *floor.* I must black *out* for a few seconds 'cause I wake up on the *floor* and start shaking my head back and forth like a cartoon character—odie, odie, odie!—and blinking erratically, *try*ing to *fo*cus, so my *eyes* can tell my *brain* what just *happened.*

Ginny had gone downstairs to comfort her *kids* when the storm started dealing its loudest blows. She darts back *up*stairs to check on *me* after the *crash.* Of course, *all* the electricity has gone out ... or, more accurately, *out* of the *house* but *into me.*

I feel disoriented in someone else's house in the *dark*, but, remarkably, I stand up without anything more *ser*ious than a minor bump on the *head.* No burns. No bruises. I think my wonky position on the end of that *bed* must have *ground*ed me somehow and saved my *life.* I come away a little *rat*tled maybe, but that would be hard to distinguish from my *nor*mal state. I had much to be rattled a*bout* in those days—motherhood, money, marriage to a man who gets more distant and dismissive by the *day. Still*, I guess my head must qualify as my sturdiest *part.* I hit a wall at lightning speed, yet mi*rac*ulously ... no harm done.

Ginny and I fear the lightning has struck the *roof* and *might* have caught the *house* on fire, so we go into the *at*tic to in*vest*igate. We find *all* of the home's antique knob-and-tube *wir*ing glowing in long strips between the joists. We don't *see* any open flames or smoke. *Still*, to be *safe*, we decide we better get the kids out of the house. Sure! *Now* we think about *safety.*

At *first*, I think *Ginny* offers to go for *help*, but we don't know who might still have phone service in the neighborhood, and her kids don't want her to *leave* them. I try to run across the street to seek help from a *neigh*bor ... in hopes of calling and checking on my *own* family, too, but the storm still rages. The rain comes down *so* hard and *so* fast I'm drenched before I take 2 *steps* off Ginny's *porch*. Tree limbs and leaves swirl all over the *street*. I have shoulder-length *hair* then. The wind spins my hair into crazy, wet whips, slapping me in the face, getting stuck in my mouth, making it im*poss*ible to see and *barely* able to *breathe*. The water and wind fly at me with such force and from so *many* di*rec*tions I have to gasp through my mouth, frantically, ir*reg*ularly, the way a drowning person might.

Wouldn't that be just *like* me ... to drown standing *up*?! ... to drown *stand*ing *up*, nowhere *near* a body of water or even a *bath*tub? ... to drown standing *up* ... *after* surviving a *lightning strike*?! I think I would be within my rights at that point to look into that stormy sky and say, *"Universe, you just like to *&#% with me, DON'Tcha?"* [PAUSE]

I make it across Ginny's lawn to the sidewalk and even to the curb, *only* to find that the storm has outpaced Evanston's no*tor*iously in-adequate sewer system. I step into shin-deep water in the *street*. Thunder booms. Lightning follows im*med*iately, *still* allowing *no* time in be*tween* ... to count *even* to ... "1,001." I have had e*nough* lightning for *one* night, so I re*treat*. We huddle on Ginny's porch to wait for the fire department.

I can't remember *how* we *not*ify them. [FUZZY EXPRESSION] Per-haps a *neigh*bor reports the strike, or *may*be they see it *all* the way from the *fire* station. *Thank*fully, Ginny has taught her kids to sit a safe *dis*tance from the T*V*, so they suffer *no* ill effects when the lightning strike fries not *only* the T*V* ... *and* the com*pu*ter ... but also *every oth*er ap*pli*ance in their home. As I re*call*, it even melts the control panel off Ginny's *mi*crowave and scrambles the circuitry in her washer and *dry*er.

The fire department arrives and declares Ginny's household *fire-free*. They declare her household *wir*ing, however, long overdue for an *up*grade and her ap*pli*ances un*us*able. It takes her *months* (and thousands of dollars) to restore *or*der. [LONG PAUSE]

Yes, as a journalism major in *col*lege, I developed a good sense of how long it would take me to produce a certain amount of writing. Too bad I didn't *al*so develop the good sense to keep my fingertips *off* a computer *key*board in a *thun*derstorm. [PAUSE]

Ginny and I miss our deadline. Still, we have a *great* cautionary tale to tell in our next *issue*.

If *you* find *your*self rou*tine*ly balancing on that procrastination/perfectionism blade, as *I* so often do, you may want to test the *"rightness"* of that for *you* ... *and* for the people who *care* about you. Does all that drama more often *serve* you ... or *scorch* you (and *them*)? How much difference does it make to you ... (or to the people who work, love and/or live with you) if you temporarily abandon your personal *hy*giene? How often does procrastinating perfectionism result in a *more*-perfect *product*?

Test the rightness of that balancing act as it impacts the quality of your *work and* the quality of *life* you want with and for your family members, friends and *co*-workers. Even if it feels un*nat*ural, *try* working a*head* of your deadline just once or twice. I *have* tested my down-to-the-wire work habits. They *work* for me (and for those who *matt*er to me), albeit *pain*fully sometimes.

Don't mistake people who work like I do for disorganized, lazy slackers. I would argue ... *we* display those qualities no more and no less than anyone *else*. You de*serve* those aspersions only if you leave *out* the key ingredient in the *for*mula ... if you don't lace your procrastination with per*fec*tionism.

Saying I work down to the wire doesn't mean I don't even *think* about a project until zero hour. I *do*. The perfectionist in me in*sists* that I spend enough time on the *front* end of a project plotting the due date on my calendar, calculating how much *time* it should take, considering what *else* will compete with that project for my atten*tion*. Then I work backward from *there* to see how *late* I can *start* and how much and how often I'll have to work to git 'er done.

I have, no doubt, tested the patience of those closest *to* me with my work process. To a *point*, I consider deadline-driven adrenaline part of the journalistic drill, and those who live or work with or near people who work the way *we* do better get *used* to that. Having *said* that, if we creative types hope to be in relationships with people who prefer more linear, more predictable ap*proaches*, we *bet*ter take steps to *min*imize the fallout and *max*imize the perks ... or at least pre*pare* those people for the odd hours, odors and energy surges that go *with* our peculiar ... *gifts*.

To this *day*, invariably, the work I attempt to do *"a little at a time"* well a*head* of my deadlines never has *quite* the same *zing* as work I produce as the clock ticks down to *zero*. That practice hasn't burned me yet. ... Well, it a*l*most did ... the day the lightning struck.

CHAPTER 26

STANDING on the Promises of God ...

Near the *end* of chapter 45, I die. [PAUSE] ... Maybe I shouldn't have blurted that *out*. Should I have issued a *"spoiler alert"* about that? ... or ... Did my introduction, the table of contents, the cover and my reference to my death in the *"... Mass Murder"* chapter give it a*way*? [PAUSE]

Bear *with* me. We have a *lot* of ground to cover before I die. You may come to think of this as a very [DEEP VOICE] s-l-o-o-o-w death, 19 chapters off. Don't *worry*; many of those chapters are *really* short, and we'll laugh almost *all* the way into the *Light*. [PAUSE]

Death ... it's the ONE thing on *everybody's "Bucket List"* ... even if we don't write it *down*. It's ... the *BUCK*ET!

Have you ever *wondered* what it *feels* like to *die* ... or ... where we go *after*? Perhaps you *wish* you could find *out*, but you'd rather not pay the *price*—in *this* case, the *ulti*mate price. If *so*, I have good news! I can offer a no-cost, no-obligation *pre*view of ... coming at*trac*tions— a peek *in*side the *buck*et, so to speak. Or at *least* I can offer a peek inside *my* bucket.

I can't claim that what *I* saw and felt at the moment of death is what *every*one sees and feels at the moment of death, but consider me ... an *"embedded journalist,"* so to speak, bringing back news from the *"front"*—news as I saw it from *my* perspective. I'm willing to won- der aloud (*and* in writ*ing*) ... *"Did I see what I saw ... because that's what I exPECTed to see?"* [PAUSE] Truthfully, I'm not sure *what* I expected. Even *so*, I'm willing to wonder *further*, *"Do we ALL see on the other side of death what we exPECT to see THIS side of it?"* ... or ... *"Do we ALL get to ... see what I saw ... and GO where I WENT?*

I can't *answer* those questions; I've died only *once*, and I didn't *stay* long enough to get the whole *scoop*. That means, like a good jour- nalist, I shouldn't speculate without ad*mit*ting, at *that* point, that I have *stopped* reporting and *started guessing*. I'll tell you if and when I *do* that as I ... *"cover"* ... *this* part of my *story*.

I consider it pretty *cool* to know what it feels like to die ... or *almost* die, I guess. Don't get me *wrong*; I don't think *I'M* cool for knowing it. I think *IT'S* cool I *get* to know it. I mean ... why *me*? Why did the Universe decide *I* should possess that fairly rare *in*sight? Why at age 29? *E*ven when the most menacing manure has hit my fan in the *past*, I haven't asked, *"Why me?"* I don't have a *"Why me?"* bone in my *body*. *More* often, I figure, *"Why NOT me?"* Should I wish *my* poop would hit someone *else's* fan? *That* doesn't seem very *nice*.

We *could* get *lost* down some big, hairy, theological *rab*bit hole here, but, for *now*, I'll trim it down to this: when *bad* stuff *happens*, I don't believe God is *pun*ishing me. The God *I* know doesn't *work* like that, and I've invested literally *thou*sands of hours of study and re*flec*tion and ... Kell-to-consciousness contem*plat*ion ... and con-sciousness-to-Kell conver*sa*tion ... to discern *how* God *works*—how God works in *my* context, anyway. That's the *only* context on which I *claim* to be an au*thor*ity ... this patch of the planet called ... Kelly *Stand*ing.

*Fur*thermore, while we're talking about death and dying and God *"stuff,"* I be*lieve* ... [ABRUPT INTERRUPTION] Did you *hear* that, *"I believe"*? *That* means, as fore*warn*ed, I'm a*bout* to *spec*ulate, so hear this as o*pin*ion. Based on my *res*earch, journalistic *in*stincts and a *num*ber of close encounters with God, the *"Bright Light"* and *death* ... I be*lieve* ... the Universe uses everything for *Good*. That doesn't mean everything *feels* good or *looks* good or *smells* good, but I believe the Universe, how*ever* we conceive of It and what*ever* we choose to *call* It, is wired for Good (good with a capital *G*). As limited human *be*ings, however, we don't always choose to *see* all the good we have a*vail*able to us, *but* I believe it's *there, if* we *choose* to tap *in*to It. [PAUSE]

NOTE: If it *both*ers you that I capitalize the word *It* when I use ... *It* to describe the Light ... or Intelligence ... or Presence I encountered, all I can say is, if you spent *any* *time* in that Light, I doubt *you'd* lowercase the *i* *eith*er. That pronoun just doesn't do ... *It* ... justice.

We *can* see Good. We *can* tap into It. Witness, once again, my dad's use of the hanging-from-a-tree, doll-in-a-*creek* incident from chap-ter 2. He had a *choice*. From the day of my hanging and forever *for*ward, he *could* have allowed me see my*self* as a *victim*. He *could* have allowed me to see the world as a *scary* place full of bullies ready to pounce from behind *every tree*. He *could* have allowed me see Baby Pattaburp as ... past her peachy prime and no longer worthy of *love* ... or ... *or* ... he could *choose* to help me see the events of that day in 1966 as ... *"Good."* I *don't* mean *"hey-THAT-was-fun; let's-try-THAT-aGAIN"* good but, in*stead*, as *"let's-look-at-this-from-a-perspective-that-won't-cripple-and-control-us-for-the-rest-of-our-LIVES"* Good.

I'll say it a*gain*: as limited human *beings*, we don't always *choose* to *see* all the good we have av*ail*able to us, but we *always* have a choice ... *I* be*lieve*.

Like a responsible *"embedded journalist,"* I keep doing my home-work about these weighty matters—checking facts, vetting sources—while attempting to report the *"Truth"* (to *me*) from the *"Front"* (of *me*). Does that make *sense*? ... This book offers *my* Truth ... to *you*. You don't have to make it *your* Truth. In fact, you couldn't if you *wanted* to. The arrangement we have is *this*: I'll show you *mine* if you'll show me *yours* ... *Truth*, that *is*. Let's *talk* about it. Get in touch. *Keep* in touch. Write your *own* book.

When it comes to spiritual matters, I have what *I* would call ... an in*formed* (but always re*form*ing) *faith*. I base my beliefs on *more* than my experience, more than one *book*, more than *one* form of prayer, more than one *brand* of *pul*pit. You know me by *now*. ... I'm a *dig*ger. If I dig for all the ponies in the piles of ma*nure*, I *bet*ter be diggin' for *wis*dom *else*where, don'tcha *think*? *I* think so. ... So I *dig*.

I don't *always* have to *dig* for wisdom; sometimes it plops in my lap with *no* effort on *my* part at *all*, except to *see* it. *Oth*er times, in the case of the *"Bright Light"* I didn't see *com*ing, wisdom swings right in and smacks me in the *face*. It smacked me in the face in 1988 ... figuratively, in the form of a few *haunt*ing words spoken by a friend, the same friend—Ginny—who happened to experience the lightning strike with me. Maybe I should have stayed a*way* from her ... or ... more *likely, she* from *me*. [PAUSE]

CHAPTER 27

One OutSTANDING Question ...

In case you hadn't *noticed*, words *fasc*inate me. String them together *one* way and they can melt your heart. String them together *a*noth*er* way and they can *break* your heart. Hear certain words *one* day and they don't even *register*. Hear the *same* words *a*noth*er* day or from another *person* and they grab you by the *col*lar. We forget *some* conversations almost before they *end*, while, right or wrong, smart or stupid, healthy or *not*, real or *im*agined, we carry *oth*er con-versations—*oth*er words—around with us our whole *lives*. [PAUSE]

Thankfully, Jeff Hubbard from junior high wasn't the *only* person to teach me *that*. I remember a *com*pliment from my *third*-grade teacher, Mrs. *Nev*ille. From my *soph*omore year in *high* school, I remember an *in*sult from a tactless *boy*friend [GRIM] (name with-*held* but *not* forgotten). I remember my daughter's *first* words and my *grand*parents' *last* words. Words. For something so *in*tangible, they sure leave *last*ing *marks*, *don't* they?

To this *day*, I carry around a conversation I had with my friend Gin-ny in 198*8*. Her words ... melted my heart, grabbed me by the collar *and* ... lasted longer even than our friendship it*self*. We both moved *on*. I moved a*way*, but I took her *words with* me.

She asked me a *question*. I remember having *actual*, ob*serv*able, physio*log*ical *symp*toms in re*sponse* to that question. Though rhe-*tor*ical, Ginny's question struck me with *such* a*ston*ishing force my stomach clenched. My brow furrowed *in*volun*tar*ily. I swallowed *hard*. I caught my breath. I don't think she *noticed*, but I shuddered, *actually* shuddered. [SHUDDER] ... Her question changed the way I approached parenting from then *on*.

In 1988, *I* was 2*8*, and my daughter, Libby, was *2*. Ginny had her *own* 2-year-old daughter, Jane ... a son a few years *old*er, Fritz. Remember them from the day of the *light*ning *strike*? ... Ginny's *spouse*, Peter, spent much of his professional life in Ja*pan*, often for *weeks* at a stretch, which left *Gin*ny ... flying *solo* on the *home* front.

She had her *hands full*, but, for the *most* part, she seemed to embrace the challenge, even with its unre*lent*ing *work*load. *Still*, I suspect her long-distance re*lat*ionship took a toll and *may* have prompted her powerful *question*.

That day, Ginny and I stood atop the wood chips at a shady neighborhood park in Evanston, Illinois. Our daughters' legs dangled through the safety straps of the toddler swings, both girls tuckered out from an earlier play group with 5 *other* mom-and-tot duos. The *girls* babbled only occasionally to each other in toddler talk, [DROOPY POSTURE, HEAVY EYELIDS] their *eyes* getting heavier by the *min*ute, [BLINK AWAKE, STRAIGHTEN] while *we* pondered ma*tern*al topics and gently pushed the girls [SLOW, RHYTHMIC] baaack and forrrrth in that slow, hypnotic, winding-down-to-nap-time rhythm that mommies and daddies have perfected and passed *on* since the in*spired* invention of the *swing*.

"*Do you REalize ...*" Ginny began thoughtfully, [SWAY FORWARD/BACK] giving Jane a gentle nudge, "*if ANYthing HAP-pened to us right now* [SWAY FORWARD/BACK] *... our kids wouldn't remember ANYthing aBOUT us?*" [ABRUPTLY STOP SWAYING] [LONG PAUSE]

[FROWN. FURROW BROW. TILT HEAD.] *Wow!* I hadn't considered *that*. [PAUSE]

"*THINK about it*," she continued, raising her voice, pressing *me* har*der* with her *point* ... while still *gentle* with *Jane*. [INDIGNANT]

"HERE we ARE ... doing EVerything for our kids at this stage—EVerything—but THEY won't remember ANY of it."

[SWALLOW HARD. SHUDDER.] Wow, a*gain*!

Ginny pressed *on, "SERiously, what can YOU remember from PREschool? ANYthing? For THAT matter, I bet you barely remember anything before ... MIDdle school! ..."*

*A*ctually, I remember a *lot* from my early years, but Ginny still *sound*ed rhetorical, so I didn't offer a re*but*tal. In*stead,* she answered her *own* question, *"I'LL tell you what you reMEMber ... not MUCH ... almost NOTHing, I bet. ... Doesn't that strike you as ... iRONic?!"*

I laughed an uneasy laugh and then ad*mit*ted, *"It never ocCURRed to me. ..."* I struggled to get my head around this a*larm*ing new thought. *"I mean, I'm 28 years OLD. I don't THINK about checking OUT any time soon ... about Libby forGETting me."*

I missed Ginny's *point. I* focused on the parent *dy*ing part ... and how un*like*ly that seemed to *me; she* focused on the kids' forgetting part and how un*fair that* seemed to *her*—not a surprising dichotomy, considering how *diff*erently we experienced motherhood and married *life: my* husband home every night, *hers* far, far a*way* ... in the days be*fore* Skype, cell phones and e-mail. Our divergent perspectives provide *fur*ther evidence, I think, of the wide-ranging, long-lasting power of *words.*

Ginny con*clu*ded, *"It's a cruel twist of nature; THAT'S what it is."* Then I think she joked that maybe Nature couldn't *let* kids remember *all* their parents did for them at that early stage because, *if* they *did* remem*ber,* they would *never* ... have children of their *own. "The human race would DIE OUT!"* [PAUSE]

I headed home from the *park* that day with the dead weight of a wilted 2-year-old in a *stroll*er and a disquieting weight on my *mind.* Even though we came at the matter from different di*rec*tions, Ginny was *right.* If anything *hap*pened to us, our kids *would*n't remember anything a*bout* us—a sobering *thought.*

I felt com*pelled* to *"do"* something with Ginny's insight. No ... what's a stronger word than *"comPELLed"*? ... I'd say I felt be*yond* compelled; I felt inexplicably *called* to do something.

Ginny's question made me realize I needed to get my *"house in order,"* so I sprang into action on 2 fronts—one *practical*, one philo*sophi*cal. I started reading up on the subject. On the *practical* side, I didn't have a *will*. [INCREASING ALARM] I needed to *get* one. I needed to discuss its contents with my family and give them a copy or tell them where to *find* it.

[NORMAL VOICE] I learned I shouldn't keep my will at *home*. Experts suggested I keep it in my lawyer's safe. *Uh, oh!* [REVVED UP] I don't have one of *those* either—a *law*yer. Experts even considered a safe-de*pos*it box a *bad* location for my will. If something happened to *me*, whomever I left be*hind* would have to go through a lot of red tape to access and open the *box*. If I in*sist* on keeping my will in a safe-deposit box, *they* said, [QUICKLY, BREATHLESS] I should keep *mine* in my *spouse's* box or in the box of a close *friend* and keep my *spouse's* will in a box we rent for *me* so *one* of us could get to a copy if, God for*bid*, we *need* to. So *now* we need 2 safe-deposit boxes we don't *have*??! [PAUSE, DEFLATED POSTURE, AUDIBLE *EX*HALE]

It all feels *very* complicated, but Ginny's *words* ring in my *ears* and spur me *on*. [VISIBLE, CLEANSING BREATH, STRAIGHTEN AS IF RESOLUTE]

Experts said we need to line up *le*gal guardians for Libby, not just cere*mon*ial guardians. Left without in*struc*tions, they warned, the court might appoint someone we don't *like*. *"Oh, my GOSH! ... Someone I don't like! ... WHOM don't I LIKE? ... I like EVERYbody."* Irrationally, I imagine the court going down the list of possibilities, in lieu of a directive from *me*, and sending Libby to grow up with some ... *mis*creant. ... Hey, like *words*, a mother's imagi*na*tion can pack a powerful punch.

Adding fuel to my frenzy, about that *time*, I remember reading an article in *Family Circle* that makes me feel like a parental putz for having overlooked so *much* critical *paper*work. I shouldn't stop at merely *naming guardi*ans, the author insists. ... What?! There's *more*? ... Yep, re*spon*sible parents re-*eval*uate their *choice* of guardians periodically, *too*, even *af*ter they've named them in a *will*.

"Are you SERious? ... I don't have TIME for this. ... Apparently, I don't have TIME to ... DIE."

The author per*sists*, urging me to ask myself, *"Has the status of the guardians you chose CHANGED in a way that would make you change your CHOICE? ... [INCREASING ALARM ...] Have they married someone you don't LIKE? ... Has THEIR family situation changed? ... Have they become ILL or moved to a place where you wouldn't want your child to be RAISED?"* [RESUME NORMAL VOICE] The *deep*er I dig, the more frantic I *feel*.

"Thanks a LOT, Ginny! The next time I SEE you, I'm gonna ask YOU some questions that will keep ... YOU up at night."

On the philo*soph*ical side, I get some nudges Ginny *doesn't* provide. In the space of a couple of *weeks*, *after* Ginny's *question*, I run across the *same* wisdom in several different locations from several *unexpected sources*. I tend to sit up and say *"Howdy!"* when that happens. It seems *every*one wants me to start keeping a *journal*— everyone from the author of an *ancient* article in my *dent*ist's office ... to a friend at *church* ... to my *car* insurance *company*!

Why would *they* care?! I don't see the connection im*med*iately. The insurance company's quarterly magazine, which, up to *that* point, I almost *never* took time to *read*, arrives in my *own* mailbox and touts the benefits of keeping a *jour*nal. A*mong* those benefits, they list ... how com*fort*ing family members might *find* those words in the case of a ... *policy holder's* ... untimely *death*. OK ... now I see why an in*sur*ance company cares about journaling. I consider it a fairly clever back-door way to market their *products*. I *also* consider it another sign I should take Ginny's question *seri*ously.

I'll ad*mit* ... our apparent lack of preparedness for our untimely deaths ... and ... my tendency to overthink back then ... send me into a bit of a *tizzy*. I suspect the wisdom that says *"What you THINK about you BRING about"* ap*plies* here, given how this story plays *out*. I ..."*tizzy*" ... a lot *less* now.

The *Family Circle* article urges parents to evaluate their insurance coverage—life and disability—for *both* parents ... and to consider setting up a fund for *college*. At *last*! ... We have *one* box checked ... saving for college. We al*ready* put aside a little bit *every* month for *that*, but we *don't* have insurance on *me*, so, at the end of all that research, I utter those *4* little *words* husbands *hate* to hear: *"We need to TALK."*

CHAPTER 28

A STANDING Argument ...

My husband and I have just purchased our first house, which leaves *very little* spending money. *Most* months, *every penny* goes to our mortgage ... and our meals. *I* could stretch *one* box of Tuna Helper to feed us for *4 days*! Long-distance calls count as *lux*uries in those *"olden"* days, before cell phones and calling plans with unlimited *min*utes. To stay within our *budg*et, I can make 10 minutes' worth of calls per *week ... max*, a de*cid*ed *hard*ship, since *every*one in my family lives back in St. Louis, 300 miles a*way*, and I have a baby do-ing *lots* of cute things I want to *share*, not to *men*tion all the news I hope to hear from *their* end. So what do I *do*? I write letters ... LONG letters.

The relationships that may have felt rocky in my *teens now* feel sol-id as a rock. In the years after high school, my mom and I reach out and recover. We bond over and talk about *every*thing—*big* things like ca*reers*, wedding plans and motherhood ... and *lit*tle things like movies, silly memories and clip-on *ear*rings (because *neith*er of us has pierced *ears*). We *rare*ly talk about *recipes*, however. Cooking doesn't qualify as a favorite feminine di*ver*sion.

My *ward*robe, in my early married days, consists of exactly *2* dress-es: I have a red plaid frock with a Peter Pan collar, oversized buttons and a faux belt that cinches in the waist ... *sort* of (*some*how, that dress manages to look *both* perky *and* pathetic at the same *time*) ... and, even *sad*der, I have a simple solid-green jumper, *home*-stitched by my *grand*mother. It prompts countless heartless, thoughtless, *clue*less people to ask, *"When are you DUE?"* ... every time I *wear* it, 2 years *AFTER* my *preg*nancy. [PAUSE]

Even *so*, in a *way*, I *love* my look. I feel like I'm taking one for the *team*. As a single working woman, I had owned a closet *full* of clothes with shoes and accessories to *match*. My priorities (and ... some of my *body* parts) *shift*ed post-pregnancy, so I settle for (and settle *into*) *mom* duds.

One bad perm, one GIANT pair of specs, one limited wardrobe, one adorable child.

I take off the *baby* weight well enough, eating a diet containing only 9% *fat*, which my doctor wholeheartedly applauds. I get up most mornings at 5 a.m. so I can meet a friend to walk 4 brisk miles in the *dark* before our spouses leave for *work*.

I had followed the Weight Watchers ma*ter*nity plan (which I'm told doesn't ex*ist* anymore) all through my pregnancy, gaining 40 pounds—a *reasonable*, un*remarkable*, *"just-a-little-more-than-we-like-to-see"* gain, according to the plan and my doctor in 1986. *Still,* I find that gain *scary*, since I have battled 15- to 30-pound fluctuations in my weight on and off since *high* school. If my body knew what fluctuation lay a*head*, it could have *warned* me, *"You ain't seen NUTHin' YET!"*

I had what *has* to qualify as one of Weight Watchers' all-time *most* imp*ress*ive weigh-ins—27 pounds lost in 2 *weeks!* (I skipped the week Libby was born—an *"excused absence,"* they a*greed.*)

Several aspiring *"losers"* in line be*hind* me hear the total without *see*ing who is on the *scale*. They gasp and crane their necks to see *who* has accomplished such a re*mark*able feat, only to see me hold-ing 9 of those *"lost"* pounds in my *arms*, wrapped in a pink *blank*et.

"Cheater! ... *CHEATer!"* they chant. Then, they joke that I won't lose the weight in that *blank*et ... for at *least* 18 *years!*

NOTE: Even back *then,* Weight Watchers' team members didn't blurt out *any*one's indi*vid*ual ups or downs from the *scale*. They *still* don't. Heck, *now* they even let you follow the plan on*line* and be a *totally stealth "loser,"* although, sta*tis*tically, those who attend *meet*ings lose 3 *times* as much weight!

At *meet*ings, they celebrate only *"cumulative"* numbers for the class each week, unless you *choose* to brag about or bemoan your re*sults*. Apparently, having a *baby* between meetings qualifies as an exception to the *"no-blurting"* rule. [SHOCKED] *"You're down ...* 27 *pounds!" I* didn't *mind*.

Over the 2 years that *fol*low, I work in*ten*tionally, *grad*ually (but not *al*ways successfully) to lose the *oth*er 13 pounds I had gained dur-ing pregnancy. With my *very* low-fat diet and *ex*ercise routine, I feel healthy and *strong* ... struggling quite a bit on the *mar*riage front ... *but* ... finding ways to be *happy,* reveling in *moth*erhood, decorating our new ... nest and doing a little freelance writing to keep my jour-nalist's *brain* cells firing.

There I *stand,* in the midst of it *all,* making arrangements for my *own* hypo*thet*ical *death,* which Ginny has so startlingly pre*dict*ed. It feels odd, out of *order,* but a*gain,* at the *same time,* strangely ... *urg*ent.

I head into the dreaded *"We-need-to-talk"* conversation with my spouse hoping to con*vince* him we need to find *some* cash *some*-where to buy life insurance ... to cover ... me.

Our talk goes *some*thing like *this*:

"We don't NEED coverage on you. I'M the sole breadwinner. Our income doesn't dePEND on YOU."

[RAISE EYEBROWS ... SMOLDERING TONE] Our income ... doesn't de*pend* on *me*?! [MILD SNEER] Hmmm. [PAUSE] I know he works *hard*. I know he works long *hours*. I *know* that his status ... as a straight-commission salesperson in a down *market* ... puts a *lot* of *weight* on his *shoulders*. *Still*, his *oft*-repeated claim to the title of [DEEP VOICE] *"sole breadwinner" stings*. It stings because ... in ad*dition* to at-home *mother*hood and all *it* entails, *I* feel like *I* work damn-near non-*stop* in support of *his* career and *our* income, *too*— serving on civic boards and joining social clubs *filled* with prospects he wants to *meet*, using my journalism degree and PR skills to write *literally hund*reds of his business notes and edit documents destined for his company's home *office*. I may not bring *home* the bacon, but I *save his* bacon ... more than *once*.

I do it. I do *all* of it, willingly, happily, a*gain* thinking I'm taking one for the *team* ... thinking we *both* think that ... thinking we are rowing the *same* boat in the *same* di*rection* toward the *same* sunny shores of prosperity and *"happily ever after."*

I believed *then*, and I *still* believe *now*, that in cases where a parent (*female or male*) exits, alters or abbreviates his or her ca*reer* to raise *child*ren (as the primary *care*giver), *that* spouse earns *half* of *every* dollar the *oth*er spouse *makes* (as the sole *bread*winner) ... at *least* half, e*special*ly if *both* spouses agree that's what they *want* and can af*ford* for their *family*, which we *did* and we *could* ... *if* we *scrimped*.

At the *time*, perhaps I should have pressed for more re*spect*. In*stead*, when he said our income didn't depend on *me*, I ig*nore* the slight and say, *"I KNOW, but you'd have to pay someone a LOT of money to DO what I DO!"*

He looks *skep*tical, but, [CHIRPY] not to worry; I'm *just* getting *start*ed.

"You WOULD have to pay someone a lot to do what I do," I in*sist*. *"We would want Libby to live the way she lives NOW, WOULDn't we? ... We'd want her to go where she needs to GO—to nursery school, to the Y, to PLAY group? We'd want her to learn the things we hope she'll learn and grow up the way we hope she'll grow UP, RIGHT?"*

Then I hit him with Ginny's *clin*cher question, *"What if I DIE?"*

[ROLLING HIS EYES] *"You're NOT gonna DIE."*

"You don't KNOW that. I'm not saying I WILL die, but I COULD. ... If I died and YOU DIDN'T, you couldn't ask a RELative to do all that I do. ... And ANYway, nobody lives CLOSE enough. You wouldn't want to MOVE ... after putting SO much time into building your business HERE."

[SIGH] *"So WAIT. ... Now YOU'RE dead, and I'M MOVING?!"*

I have to admit it sounds far-*fetched*. After *all*, I'm 28 years *old*.

"All I'm SAYing is ... you'd have to PAY someone a LOT to do what I do ... OR ... you'd have get re-married AWfully fast." [SMIRK]

"Now YOU'RE DEAD, I'VE moved aWAY ... AND ... I'm reMARried?!" [PAUSE/SHAKE HEAD IN DISBELIEF]

In my experience, this qualifies as the kind of discussion *most* men HATE—an *un*likely hypothetical ... posed by an alarmed spouse ... prompted by something a *friend* said ... fueled by some *fleeting* article ... in a *women's* magazine ... drafted by a *dubious source*. I know he's losing his *patience*, but I feel what I can *only* describe as Divine prompting to plead my *case*.

I joke, *"For the RECord, I hope you'll wait an apPROpriate amount of time before you rePLACE me."*

[DISGUSTED] *"I'm goin' to BED."* End of discussion.

CHAPTER 29

STANDING (and Sitting) on Thin Ice ...

My spouse may silence *me* the night we have *"the talk,"* but my Divine internal *wood*pecker won't shut *up* about the arrangements I need to make for my untimely *death*. I decide to approach it as a *jour*nalist, on behalf of *all* at-home mothers and fathers. I decide to *write* about the subject and share Ginny's provocative question and its practical *and* philosophical implications. I write a 2-part series for that tiny-but-meaty monthly parenting newsletter Ginny and I co-edit.

Looking *back,* I gave the first installment a pretty *gloomy* title: *"What Will My Daughter Know of Me If I DIE Before She's Three?"* Morbid? *May*be, but, for my *readers*—the parents of *toddlers*—you gotta ad*mit* ... it's a *grab*ber. And ... I consider it *bet*ter than *"What Will Your Daughter Know of YOU If YOU DIE Before She's TWO?"* [PAUSE]

In the article, I pose Ginny's question and write about feeling nudged *ever since* to keep a *jour*nal. I say I have started recording things I want Libby to know about herself and about me if, God for*bid*, I don't live to tell her my*self*. I urge readers to do the *same*. In *truth*, I think I *mean* to journal more often than I actually *do* it, but today I *do* have several Rubbermaid bins stuffed to overflowing with old journals, so I must have taken the assignment seriously enough *not* to rank as a *total "prepare-as-I-SAY-not-as-I-DO"* hypo-crite.

The articles I had read about journaling say it doesn't matter *what* we write, just *that* we write. Often too tired by the end of the day to face an entire blank *page*, I remember using a special *cal*endar at first, just to write a *few* words in *each* day's square. I jot down new *foods* Libby tries and re*jects* ... or ... new *words* she pronounces in funny *ways*: *"spec-tac-LEE-ar."* Leave it to *my* kid to attempt a 4-syl-lable word only 2 years out of the *womb*.

A Test of Wills

I've always loved hypotheticals. I used to drive my mother crazy playing the "What Would You Do If. . ." Game.

"What would you do if you found a million dollars in the street?". . ."What would you do if someone left a baby on our door-step?". . .and, my mother's all-time, most-hated question, "What would you do if I died?"

Her response was usually, "Oh, Kelly! Don't *say* that! Don't be so morbid!"

Morbid, maybe. But now, my "What Would You Do If" Game has taken on a whole new meaning. Back then, it was just a hobby to consider "What Ifs." Today, as a parent, it's a responsibility.

Writing a will, naming guardians for your children and making sure the people who need to know your intentions know them is part of that respon-sibility.

Of course it isn't something any of us *wants* to think about, but, the reality is, if you and your spouse should die without a will naming legal guardians for your children, the court will appoint someone to care

for them— someone who may not be your first choice, or even your second. How awful!

A lawyer can draw up a simple will for about $25 to $150. The library even has plenty of refer-ences to help you prepare a will yourself, although having a lawyer review it still is a good idea.

But parental responsi-bility doesn't end merely with *writing* a will. Having one won't do your children any good if no one knows where it is or what it says. A Feb. 1, 1989 *Family Circle* article offered these tips:

–Tell your family where your will is located!
–Discuss its contents with the people who would be involved upon your death.
–Store your will in a safe place. *Don't* keep it at home where it could be lost, stolen or destroyed.
–Your lawyer's safe may be the best place for the original copy of your will, experts say.

–A safe–deposit box is *not* an ideal place for your will since it might not be available immediately upon your death. If you *do* store it there, however, be sure someone, in addi-tion to your spouse, knows where you keep the key. And, consider keeping your will in your spouse's box and his/her in yours to avoid delay should one of you die.

After you've gotten these unpleasant legal hypotheticals out of the way, you can sit back and consider some happier hypotheticals:

What would you do if you got to sleep late every day for a month!. . . What would you do if your children were *born* potty– trained? . . . What will my children be like when they're my age? It's not such a bad game after all.

Remember, we'd be interested in your thoughts and experiences regarding wills, insurance and the "legacy" you hope to pass on to your children.

I title part 2 of my series *"A Test of Wills,"* about the legal and finan-cial side of young parents preparing for *death* ... and ... the mild ar-gument it had prompted between my *spouse* and me. A very *punny* title ... but practical, *too*, I hoped.

Those articles appear in November and December of 1988. By Au-gust of 1989, just 9 months *later*, I start exhibiting a *mild* but dis-quieting symptom—rectal *bleed*ing. No big deal ... *except* ... by *then* we're trying to conceive a second *child*, and this seems unlikely to *help*.

[VAMPY] *"Hey, HONey ... c'MERE!* [INSERT COME-HITHER FIN-GER CURL W/ AMOROUS EYES & SLIGHT SMILE ... PAUSE ... FOLLOWED BY ABRUPT EYE POP AND *VISIBLE BUM* CLENCH. LOOK QUICKLY FROM SIDE TO SIDE, FROZEN, AS IF AFRAID TO *MOVE*.] ... *"Oops! Nope. On SECond thought,* [HOLD UP "STOP-SIGN" PALM] *DON'T c'mere, HONey."* [PAUSE]

Though inconvenient and slightly embarrassing, my symptoms don't seem *serious* enough to launch a *full-blown* tizzy. You have to remember, in *those* days, we didn't *have* every pharmaceutical company on the *planet* filling our magazines and TV screens with the vile and invasive side effects of their *products. "Rectal bleeding"* wasn't ready for its close-up; it had *not* yet entered our everyday lexicon. *Still,* I know the situation *does* deserve a call to my doctor, who happens to be on vacation. Good for *him ... bad,* as it turns out ... for *me.*

I tell the nurse, *"SURE, I'll see whoEVer's covering for him. This is GROSS; I'd rather not WAIT."*

And so begins my descent into what my lawyer friend from college later calls *"the worst case of wrongful diagnosis"* he's ever *heard.*

The fill-in doctor refers me to an *aging,* bow-tie-wearing, conclu-sion-*jump*ing, egotistical gastroenterologist whose name I change *only* so I don't have to *look* at it again. Let's call him ... hmmm ... Dr. *Dolt.*

Over the next 8 months, he nearly lets me *bleed* to death. I see him for the *first* time in the *private* consultation side of his office—*less medical,* more mahogany. At *first,* meeting that way strikes me as kinder and smarter than making me sit on a *cold table* in a *sterile* exam room while I wear a *hospital gown.* I *still* prefer doctors who meet me with my clothes *on ... first.* So far, so good with Dr. Dolt.

That positive first impression doesn't *last.* I *sit* there, fully clothed, in a leather chair, surrounded by diplomas on his walls and plastic models of colons and rectums on his credenza. I size him *up.* He strikes me as a little gruff ... maybe a *lot* gruff. I have a high thresh-old for *"gruff."* I tend to take *"gruff"* as a challenge to see whether I can soften up the surly among us. *U*sually I *can.* Witness my dearly departed crusty old Edna, from Pope's Cafeteria. I softened *her* up.

Still, this doc seems like he has a deeper layer of crust than *she* did ... and an ego the size of an Illinois *governor's.*

"Maybe I'm rushing to JUDGment," I tell myself. *"Give him a CHANCE. Look for the GOOD in him. Maybe he's just ... BUSiness-like ... or OverBOOKED. After ALL, his nurse got me in on short NOtice. Maybe he's ticked at HER."* I wonder whether maybe I'm projecting my dislike of my *symptoms* onto *him.* ... *Who knows?* I decide to *like* him. [PAUSE, TILT HEAD] ...

[ABRUPT] Nope. I was right. It's official. Dr. Dolt gives off a brusque, bored, too-good-for-you vibe. *Obviously,* he doesn't *say* he thinks I'm be*neath* him ... to my *face* ... with *words;* he *says* it with his clipped, impatient tone and dismissive *body* language. I *hate* it when doctors *do* that ... or when *any*one does that ... to *any*one.

Still, playing the Pollyanna part I know so *well,* I squelch my intuition. I figure, *"This might not be an enTIRELy bad thing.* [LOOKING AROUND] *He has all these diPLOmas on his wall. He must know a lot about SOMEthing ... even if it ISN'T MANners."*

My internal voice adds charitably, *"Maybe I would behave that way if I went to school that long."* ... Nope. *Scratch* that. Lois and Kip *never* would allow me to get away with *any* version of Dr. Dolt's haughty attitude, no matter *how* many diplomas I ac*cum*ulated. My mom often jokingly quotes Winston Churchill about social blunders like the ones Dr. Dolt commits, saying, [MOCK, DEEP] *"That is preCISEly the kind of impertinence ... up ... with ... which ... I WILL NOT PUT!"* [PAUSE]

So *now,* in the space of a *nano*second, I go from per*turbed* to *pity* because the man didn't have *my* parents. *"Poor guy: if he KNEW better, he'd DO better."* Looking *back,* I find it alarming how quickly I abandoned my instincts for self-preservation, how quickly I gave *oth*er people the benefit of the doubt—even people who treated me less well than I de*served.* For a long time, I displayed an unhealthy hybrid of pride and humility—perhaps too proud of my *parents* and my *up*bringing, too ashamed of my*self.* I strike a better balance *now,* but, back *then* ... [VOICE TRAILS OFF ... SHAKE HEAD]

As I relate my symptoms to the dismissive Dr. Dolt, he takes *notes—* nothing odd about *that*—but the longer I *speak,* the more I notice a subtle and in*congruous shift* in his de*mean*or. As *I* share, in di*stressed* tones, what *I* consider at *least* inconvenient, if not a*larm*-ing, symptoms, *he* seems oddly ... *pleased.* Then, seeming to form a preliminary medical o*pin*ion, he asks whether anyone in my *family* has ever had something called "in*flam*matory *bow*el disease."

He asks his question in an odd, almost *hope*ful way, as if to say, *"Pleeeeze, bring me an interesting case. If you can't be interesting, don't BOTHer me."* Or ... wait ... maybe I'm giving him too much credit. Maybe he doesn't *care* about an *in*teresting case at *all*, just a *lu*crative one. *Eith*er *way*, I find his *al*most-gleeful, *ghoul*ish response to my symptoms off-putting from the *start.* And *yet*, I *choose* to sit there. I *choose* to return. I choose not to *say* anything ... back *then.*

I tell him I'm not *sure* about my family history but that my *sis*ter mentioned *some*thing recently about some gastrointestinal symptoms *she* was having. *"It MIGHT be that. WHAT did you CALL it?"*

Dr. Dolt seems even *more* pleased, repeating, *"Inflammatory bowel disease ... I-B-D."*

"I'll call her to find OUT."

I'm due back in his office the next day for a sigmoidoscope exam so he can see for him*self* what's going *on "up there."* Over*night*, I call my *sis*ter. She says that, *no*, the worst she has *ev*er encountered is something called *"IRritable bowel."*

Before my scope, we meet again in Dr. Dolt's private of*fice*. When he *sees* me standing in the *door*way, he dispenses with *"Hello"* or any *oth*er pleasantries and gets *right* down to *bus*iness, saying, [EXPECTANTLY] *"Well ..."*

I'm *so* startled by the lack of *greet*ing I look at him blankly.

[PUZZLED] *"Well ...?"*

"WELL... did you talk to your SISter?"

"Oh! ... YES. She says she doesn't have inFLAMmatory bowel disease. She said what she has MIGHT be ... IRritable bowel."

With *that*, the seemingly dis*gust*ed Dr. Dolt *lit*erally tosses his expensive pen in the air and lets it fall and clatter loudly onto his *desk.*

[IMPATIENT, DISMISSIVE] *"Is THAT all?! You mean irritable bowel SYNdrome. And that's just a little nervous diarrhea. ... Half the popuLAtion has THAT."*

I feel almost apologetic. *"I'm sorry to disapPOINT you, doctor. I'm sorry my sister doesn't SUFfer MORE. I'm SORry my case isn't more INteresting or more potentially PROfitable for you."* No, I didn't actually *say* that ... or say *anything*. I did *think* it, though. What an *ass*! At least he works on the right part of the *body*! I guess it *takes* one to *know* one.

For the *record*, I have *since* met *many* gastroenterologists—fantastic doctors who manage to pre*serve* my *dignity*, re*spect* my in*tel*ligence *and ease* my an*xi*ety, *all* while saving my *life*. Not *ALL* doctors resemble the organs upon which they *work*. [PAUSE] For whatever *reason*, I fall into the hands of one who *does*. If I had it to do *over again* ... if I had the wisdom *then*, at 29, that I have *now*, at 51, I would have left the office right then and there, be*fore* Dr. Dolt fired up the old sig*moid*oscope. I would *heed* the red flags my intuition kept waving about him. Then a*gain*, looking on the *bright* side ... (if a sigmoidoscope exam *has* a bright side) ... if I *had* walked out ... I wouldn't have this *story* to tell, and you know by now how my family *loves* a good story ... as long as you live to *tell* it.

Dr. Dolt performs the test, but he seems to view it as a rote, obligatory-but-no-longer-interesting *chore*. I half expect him to play a round of solitaire with *one* hand while conducting the *test* with the *oth*er. He travels 10 centimeters up, *"where no man has gone beFORE."* He finds nothing and says so with a tone that conveys, *"What a waste of my TIME!"* He seems to for*get* that I didn't seek him out hoping he *would* find something. *I* hope he *won't*. I can't believe I seem at cross-purposes with my doctor ... because I'm not sick *enough*. I don't *want* to be interesting. I have *no* de*sire* to end up a fascinating medical *footnote*. I want *answers* ... ad*vice*.

"You probably just have HEMorrhoids."

I hadn't even had *hem*orrhoids when I was *preg*nant. The women I knew who *did* have them didn't seem to think there was anything ... *"just"* ... a*bout* them. Before I even called my *reg*ular doctor, I had done the *"chick thing"* and compared notes with my close *friends*. *None* of them had experienced *any*thing like *my* symptoms.

I let all those diplomas on Dr. Dolt's *wall* blind me, thinking he must know *better. Still,* I muster the courage to *challenge* him, *"Wouldn't I KNOW if I had hemorrhoids?"*

[CLIPPED] *"Not necesSARily; they might be inTERnal hemorrhoids. ... Sit on ice cubes."*

"ICE cubes?!"

"Yes, that's what I would suggest. Sit on ice cubes ... several times a DAY ... until your symptoms subSIDE. It's nothing SERious." He *says* this with his *back* to me, over his *shoulder,* as he walks out the *door.*

In *retrospect, this* is where the comedic news team on *Saturday Night Live* could unleash one of its *"Really?! ... Really?!"* segments.

"Really, Dr. Dolt?! REALLY?! Nothing SERious?!"

I leave his office feeling like he has patted me on my feminine little head and sent me away with a *lolli*pop ... or, more *a*ccurately, a *popsicle. In fact,* my husband and I attempt to keep our senses of *humor* about it all and jokingly refer to *me* as *"frigid" and* to this period in our *mar*riage as *"The Ice Age."* I keep my ice packs carefully *seg*regated in our freezer and call them *"ASSicles."* [PAUSE]

My symptoms in*ten*sify—with more frequent and heavier *bleed*ing. I call Dr. Dolt's office. He asks me to *quanti*fy my blood loss. He sounds *skep*tical, even *angry, "Is it just a little on the TISsue, or is the whole BOWL red? ... Because a couple of DROPS can LOOK like a LOT of blood. ... Is it EVery time you GO or just once in a WHILE?"*

"It seems like a lot to ME ... the whole bowl, I guess, and, YES, EVery time."

"If you start losing more than a cup a DAY, CALL me." He clicks off the line. What am I supposed to *do*? Hold a measuring cup under my *bum*?

He told me to call, so I *do* call, every few *weeks*. I call to say I'm losing even *more* blood. I call to say *now* I'm having diarrhea *with* the bleeding. I call to say *now* I'm having cramping *with* the diarrhea *and* the *bleed*ing.

"You're probably eating too much FRUIT. Stop eating FRUIT. ... Are you sitting on the ice cubes?"

"Yes, as much as I CAN with a 3-year-old at home. The ice ISN'T HELPing."

Halloween 1989. Libby's costume hit the right note, but my health fell flat.

This goes on for 4 months—calling, being told to sit on more ice cubes, being told not to worry, being told it's ... *noth*ing. In December, I call Dr. Dolt a*gain* to say I don't mean to be a *pest*, but I *really* think something may be *wrong*. I'm *tired*. I'm losing weight—*never* a cause to complain in the *past* but alarming at this *new* rate.

[IMPATIENT] *"We did the scope in my OFFice. Nothing's WRONG."*

"You did the scope in AUGust. It's DeCEMber ... and ... NOW ... I'm not always making it to the RESTroom in time."

[PLACATING] *"These things take TIME. Give it TIME. You had a big BAby; that can put PRESsure on things ...* [WHISPER] *down there."*

Down there?! Was he *kid*ding? Where *are* we, in *kin*dergarten? I begin to wonder whether someone *forged* the signatures on all those dip*lo*mas.

[ARGUMENTATIVE] *"I had my daughter 3 YEARS ago. Wouldn't this have shown up THEN if that's what CAUSED this?"*

[OVERLY PLACATING TONE] *"Not necesSARily. Give it more TIME."*

*Mean*while, my husband earns a trip for two to Mexico for exceeding his sales goals for the *year. Olé!* At the *time*, Mexico's water, produce and sidewalk vendors have a reputation for inflicting *"Montezuma's revenge"* on even the *healthi*est travelers. In light of that rep*ut*ation *and* my con*dit*ion, I call Dr. Dolt and ask whether he considers it wise to take the *trip.*

"Pass up a trip to MEXico because of a little diarRHEa?! Don't be riDICulous! GO! Have a good TIME. If you feel WORSE, you can always call me when you get BACK ... AND," he adds brightly, *"just THINK ... you'll come home with a TAN."* [PUZZLED EXPRESSION ... LONG PAUSE]

CHAPTER 30

STANDING on a Beach in Mexico ...

I go to Mexico. I am de*ter*mined *not* to rob my husband of his hard-earned *trip*. I tell myself I will be *fine*. After *all*, Dr. Dolt *said* so ... for whatever *that's* worth.

I do fairly *well* in Mexico, better than *many* on our trip, in fact. The sun feels *so* good on my skin. The waves sound so *sooth*ing. I see the sights, in*clud*ing the beach near Puerto Vallarta, where locals claim Maria Shriver and Arnold Schwarzenegger spent their recent honeymoon—an omen, perhaps? We see pageantry and poverty in equal measure—toddlers begging while their mothers wash clothes on river rocks, little girls of the mid-'80s dressed in starched white *pin*afores and *ruf*fles like the ones *we* wore in the '60s. We see tourists taking their photos with 9-foot-long iguanas and 6-foot-tall warriors wearing feathered masks, war paint and not much *else*. [RAISE EYEBROWS ADMIRINGLY—COUGAR PURR]

So far removed from my typical Chicago *Feb*ruary, I feel *en*ergized. I try *every*thing—every ac*tiv*ity, that is, *not* every food or every cocktail with a salted *rim*. I ain't loco, Amigo.

I *do* attempt a hilariously jarring brand of tropical *po*lo. Players sweep full-size brooms at a volleyball ... heading for opposite goal-posts ... on the *beach* ... while riding on the backs of *buck*ing, *barely* willing *don*keys.

The final score? I have *no* idea. I meet *my* goal by staying *on* my donkey. *La*ter, *pool*side, I cheer on some of the company's *top* executives, as they fight—and I mean wage *war* against each other—over a greased watermelon in the *pool*. I can't say I recom*mend* Water-melon Water Polo as a spectator sport, unless you *like* the sight of middle-aged white men with their chest hair sculpted into Vaseline peaks and pasty skin dotted with *water*melon seeds ... swim trunks askew. [REPULSED FACE ... PAUSE]

Still, I *love* the trip! I play a little tennis. I even win the prize for ... *worst play*er. I hadn't played since *high* school, and, given the months of embarrassing symptoms I have en*dured*, I accept my award *proud*ly ... as a badge of *cour*age ... just for stepping onto the court in *white* tennis togs. I do *all* that *not* without *fear,* but *thank*fully without *in*cident ... gastro or *oth*erwise. [WIPE BROW, RELIEVED]

Then, at dinner on the last *night*, fellow travelers start dropping like flies, thanks to a week's worth of forgetting to use bottled water to brush their *teeth*, a week's worth of putting local-water *ice* cubes in their *drinks*, eating *ques*tionable churros from *street* vendors and eating lettuce rinsed in *un*filtered water from the buf*fet* ... *all* of which I carefully a*void*. On the plane on the way *back*, when the pilot turns off the fasten–seat-belt sign, we hear frantic clicks up and down the *aisle* from passengers *des*perate for a lavatory. Again, mi-raculously, *I* don't happen to be *one* of them, but, *boy*, can I *sympa*-thize! The shoving in the aisle recalls the violence of Watermelon Water Polo but with higher *stakes* and with*out* the Vaseline.

Good thing I enjoy that week in Mexico, what I *now* see as the calm before the ... storm—the *shit* storm—*lit*erally.

CHAPTER 31

STANDING at Sears with Big Bird ...

Mexico throws me *off*. I feel relatively *well* there. I had told myself I *would* be, so I *am*. I tell myself I won't ruin my husband's trip, so I *don't*, but I can't main*tain* it. Within a *week* of *our* return, my *symp*toms return with greater force and frequency than *ever*. Up until *now*, Libby hasn't *not*iced my frequent trips to the bathroom. Those must strike her as *nor*mal, in light of her fairly recent potty training.

"Don't WAIT, Mommy. If you gotta GO, GO!" she says, as if mentoring me on best potty *practices*.

Her encouragement turns to im*pat*ience when *my* trips to the bathroom force me to cancel or delay some of *her out*ings. I explain that I picked up a bug in Mexico called *"Montezuma's re VENGE."* She doesn't yet know how to be dis*creet*, so we have many teachable *mo*ments related to my con*dition* ...

A few days *after* we return from Mexico, I have to take our car in to Sears for new *tires*. I have to take Libby *with* me. We have to *wait*. That doesn't bode well. They tell me it will take 2 *hours* (an e*ternity* with an active toddler) ... but ... *fortunately*, Sears provides 2 amenities that put me at *ease*: a TV tuned to *"Sesame Street"* and a restroom located *right* off the *wait*ing area. I tell myself, *"We can DO this."* Almost as quickly, I realize, *"We canNOT DO this. I have to GO ... NOW!"* I lean down to Libby, al*ready* engrossed in Big Bird's latest *antics*.

[WHISPER] *"C'mon, Libby. I have to go to the BATHroom."*

"No! I don't WANNA go."

"I KNOW, Sweetie, but we HAVE to. I HAVE to go. C'mon ... PLEASE."

"I'm WATCHing!" she argues, without taking her eyes off the set. She points to the TV and stares at it *so int*ently you'd think she fears she'll miss another ... *moon* landing or ... a declaration of *war* or something if we step a*way*. She plants her elbows on her knees

and curls her fists up on her cheeks and, es*s*entially, *dares* me to make her *budge*. She *pur*posely avoids my *glare*, but everyone *else* studies *us*. The *oth*er Sears customers shift in their *chairs*. We share a *small room*, and this looks like it may become a *big bat*tle.

"You can watch when we get BACK. 'Sesame Street' *will still be ON."*

[LOUDER] *"No! I don't WANna go."*

[MORE ADAMANT] *"I KNOW you don't, but we HAVE to. I'm NOT KIDding, Libby. We have to go ... NOW!"*

My body tells me in *every* way possible I have NO time left for negotiation. I stand *up* ... *carefully* ... take Libby's hand and start to *pull* her toward the *rest*room. She *yanks* it away, something she wouldn't normally *do*, but *noth*ing works normally lately. She knows we have an audience; maybe *that* drives this *un*characteristic be*hav*ior. Maybe this qualifies as pay-back for our time away in *Mex*ico. I don't have *time* to *won*der. I take a *baby* step ... (the only kind I *dare* take) ... toward the restroom *door* ... about 15 feet a*way*.

"Nooooo!" she screams, abandoning her *"inside voice"* and alerting *every*one, all the way back, *past* the counter, through the tire center's cinder-block wall, to the mechanics out in the *ser*vice bay. *E*very head turns. All eyes (and all *ears*) are on *us*. Some bystanders look sympa*thet*ic. Some seem a*mused* ... some more an*noy*ed, even disap*prov*ing. I shoot them a look that says, *"I'm sorry; I'm doing the best I CAN."* I'm thinking, *"You have NO iDEa ... how much worse this could GET ... if I don't MAKE it to that BATHroom!"*

"No!" Libby repeats, as if I've stuck her with something *sharp*. She goes limp the way only a toddler *can*. I smile a weary, *very* pained mother's smile at the room packed with *on*lookers [SMILE, SCAN CROWD] and clench my bum cheeks together with all the force I can *mus*ter. [MAKE CLENCHY FACE] I literally *drag* Libby across the room. *She* flails. *I* flinch. I have her suspended by one *arm*, off the *ground* ... but facing the *floor* now ... with the toes of her shoes leaving vivid *skid* marks across the linoleum.

"No, no, no, no, no," ... she says in time with the bumping of her toes across the *floor*. She has an ad*van*tage. *Nor*mally, I could cross a room that size in *seconds*. *This* time, in *this* room, I have to move

very slowly, sliding Libby *then* shuffling my *own* feet … sliding Libby … then shuffling my *own feet* … a few *inch*es at a *time*.

We're *al*most to the restroom *door*, the Promised Land within *reach*, when Libby fills her lungs with one e*n*ormous *in*hale. She kicks and catches her ankle in one last-ditch effort to *teth*er herself to the nearest *chair* leg. She digs in *one* toe and explodes, *"Noooooo. I don't WANNA go! You'll have DI-UH-REE-UH!"* [LONG PAUSE]

*In*stantly, my face takes on the hues of a Mexican *sun*set … in re*verse* … traveling from my collar-bones *up* my face to the tips of my *ears. Se*veral Sears patrons nearly spill their *cof*fee. At least *2* laugh out *loud.* One *old*er woman wrinkles up her *nose.* Several pretend not to hear and keep reading their *mag*azines and *news*papers. The clerks at the counter stop dead in their tracks. Is it just my imagi*na*tion, or does one of them call out, *"Number 2!"* as the door swings shut be*hind* us? … Ugh! [BOW HEAD IN SHAME]

Mir*a*culously (and I *do* mean mir*a*culously), we make it into the restroom without *mis*hap. I hesitate to emerge since *every*one heard *every*thing—before, *during and af*ter our *test* of *wills.* … We take a *long* time washing our *hands.*

By the time we tip-toe *out,* someone has changed the channel on the T*V.* I'm *grate*ful. I decide we'll head into the mall to wait out the *rest* of our *2* hours. I find a *"safe"* place to sit—near a*noth*er restroom and a *foun*tain with a raised edge and lots of little kids running around in *circ*les. *Perf*ect! Maybe Libby can *join* them and burn off a little *steam.*

She does just *that.* Almost *never* shy, she joins the fun already in *pro*gress. She and her new playmates run rings around the fountain. They stop *sudden*ly. … [SQUINT AT DISTANT HORIZON] I see her holding *forth* with some children and their *moth*ers on the far side of the *foun*tain. She looks over at *me, points* and says, *"MY mommy can't run 'cause SHE went to Mexico, and she got … um … SHE got … hey, MOM! WHAT did you get in Mexico aGAIN? … Oh, I know. … She got … Montezuma's AVENGE!"*

CHAPTER 32

STANDING in an Ambulance ...

By *now*, you *may* feel like shouting, *"C'mon! DIE already."* After *all*, I promised *6 chapters* ago to kick the bucket. *Since then*, I've *dragged* you to a *park* ... stopped off to write my *will* ... made you wade through my wedded bliss (*or* ... *blist*ers, as it were) ... taken you to *Mex*ico ... introduced you to the doctor from *hell* (which froze over, by the way, complete with front-row seats to my own personal *"ASS Capades"*). I even hauled you to *Sears*.

Here I *am* ... 27 pages *later* ... *still* Standing. Well, sit *tight*. It's *almost* time to call a *chap*lain ... [PAUSE] or at *least* an *am*bulance.

My health declines *so* gradually from August of '89 to February of '90 I don't *real*ize how *sick* I am. I don't notice how *weak* I feel ... how much I'm *not* able to *do*. Where I would *nor*mally plop down on the floor to play *with* Libby ... or ... chase her around the neighborhood at high *speed*, by early *Feb*ruary, I find myself sitting on the *couch* merely *watch*ing her play and, then, eventually, lying *side*ways on the couch like a *droopy rag* doll, barely able to keep my *eyes* open. I rally enough to handle meals ... *bath* time and *bed*time, but I get up *count*less times every night with ex*cru*ciating waves of ... diar*rh*ea.

It *fi*nally occurs to me that we're in *cris*is mode when Libby brings me one of those little cardboard *Golden* Books. *You* know the ones ... *The Pokey Little Puppy, The Little Engine that Could, The Three Little Pigs* ... the books we used to buy at *dime* stores for 59 cents *each* ... the ones with the colorful *draw*ings and gold tape binding *run*ning along the *edge*. Each one *could*n't weigh more than a few *ounc*es, but, by *Feb*ruary, when Libby asks me to *read* one to her, I can't *lift* it. [PAUSE] In *my* book ... my little *Golden* Book ... *that* spells *cris*is.

I call Dr. Dolt *one last* time and beg him to take me *seriously,* to look closer, to *do some*thing.

"I can't LIVE like this."

"OK, I tell you WHAT. ... I'm going away for a long WEEKend," he says. *"I'll be back in the office on TUESday. If you're not better by THEN, we'll have you come IN, and I'll do aNOTHer scope. In the MEANtime, get some REST. ALL moms get tired when they're chasing after toddlers."*

[EXASPERATED SIGH!!!]

I spend a grueling weekend during which I lose more and more *blood ... and ...* more and more *sleep.* I call the *min*ute he said he would return. Dr. Dolt's postvacation schedule is booked *solid,* so his nurse puts me off for ... a*nother week.*

That night, I don't sleep at *all.* We have a tiny Cape Cod house, but, *thankfully,* it has 2 bathrooms. I have to go *con*stantly now.

God for*bid* someone might be *in* there when *I* have to go. *That* night, I try to use the bathroom down*stairs*, so I won't disturb Libby and my husband sleeping *up*stairs. *E*very time I *go*, I have blinding cramps in my gut that make me double *o*ver.

You know the agonized sound you make when you throw up *vio*lently? ... the intense way your abdominal muscles contract as your stomach contents lurch *up*ward? Well, *I* have the e*qui*valent going on down be*low* ... the same tortured sounds and the same violent lurching but *low*er and *down*ward. It *feels* and *sounds* like someone is twisting and wrenching and *wring*ing *out* my colon like a drenched *mop* ... a mop that *looks* like it's soaked in *blood* and *smells* like ... well, I won't even *take* you there. I feel dizzy but I wait until my husband wakes up to tell him I think I need to go to the *hos*pital.

Libby's up. I make her breakfast, all the while steadying myself against the edge of our kitchen *sink*. I plant my elbow on the countertop next to the *sink* and rest the *left* side of my *head* on my *fin*gertips as I wait for the *toast* to pop up. I get Libby settled ... then I rush the few feet to the downstairs *bath*room for a*noth*er particularly bad bout.

I fear I might *faint*, so I sit back down on the toilet lid and double *o*ver, wincing and gasping as if I've just run a *mar*athon. I consider yelling for *help*, but I don't want to frighten *Lib*by. When the dizziness sub*sides*, I make my way to the *bot*tom of the *stairs* ... at the *front* of the *house* ... to call up to my *hus*band. I can *see* him shaving up there with the bathroom *door* open. He *sees* me and wonders what the *heck* I'm doing. He takes one puzzled step out of the *bath*room, with his razor still poised in the air. He watches as I hunch over *al*most in slow *mo*tion. He tells me later that he *won*dered why I was looking *so* intently at the *stairs*. He as*sumes* I'm leaning down to pluck some *lint* off the *car*pet ... un*til* ... he sees my *face* ... hit the *step*.

He *bolts* down the stairs, his *own* face still covered in shaving cream, except for *one* long foam-free stripe down his *cheek*. He helps me to my *feet*, and I say, [URGENT, LABORED] *"Hurry! Get me to the BATHroom!* ... and [WEAKLY] *Call 9-1-1. I had a REALLY ... BAD ... NIGHT."*

He gets me to the *bath*room, and I close the *door. Thank*fully, Libby's ob*liv*ious, playing down the hall in our *fam*ily room. I finish *up*, flush and open the door but leave my hand on the knob because I can't *focus* and don't *dare* let *go*. Wobbly, using my *right* hand, I steady myself on the *toi*let tank. I *faint*, hitting my head on the tank or the toilet bowl as I *fall* ... I'm not sure *which*. I end *up* with my head on the floor in the *hall*way ... *out*side the bathroom ... and my *body* twisted around the toilet on the bathroom *floor*. Libby hears the crash and, like the curious little miss she *is*, comes to investigate.

As I come *to*, I see her standing in the hall with an absolutely *strick*en look on her face. They say a toddler's greatest fear is losing a parent. This is as close as Libby has ever *come*. I see sheer terror in my daughter's *eyes*, as if she can't make sense of the scene (which, of course, she *can't*). *I* can't even make sense of it.

In my e*x*perience, when people, especially *child*ren, come face to face with their greatest *fear*, it literally transf*orms* their *features*. Something happens in their *eyes*. You can almost *see* the veil of shock descend to protect them from whatever they don't *want* to *see*.

With me on the floor at her *feet*, *Libby* has that look. In fact, *today*, when I look at pictures of her from be*fore and af*ter that point in her *child*hood, I can see that shift in her *gaze*. It breaks my *heart*, and it strikes me that *some* of her innocence and optimism evaporated right out of her e*x*pression that day. I hope she re*claims* it, if she hasn't al*ready*.

A*long* with that image, Libby lets out this uneasy, dis*turb*ing, halting kind of *laugh*, [DEMONSTRATE] as if she thinks I might be playing some *sick* kind of *game* and I just haven't let her *in* on it yet.

She laughs, as if to say, *"Make this FUNny, Mommy. Make this FUNny."*

I can't get *up*. Yes, at 29 years *old*, I'm *living* the geriatric com*mer*cial, *"Help! I've fallen and I can't get UP!"* Sur*real*? *Yes*. Survivable? I'm not so *sure*.

My husband arrives, hastily dressed and *still* with only one stripe of whiskers shaved a*way*. He finds me on the *floor*. He barks at Libby, standing there *dumb*struck ... to hurry and get *dressed*. She doesn't *move*.

As human *beings*, we exhibit one of 3 reactions to *crisis*: *fight, flight* or ... *freeze*. In *this* crisis, Libby *freezes*.

[EYES WIDE, FEARFUL] *"What's wrong with MOMmy?"*

I say, [SOFTLY, WEAK BUT REASSURING] *"I'm OK, Libby. Mommy's OK. Go get DRESSED."*

She won't leave my *side*. I find it hard to be reassuring from that *angle*. I *force* a smile and look *right* into her *eyes*.

[WHISPER] *"It's OK. ... Go aHEAD. ... Get DRESSED."* I *whis*per my in*struc*tions, perhaps in the same *way* and for the same *reasons* my *dad* whispered to *me* when he saved me from *hang*ing—to calm her *down* and break the *spell*.

The paramedics are on their *way*. The dispatcher urges my husband not to *move* me, in case I have injured my neck or my *spine* in the *fall*. Sometime in the midst of all the com*motion*, I lose control of my bowels—*in*side my robe. *Lovely*, just *lovely!*

While I'm lying on the floor and drifting in and out of consciousness, the lingering smell of toast and scrambled eggs reaches my *nostrils*. I find it oddly *comforting*. *"At LEAST I fed Libby before I FELL and pooped in my PANTS. That's SOMEthing."* There I *go*, diggin' for the pony in the pile of ma*nure* again. Leave it to *me* to smell *toast* when I've just crapped my *pants!*

The ambulance arrives. A crowd of neighbors gathers outside our *house*. The paramedics strap me to a *back* board, although I'm *fairly cer*tain I have *no spinal injuries. "Gentlemen, my problems lie somewhat SOUTH of my SPINE, thank you very much."* A neighbor says Libby can stay and play with *her* daughter while they rush *me* away in the *ambulance* ... or ... *"am-BLEE-ance,"* as Libby calls it. My husband says he'll meet us at the hospital once he gets Libby settled with the *neigh*bor.

Libby says she remembers parts of that morning *vividly*. She watches the paramedics bark up our front door with the metal edges of the gurney on the way *out* and thinks to herself, [LIKE A TATTLE-TALE] *"Ummmm. Daddy's gonna be maaaad!"*

In the ambulance, I hear myself describing the months of symptoms that led up to the 9-1-*1 call*. I feel *stupid*. I waited too long.

I persevered through too *much*. I tried to be the stoic little Standing my parents *raised* me to be. I tried to be the perfect *mom,* the perfect *wife* ... but *this* ... *this* is *perfectly horrible.* At least I allow myself to hope I will finally get the help I *need.* ...

CHAPTER 33

STANDING in the ER ... Disrobing ...

At the *hos*pital, wouldn't you *know*, I encounter a nurse who could qualify as Dr. Dolt with*out* the di*plo*mas—brusque, thoughtless, compassion im*paired*. She can *see* I need to get cleaned *up*. And it no longer smells *any*thing like *toast* anywhere *near* me. There wasn't much *left* in my digestive tract when I lost control at *home*, but, now that I've been stretched out, strapped down and transported, I have quite a bloody *mess* running down my *back*, al*most* from my *arm*pits to my *knees* and twisted into the tangled, soggy folds of my *robe*.

[PERKY] Not to *worry*. My *robe* features a *long*, handy *zipper* in *front* ... one that runs *alllll* the way from my neck to my *knees* ... *so* ... I *fool*ishly as*sume* ... it shouldn't present a *problem* to *un*zip it, slide it *off* my *shoul*ders ... *un*der my bum and *off* ... past my *feet*.

Does my cruel or merely dim-witted nurse *choose* that route? *No* ... of *course* not! In*stead*, inex*pli*cably, she unzips the robe only *part*way, and, before I can *protest* or suggest an al*ter*native, she pulls it off ... *OVER MY HEAD* ... dragging its *"aromatic"* contents across my *face* ... [GRIT TEETH] and into my ear and *hair*. Let me *say* ... I *don't* happen to *be* one of those people who thinks her poop doesn't *stink*. I *know* better.

My nurse then, realizing (or *reveling* in) her miscalcu*la*tion, without a *word*, sets the of*fend*ing garment down on the end of my gurney by my *feet* and *leaves* me like that—face smeared with poop and blood—while *she* goes to fetch *clean*ing supplies ... I *hope*. [DUMBFOUNDED EXPRESSION] ... *or* ... Has she gone for a *coff*ee break? I can only *wonder*.

Let me be *clear* here. I *love* nurses. They have held my *sorry* hide together better, more thoughtfully and more pro*fess*ionally than many, if not *most*, of my *doct*ors. I look for the *best* in *nurses* ... just like I look for the best in everyone *else*, and I often find it easier to *see* in nurses. They're so ... *nursey*. Maybe that's why *this* ER anomaly stands *out*.

I understand nurses have a tough *gig*—wading through the dregs of the human *body* ... *day* after *day*. I *get* it. My friend Linda has a *sister*, Mary, who's an ICU nurse *man*ager. Mary says she does *fine* with *most* of the dregs she encounters on the *job*, but ... she can't stand 2 things: *"snot ... and bloody stool."*

"Snot makes me GAG," she admits. Then, with the detachment only a nurse who has spent *years* in the trenches could dis*play*, with a *straight* face, Mary says, *"And you KNOW ... poop doesn't smell that good to START with ... so ... when you add BLOOD TO it, it's REALLY AWFUL!"*

Unfortunately, just like *any* profession, nursing has *its* share of bad apples, *too*. A rare few go *into* it because they *like* inflicting pain or they like to see people *suf*fer. It appears I got *one* of them in the *ER* that day. She re*turns* with a plastic *basin*, a bar of *soap* and a few washcloths draped over her *left* arm. Right off the bat, I can *tell* ... it *ain't* gonna be e*nough*. Be*fore* she takes *any* more steps to *de*-muck me, she scoops my wadded-up robe into *one hand*, frowns and wrinkles up her *nose*; she's seemingly *un*sure which way to *go* with it. Standing at the end of the gurney with her *back* to me, she shifts *left*, then *right*, then left a*gain*, like a basketball player hoping to hand off the *ball*. She finally spins to *face* me, holds the nasty bundle practically in my *face*—*again!*—and asks, *"What do you want me to do with this?"* [PAUSE, SNEER]

"Oh, Honey! I'll TELL you what you can DO with THAT."

I'd *like* to respond that way ... but ... knowing she holds my life (*and* my access to *soap*) in her *hands*, I think *bet*ter of it. In*stead*, I choose to say, [WEARILY] *"Just throw it a WAY."*

"Really?!" she says. *Now* she no longer seems dis*gus*ted by it, as if to say, *"Hey, cool! A FREE ROBE! ... If YOU don't want it, maybe I'LL take it. ... Really? You don't WANT it?"*

"No. Really. I DON'T WANT it. I don't ever want to SEE it aGAIN."

*Thank*fully, a more com*pas*sionate nurse hooks up my IV and pumps me full of fluids to replace all I lost over*night ... (and some* of what I lost over the preceding 8 *months*).

They alert Dr. Dolt, who arrives 3 ½ *hours la*ter, all breathless and tan ... from God knows *where*. Before he sees me *or* my chart, he calls to me from across the ER, *"This is UNrelated to what I've been TREATing you for. This is UNrelated to what I've been TREATing you for,"* saying it *twice*, as if to convince him*self* and anyone *else* within *ear*shot.

He's not *close* enough to hear me re*spond*, [VOICE RISING] *"This is preCISEly what you HAVEN'T been treating me for."*

He arrives at my gurney all smiles.

"So, you had a rough NIGHT, huh?"

"She's had a rough several MONTHS," corrects my husband, meeting Dr. Dolt for the first *time*.

Dr. Dolt deflects the thinly veiled criticism. *"Didn't you say you'd been to MEXico recently? I bet you picked up something THERE."*

I think, *"You IDIOT!! You TOLD me to GO there. Knowing my symptoms, you TOLD me not to pass up a trip to Mexico because of* [MOCKING] ... *'a little diarrhea' ... and NOW I'm in the ER ... and YOU claim this is 'unrelated' to what you've been TREATing me for??!"*

I shriek all of that in my *head*, but the *only* part I have the *guts* to say *out loud* is, *"This started beFORE Mexico, Dr. Dolt ... WAAAY before."*

[LIGHTLY BOMBASTIC] *"I'm STILL inclined to think you just picked up some TROPical BUG. [AS IF TALKING TO A CHILD ...] Let's get you HYdrated ... send you HOME ... and see how you do after a few days' REST."* Other than vitals, Dr. Dolt doesn't order *any* other *tests*.

I don't *ar*gue. I *should*, but I *do* feel *bet*ter after several bags of fluids ... *and*, at *home* that night, I sleep better than I have in a *long* time, although *still* plagued by frequent bouts of diarrhea, but ad*mit*tedly, *mea*surably—if only temporarily—better.

The next *morn*ing, already starting to de*cline*, I replay Dr. Dolt's ER performance in my *head* and *fin*ally act upon the uneasy intu-ition I had *had* about him from the *start*. I call my *reg*ular doctor, the one who had been on vaca*tion* back in *Aug*ust when my health *start*ed to un*rav*el. To his *cred*it, he ad*mits* that he doesn't like what he *hears* but says Dr. Dolt has always been his *go-to* ... *gas*tro guy ... and he wants to believe my experience is an aber*ra*tion.

Just to be *safe*, however, since I have been losing what *I* describe as *"a lot"* of blood ... and ... since Dr. Dolt hasn't *or*dered any *blood* tests, *my* doc sends me to the lab at the hospital to check my *hemo*-globin level. *May*be we'll i*dent*ify this mys*ter*ious Mexican bug I have sup*pos*edly con*tract*ed, too—even though I felt *fine* in Mexico. *My* doc alerts Dr. Dolt about the order as a *court*esy and promises to share his *find*ings with him—a courtesy Dr. Dolt has *not* seen fit to observe in re*turn*.

My doc says to me, *"I'll have them rush the results so YOU don't have to spend aNOTHer night worrying."* Nice! What a *novel*ty—compassion from my *care*giver. I tell him I suspect ... if *he* had been on the case in *Aug*ust, I wouldn't be in this pickle *now*.

I can barely *drag* myself to the lab, and then we wait at home for the re*sults*. Instead of hearing from *my* doctor, I hear from Dr. *Dolt*. It seems he doesn't want *any*one looking over his shoulder on my *now*-precarious case, so, without a word to me *or* my husband, he takes over, and I never hear another *word* from my regular *doc*tor. *Very* casually, without even the *slight*est note of a*larm* in his voice, Dr. Dolt says he wants me to return to the *hos*pital, probably for *"a day or 2."* As it turns *out*, my hemoglobin level is *"low,"* he says, and we should get to the *bot*tom of it. Bottom, in*deed*!

He plays it cool ... *so* cool, in fact, I don't really understand how *ser*ious my condition is until I'm sitting across the desk from the triage nurse in ad*miss*ions. She looks at a piece of paper in front of her—apparently my *lab* results—and does a discreet double take. A subtle expression ... *some*thing ... crosses her face. Is it con*cern*? ... a*larm*? ... a *gas* bubble from *lunch*? I'm not *sure*.

"Are you all RIGHT?" she asks.

"No, not REALLY." I half smile. *"That's why I'm HERE."* I try to be friendly, the way I was *raised* to be when meeting new people—

asking how *her* day is going, trying to take a genuine *in*terest, cracking jokes—but I can't quite pull it *off.* I'm fading *fast.*

"Do you feel FAINT?"

[WEAK] *"Well, I fainted YESterday a couple of times. NOW, I'm just REALLY tired."*

She says, *"I don't DOUBT it. You have a hemoglobin level of 5.5."*

"Is that BAD?" Hey, I studied *jour*nalism, not *ju*gulars.

She says, *"A NORmal hemoglobin level is 12 to 13, so, YES, 5.5 is NOT where we want YOURS to BE."*

I *never have* been *great* at *math,* but even *I* can tell that means I have less than *half* the blood of a normal *person.*

I slump in my chair. [BLINK HEAVILY] *"I feel like I can barely hold my HEAD up."* I lean on the edge of her desk and support my head with my *hand.*

"... Let's get a wheelchair in here and get you to a ROOM." Very professionally, she asks, *"WHO'S your DOCtor?"*

I *tell* her. ... Despite her diplomatic poker face, I can *tell* she disapproves.

She's not the *only* one.

CHAPTER 34

Generating OutSTANDING Headlines ... for Someone *Else* ...

I don't know about *you*, but *I* find that ... the circumstances I rail against *most* ... often bring my greatest *bless*ings ... in the *end.*

As a *child*, I rail and wail against the *bul*ly who hangs me from a tree ... but ... in the *end* ... I see myself as the *"luckiest little girl on the BLOCK."* ...

As a *teen*ager, I rail, *in*wardly, about switching *high* schools right before my *sen*ior year and having to *for*feit my sports eligi*bil*ity ... un*til* ... I *rea*lize ... in the *end, that* sacrifice *frees* me *up* ... to join a *dif*ferent kind of *team*—the speech and de*bate* team—a nerdy-but-nice assemblage that launches ... more *true* friendships, garners *more troph*ies, bestows more con*fid*ence and leads me to a more satisfying ca*reer* than ... *field* hockey, *vol*leyball, *soft*ball and *bas*ket-ball ever *would* have ... had I *stayed* at my other *high* school. ...

In my late *40*s, I rail and wail, a*gain* ... *most*ly *in*wardly, about a *friend* who stands me *up* at the last *min*ute for a live performance I have talked about for *months*, which she *knows* I can't *wait* to at-tend. ... In the *end*, the person I ask to take her *place* pulls some un*expected strings*, and we get to *meet* the performer (my *all-time* favorite) *face-to-face* ... one-on-*one* ... behind the *scenes* ... at a *big* party ... *after* the *show!*

Yes, I rail, but, *some*how, the Universe never fails to deliver an *up*side ... to my *up*set. When bad things *happen*, I may not *see* the cor-responding blessing for *days*, weeks or even *years*, but that belief in all things happening for *good* ... really *does* play out in my life. Once again ... always ... I learn, *"If you don't get what you WANT, find a way to love what you get ANYway."*

I don't get what I want in one of my early PR jobs after *col*lege, either. I forget the *"love-what-you-get"* lesson and rail once *more*.

Who *wouldn't*? I work with people I consider *difficult* ... making calls I consider em*bar*rassing ... to elusive media people I find un*receptive* ... for a salary almost *anyone* would consider in*sulting*. Reporters don't want to *hear* about, *write* about or *talk* about my client's re*volt*ing array of medical products ... products that deal with *THE* most *personal* bodily functions ... or ... *mal*functions ... you can *name*.

One reporter stays on the line long enough to ask, [REPULSED] *"Do you get PAID to TALK about this stuff?"*

[INCREDULOUS] *"Do you THINK I would DO it if I DIDN'T?!"*

After several of those rude and/or dismissive encounters with local and national media on behalf of one par*ti*cularly *odious* product, I ... finally find a re*ceptive* re*porter*. He returns my call—a mini *miracle*. He requests *more* details and pumps me for scoop be*yond* our media kit. He *prom*ises a full-page spread on the front of his newspaper's *features* section. I can't be*lieve* my good fortune. Quickly cocky, I credit my perse*verance* and good *sales*manship. Then he sends me all over *town* to find stats he *claims* will make the piece even *more* compelling.

In keeping with my lifelong *pat*tern, I don't detect his ill in*ten*tions; I don't catch the whiff of de*ceit* in his *voice*.

I hold this seemingly unfortunate job in the days *long* before the Internet. Back *then*, reporters have to make more *calls*, crack more *books* and consult what *we* would consider prehis*toric* to*day*—microfiche *archives*. Without ad*mit*ting it, the *lazy* reporters (and even some hardworking, res*pon*sible journalists) rely pretty heavily on PR rookies like *me* to dig up *facts for* them.

It feels symbiotic: *they* get the background *they* need; *we* get the coverage and third-party en*dor*sements our clients *crave* and advertising dollars can't *buy*. *They* have the column *inches*; *we* have the dollars, the *"purdy"* graphics and the carefully crafted messages to help *fill* them. That serves the *public*, howe*ver*, only *if* the reporter taps more than one *source* ... *if* he or she doesn't just write a lop-sided piece, filled with whatever *one spin* doctor chooses to dis*close*.

I seem to re*call* that the industry stats of the time confirm that at *least* a *third* of what passes for *"news"* ... on the air and in *print* ... is *put* there by a public re*la*tions person. Don't hear me suggesting that qualifies as a *bad* thing necess*ari*ly; it *doesn't*. Pre-Internet, how would people know about good products (or *bad* ones) if *no one* gets the *word* out?

In journalism school, our professors told us ... the best way to drive a *bad* product *off* the market ... is to promote the *hell* out of it. They were *right.* PR people can get *lots* of consumers to buy a product ... *once.* After *that,* the product stands or falls on its own *me*rits. A *bad* product falls *fast*er if it has a big budget be*hind* it.

Companies or causes with PR budgets often could and still *can* afford to conduct expensive *re*search no one *else* will *do*—not just the fluffy stuff like *"Who has the most kissable lips?"* but *weight*ier questions like *"Who's making cancer treatment more comfortable?"* ... *"How can I protect my kid from a bully on the PLAYground ... or* ... *germs on a TOOTHbrush ... or ... oBEsity in the LUNCHroom?"* ... *"Where should I park my investment dollars for reTIREment?"*

Public relations practitioners dig for and draft *a*nswers to those questions. Money spent on public re*la*tions (*or* ... [LOFTY] *"reputation MANagement,"* as the industry calls it *now*) ... supports no *end* of worthy causes. Corporate sponsorships pay for a lot of the *facts,* a lot of the *fun,* and a lot of the *fund*raising the *not*-for-profits *need* to stay up and *run*ning. Theo*ret*ically, journalists keep those efforts *hon*est; they provide the *bal*ance so the public doesn't get herded toward a product or a cause like a slack-jawed tourist with his or her *pocket* gaping open ... ripe for *pick*ing.

Back *then,* in 1985, the reporter *I* reach takes a *dif*ferent path. After gobbling up every *bit* of background I *offer,* he *does* produce the full-page article he *p*romised, but he provides *no* balance at *all.* In*stead,* he devotes *all* of those precious paragraphs ... to my *competitor!* [PAUSE]

When I ob*j*ect, he says, *un*apologetically, *"I never SAID I would devote a whole page to YOUR PROduct. I just said I would devote a whole page to ... the ISsue."*

The *"issue"* to which he re*fers* is ... colorectal *c*ancer. *No* one wrote about it or talked about it much back then, in the days BE*FORE*

Ronald *Reagan* and Katie Couric's *husband battled* the dis*ease*.

[OUTRAGED] I challenge him. *"That's disHONest! You KNEW I thought you were writing about my client! ..."*

I have to be *careful*. ... I can't afford to tick *off* the reporter for fear he'll write something damaging about my *client*, but, c'mon—he hadn't mentioned the *client* at *all*.

"Why didn't you just get the research you needed ... from the company you DID feature in the article—quote THEIR experts, use THEIR stats, abuse THEIR PR people?"

[SOFTLY, DISCOMFITED] *"They don't HAVE any. THEY don't HAVE the research or the PR budget your CLIent has."*

"Maybe that should tell you their product isn't as GOOD ...," I suggest *bold*ly.

You done me wrong, Mr. Reporter!

Then comes the *kick*er. *"Oh, it probably ISN'T as good. I can almost guaranTEE it isn't,"* he admits, *"but my BROTHer-in-law WORKS for THEM. I was doing HIM a FAvor."*

[INSERT ICONIC DORIS DAY OUTRAGED EXHALE.] *"Ooooooh!"*

My client (and, ap*par*ently, his *brother*-in-law's *company*) *both* have revo*lu*tionary, potentially lifesaving products that make testing for an early symptom of colorectal cancer less cumbersome and less embarrassing than *previous* versions. The symptom? Blood in one's stool, an early, often-overlooked symptom of the dis*ease*.

I feel *glad* the *"issue"* gets the coverage it de*serves*, but I can't *help* feeling *cheat*ed that my com*pet*itor gets the *cred*it. *Truth*fully, I find it sur*pris*ing that the reporter's willing to *have* even *that* much of a conversation about it *after* the fact. *Most* reporters wouldn't deign to *jus*tify their coverage (or *lack* thereof) to a lowly PR *flack.*

In that *mo*ment, I fall *out* of love with public re*la*tions. I feel like a beggar ... a *blind* beggar ... one who has climbed *out* ... on that hu*mili*ating *street* corner ... with my cup in *hand* ... *plead*ing for some *crumb*s of *cover*age. Rather than just walk *past* me, that reporter leads me to believe he will *fill* my *cup* ... to the *brim. Then,* without *warn*ing, he flips a figurative *bottle cap* into my cup ... in*stead* of all the *coins* he led me to ex*pect.* Did he think I wouldn't *notice?* Did he *care?* [PAUSE]

That taught me a valuable *les*son: when you try to get something for *noth*ing ... like coverage in a *news*paper ... you have NO control, and you can't com*plain* if it doesn't come *out* exactly the way you *hoped.* I didn't realize it be*fore,* but, in that *mo*ment, when I see that beautiful full-color, full-page spread—*my* work—attributed to my com*peti*tor ... I realize ... I ... am, in*deed,* a *beg*gar. E*ventu*ally, that experience spurs me toward my speechwriting *specialty,* where I imagine I have more control over the finished *product.*

In *that* moment, however, I feel be*trayed.* I feel em*bar*rassed in front of my *boss*es, whom I have un*witt*ingly led to believe a *lie* ... that *big* coverage is coming our *way.* I feel *stupid* and *angry* ... angry at my*self,* mostly, for having allowed that reporter to *use* and a*buse* me that way.

Where were my journalistic *in*stincts?! Have they e*vapo*rated? Did I ever *have* any in the *first* place? I *wonder* ... and I *fume.* I have nowhere to *go* with all those emotions ... nowhere except where I *al*ways go ... to God, a different *kind* of God than I know to*day* but the God I understood at the *time.* But, *this* time, I go to God in a new *way* with an un*fami*liar *at*titude ... disheartened and *angry.*

[CHOPPY, AGITATED] *"Why do I have this AWful job?!"* ... *"Why do I work with these AWful people?"* ... *"Why did I leave a BETter job and BRILLiant people and move away from my FAMily ... to make LESS money ... and to MARry someone who doesn't even seem to LIKE me anymore, much less LOVE me?"* ... *"What, God, do you want me to learn from THIS?!"*

I come awfully close to asking God a question I almost *never* ask: *"Why ME?"* I almost forget—almost outright re*ject*—what Baby Pattaburp taught me so long be*fore* ... that *bad* things are actually *good* things in dis*guise* ... *if* you choose to *see* them that way. In *this* case, under *these* circumstances, I re*fuse*. I rail at God about my miserable job and my mistreatment at the hands of that wily reporter ... un*til* ... 5 years *later*, when I get the greatest evidence *ever* that things happen for a *rea*son ... and the Universe really *does* use ev*erything*—even a *sucky* job and a *slimy* re*porter*—for *Good*.

[PAUSE]

CHAPTER 35

Sacred MisunderSTANDINGs ...

Shortly *after* my disillusionment with public re*lations*, I get a ticket *out* of my awful *job*. I had been the primary breadwinner for those months while my spouse completed his company's sales training and got his business off the *ground*. Fortunately, at about the time of *my* professional *set*back, *his* professional efforts start paying *off* ... well enough that he needs my help in his office. *"Uh, oh! BAD iDEa!"* But I can't *see* that at the *time. I* just feel thankful I can kiss all those em*bar*rassing assignments related to colons and rectums good-*bye*.

Eeew! Did I actually *say* I ...*"kissed a colon good-BYE"* ...?! I would *like* to have asked that re*port*er to kiss my ... well ... close e*nough*. ... [PAUSE]

My grandmother always said, *"Whenever God closes a DOOR, SOMEwhere He opens a WINdow."* This seems like a Divinely de-livered case in point—a new *job*, firmer financial *foot*ing, brighter prospects—and *yet,* I rail at God at least *one more* time ... *this* time about something I consider nearer and dearer to God's *heart. This* time, I rail about re*lig*ion it*self*. [PAUSE]

When I met my husband, he did *not* attend church and hadn't for *years*. He described himself as an *"N.P.C."*–Non-Practicing Catho-lic. In *fact*, when his *very* Catholic mother (pre–Vatican II Catholic) visits him in St. Louis during the year we *date*, he calls *me— Meth*-odist little *me*—on the *sly* ... to ask where she might find the nearest *mass* ... because *he* doesn't have a *clue*.

He jokes, *"How would I know? ... I go to St. MATtress every Sunday."* [PAUSE]

I find that *funny* ... a *lit*tle bit funny ... un*til* ... *Lib*by comes along and I get *ser*ious about taking her to *church* every Sunday ... *my* church ... the *Meth*odist Church ... the kind of church I remem-ber from *child*hood, the kind of church in which we got *married,* without a Catholic priest and without objection from my husband, even without objection, as far as I knew, from his mother.

Note: Let my experience serve as a cautionary tale. Just because someone doesn't voice an objection when invited to ... "speak now or forever hold her PEACE" doesn't mean she doesn't harbor an objection ... or several. It doesn't mean objections won't come to light later, but I don't have time to dwell on that now. I'm about to die, after which, according to my former mother-in-law, I will go to hell and drag her son, our "illegitimate" daughter (according to her) and maybe even her ... with me—damnation by association, I guess.

I don't share her perspective, but I don't feel the need to take her on about it, either. In fact, when it comes time to baptize Libby, more than 2 years into my marriage, aware of an emerging objection to my non-Catholic status, I ask the pastor—the Methodist pastor—to be very sensitive to the ecumenical mix in my new family. As he dips his fingers into the baptismal font, he helpfully explains that, within Christianity, when it comes to the sacrament of baptism, even Catholics observe no distinction between denominations. Jesus didn't then. We don't today. I suspect my mother-in-law doesn't buy it, but I applaud myself for making the effort, anyway.

And so, early on, the Catholic "Hatfields" and the Protestant "McCoys" choose to live and let ... die ... so to speak. [PAUSE]

I start taking Libby to church with me when she's 6 weeks old. Unless one of us is sick or we all go out of town, we never miss. I teach Sunday school while Libby plays (or naps) in the nursery. I feel at home in the community and in the theology (at least I did back then).

I hear people say ... "This church or that church ... just doesn't DO it for me." That attitude mystifies me. I want to ask (but usually don't), "What do you think church should 'do' for you? Shouldn't there be a place—ONE place every week—where you go to put something IN and soak something UP, not just take something OUT or get something BACK?"

As for me, I didn't and I don't go to church to be entertained, even though I often find it entertaining ... and much more. I once heard a speaker say, "If the church you attend isn't what you think it

SHOULD be, DON'T LEAVE. STAY ... and make it BETter. FIX it!" I drank *that* Kool-Aid.

I think of worship as something *I* do for *God*, not the other way a*round*. It may sound simple and a little sancti*mon*ious, but I go to church to say *"Thank You"* and to say *"How can I help YOU, God? ... Where are my rough EDGES? ... What's NEXT?"* I want to culti-vate the relationship I have with that my*sterious "Something Big-ger than MySELF"*—a *Som*ething ... a *Some*one ... whose Company I have known, enjoyed, sought and counted on *practically since birth*. And I *do get* something. Back *then*, that weekly dose of Meth-odist fellowship feeds the part of *me* that's *starv*ing.

My *spouse*, on the *oth*er hand, must not feel *hun*gry in that *way.* He maintains *his* membership at ... *"St. Mattress."* I urge him and invite him to attend *with* us, but he de*clines*, saying that going to the Methodist Church doesn't represent enough of a *com*promise on my part. I didn't *re*alize we were negotiating. He says he doesn't ex*pect* me to attend a *Catholic* church, *but*, if I want *him* to go *with* us, we can*not* attend a *Meth*odist one. *I* will have to find what *he* calls a *"COMpromise church."*

I *do* it. It *irks* me, but I *do* it. In the interest of family *u*nity and mari-tal *har*mony, I set out in search of some ... *common ground. I* would attend *once*, by my*self* (with Libby in tow), to get the lay of the ... *ho*ly land, so to speak, so *he* doesn't have to visit congregations I *know* he won't em*brace.* Then, if a church clears *that* hurdle, I invite *him* to take an ecclesiastical ... *"test-drive."* He rejects *sev*eral pos-si*bil*ities. I fear I won't *find* one that makes him as comfortable as St. *Matt*ress does. How *could* I?

*Fin*ally, we settle on a church in northwest *Ev*anston. I*ron*ically, its initials are ... N.P.C., *not* for Non-Practicing *Cath*olic, as my spouse *hum*orously sug*gests, but* for Northminster Presby*ter*ian Church. Why Presby*ter*ian? What tips the scale? My husband sees the words *"Confession of Faith"* in the bulletin and as*sumes* there *must* be some *o*verlap with his long-dormant Catholic *roots.*

Too filled with joy and relief that I seem to have found a con*tend*er, I choose *not* to point out that Presbyterian *"confessions,"* whispered silently between one*self* and God in a *sanc*tuary, bear *little* resem-blance to *Cath*olic confessions made to a *priest* through a screen in

a con*fess*ional. At *this* point, *I* don't *care*, and I hope *he* won't *notice.*
He doesn't.

Adding incense to *in*jury, he admits he *also* likes this par*ti*cular
Presbyterian church because he knows that a lot of promising *busi*-
ness prospects live nea*rby* and probably at*tend* *re*gularly. *That*
mercenary observation of*fends* me, and I *tell* him so, even as I acknowledge the *truth* in it. *Can* people make business connections
at *church?* Of *course*, but I consider it a bit crass to base even *part*
of our decision about where to *worship* on *that.* I feel, at *most,* it
should rank as a happy, or*ganic, un*forced *bless*ing ... *if* it material-
izes at *all* ... down the *road.*

I choose *not* to quibble ... un*til* ... he chooses not to at*tend.* Before
too long he returns ... to St. *Mattress.* Even *then,* I take my com-
plaints about that more to *God* than to my *hus*band—a decided *mis*-
step, I now *see. I should* have con*sulted* One and then con*front*ed
the *oth*er, but I execute only *half* of that game plan. It takes me
years to emerge from that *un*healthy, *people-*pleasing, *go-*along-to-
get-along *pattern.*

I rail ... to God. After *all,* I have granted what I consider a profoundly un*reasonable re*quest. I have left a church I *love,* a church
filled with young families and
thriving women's and children's *mini*stries. I uproot my
routine, abandon my roots,
rock my *soul.*

Let's not for*get* ... growing up,
it was the *Catholic* kids on
my block who told me *I* was
going to *hell,* but it was OK
if they played with my *toys* ...
so spake their *mothers*—and
their pre–Vatican II *Church*—
so this *feels* like fourth grade
and Fernbrook Drive *all* over
again.

"Why, God," I ask, *"must I
change MY religion when
HE doesn't even PRACtice*

Working in the church nursery.

HIS???!! This feels SO wrong ... so unREAsonable. ... This makes me ... SO ... MAD!"

God doesn't provide an answer I can *hear,* so I decide to *stop whin-ing* and *start digging* ... to find the pony in this *fresh* pile of ma*nure* ... to put down roots ... to bloom where I'm *plant*ed. I throw my-self into my new *setting.* I take classes, work in the *nurs*ery, write for the church *newsletter,* join one particularly memorable book-discussion group called *"The Styrofoam-Cup Task Force,"* devoted to living out our values and seeking sim*plic*ity in a ma*ter*ialistic, *throw*-away society (how simul*taneously pompous,* pious and po-litical *that* sounds *now!).* ...

And ... almost as an act of defiance, I remain active in *one* of the groups from my *Meth*odist church, a circle of dear, devoted women who make and serve a *huge* charity dinner for the com*mun*ity every *year.* I just can't and *won't* cut those ties com*plet*ely. What a *re*bel!

Within a few *years,* I find myself in Evanston *H*ospital, where the Universe uses *both* of my agonizing setbacks—the job I had *hated* and the ulti*ma*tum I re*sent*ed—for my own *good.* In the *end,* they *both* help keep me a*live.*

CHAPTER 36

Reaching an UnderSTANDING about My Colon ...

In the hospital in 1990, nearly 5 years *after* that awful, embarrassing *job* and nearly 5 *weeks* into a hospital stay Dr. Dolt had as*sured* me would last only ... *"a day or 2,"* he and several other doctors stand at my hospital bedside and say, *"Kelly, we don't know WHY, but your colon ... is trying to KILL you."*

I say, *"Yank that sucker OUT."*

They say, [STARTLED] *"You don't know what you're SAYing."*

I say, [JOKINGLY SMUG] *"Actually, I DO. I know quite a LOT about colons. If mine is KILLing me, yank it OUT."*

I can *say* that with confidence pre*cisely* be*cause* I *had* that *mortify-*ing job 5 years *ear*lier ... pre*cisely* be*cause* ... that dirty, rotten *rat* of a re*porter* sent me all over *town* to get to the *bottom* of ... *bott*oms. It ap*pears* my *tor*mentor has be*come* ... my *body*guard. How's *that* for a headline?

Back *then,* on the *job,* I gathered all that information to help colorectal *cancer* patients detect their condition *early* enough to *save* themselves. *Now, here* ... in the *hospital,* I *need* that informa*tion* to save *my*self. I don't *have* colorectal cancer—at least we don't *think* I do. We don't know *what* I have, but we *do* know my colon appears to be dis*integrating ... rapidly. *Now, thank*fully, when I have *no* time to crack the books, *no* time to track down *facts, no* access to *micro*fiche ar*chives,* I already *know* what I need to *know* about colons. How *handy!*

"I GET it, God. ... THANK You! ... When I find myself in difficult cir-cumstances in the FUture ... if I HAVE any future circumstances, given how SICK I am ... I will TRUST You. From here on OUT, when I face something DIFFicult, I will asSUME ... no, I will beLIEVE ... no,

I will KNOW ... SOMEhow ... the bad will lead ... to good. No, the bad already conTAINS the Good. I will KNOW ... You are eQUIPping me ... for SOMEthing. I will ... NOT ... rail."

I *don't* say that as a *bargain* ... *"If You get me OUT of this, God, I'll change my ATtitude."* No, I *say* it to acknowledge that my attitude al*ready has* changed ... back to what it *used* to *be*. I reclaim my *for*mer under*stand*ing. Thanks to a head full of long-forgotten but recently urgently resur*rected* facts about *col*ons, I see *clear*ly, *a*gain, that ... *soon*er or *later, "bad things become BLESSings"*—the wisdom imparted to me by Baby Pattaburp and my dad *so* many years be*fore*.

I say all that (or, actually, *pray* all that) *si*lently to *God*. To my *doc*tors, I re*peat, "Take out my COlon."*

"But you're a young WOman, and that's a ... DRAStic LIFEstyle change."

"I'm DYing; THAT'S the most DRAStic ... 'LIFEstyle change' ... there IS. TAKE ... OUT ... MY COlon!"

Under*stand*, I'm *ask*ing for a *col*ostomy ... a fairly *com*mon surgery that would divert my body's waste from its *nor*mal *path*—through my in*test*ines—to empty, in*stead*, through a surgically created opening in my abdominal *wall*. If success*ful*, from then *on*, I will have to attach a pouch or bag to that opening to collect a new ... *cal*iber ... a new con*sis*tency of ... poop. [PUZZLED] Does poop *come* in calibers? [PAUSE]

Anyway, I don't *love* the idea of a *col*ostomy. Given a choice, who *would*? I'll have to clean and maintain the site and empty and change the pouches, probably for the rest of my *life*. ... To*day*, they can perform this kind of surgery with*out* an external pouch and, in *some* cases, even re*verse* it once the patient's gut cools down, but in *my* case, in 1990, a traditional colostomy appears to be my *only* option. I *want* one. I figure ... it beats *dy*ing. [PAUSE]

The hospital has a colorectal surgeon standing *by*—Dr. *Lar*sen. Did you hear birds chirping and harps humming at the mention of his *name*? You *should* have. I use his *real* name here because he stands out as a true *he*ro, although I'm not sure about the spelling or even his first name. I was too sick for the short time I knew him to retain every detail. Still, from day *one*, he follows my case with keen and caring *interest.* He tells me he's ready to perform whatever surgical procedure I need when*ever* I *need* it ... *but* ... he cautions, *"That's not something you RUSH INto,"* ... *and* ... he can't do *any*thing until the *lead* doctor on my case, Dr. *Dolt, says* he can.

Always the consummate pro*fes*sional, Dr. Larsen *never tells* me he disap*proves* of Dr. Dolt's ap*proach* ... but ... I detect what strikes me as an *un*common *pat*tern. They *never* make rounds to*gether.* I *could* chalk that up to co*in*cidence—busy schedules, conflicting *cal*endars—but I sense there's more *to* it than *that.* Dr. Larsen does something busy surgeons don't often *do*: he returns to my room fre-*quent*ly—sometimes several times a *day*—*es*pecially after he knows Dr. Dolt has *vis*ited. He *though*tfully, *gen*erously, *pa*tiently explains my *op*tions—even *non-sur*gical options that wouldn't in*volve* him—including details Dr. Dolt *om*its and a degree of compassion Dr. Dolt *lacks.*

I *like* Dr. Larsen. I *trust* him. He has my *back.* Good *thing*, since he *may* have to dissect my *front.*

CHAPTER 37

WithSTANDING Medical Residents ... and Setting Unfortunate Precedents ...

Doctors argue the colon/colostomy thing with me *so* long I nearly *bleed* to death while rushing to the bathroom every *6 minutes*—multiple I*V* poles in tow, modesty and underwear long since a*ban*-doned.

The closer I get to *death*, the more *pop*ular I be*come*—a *ce*lebrity of sorts. They make me the *"Case of the Day"* several times a *week*, when *all* of the doctors—from newbies to neurosurgeons—gather in an auditorium after rounds to discuss a rare or troubling patient, even one whose case falls *out*side their *special*ties.

That's *me*! I qualify on *both counts*—rare (because I'm so *young*) and more troubling by the *min*ute (because I'm so *sick* ... and not responding to *any*thing they're doing to get me *well*). In *fact*, not normally a delicate flower when it comes to medical inter*ven*tions, I exhibit allergic reactions to practically *every* test and treatment.

At *one* point, we find out too *late* I'm allergic to the iodine they use in *CAT* scans. We discover this important little tidbit only *af*ter they inject the iodine into my *veins* ... *af*ter it pollutes my entire *blood*stream, so I react *vi*olently, from the *in*side *out*. My face bal-loons up like a *bas*ketball, and my *lips* inflate like *in*ner tubes.

A nurse comes in, does a *dou*ble take, tilts her head quizzically and asks, *"I haven't SEEN you before. Are your lips ALways ... um ... FULL like that?"*

I don't have a *mir*ror, so I don't know what she *means*, but I'm not *known* for my ... *thick lips*. In *fact*, under *nor*mal circumstances, my upper lip disap*pears* like a *win*dow shade when I *smile*. Within *sec*-onds, even *I* know something's wrong, waaaay wrong, because I can *see* my lips sticking out past my *nose*, and my *fin*gers look like an assortment of Johnsonville *brats*. I feel itchy hives erupting in my mouth, down my throat and under my *skin*. Then my eyelids swell so *much* and so *fast* I can't *see*. The nurse bolts out and returns with something she shoots into my IV to restore order to my *face*.

After the crisis *pass*es, the nurse laughs, *"I thought you couldn't POSSibly be that ugly, but ... you NEVer KNOW."* She adds, *"I wasn't sure how to ASK. ... Do you ALways look like a FROG?"* We giggle together.

The *"Case-of-the-Day"* doctors meet, hoping to brainstorm a less disfiguring *treat*ment. *First*, they go with the picked-up-a-parasite-in-Mexico theory. I spend several days in iso*lat*ion. No one can *vis*it me without full infectious-disease pro*tect*ion, so everyone enters and leaves shrouded from head to toe in yellow anti-microbial *scrubs*. My husband jokes that they only *dare* serve me pizza and pancakes from the hospital cafe*ter*ia because *those* are the only foods ... they can slide under my *door*.

After a few days and what *seems* like a few *thou*sand tests for all manner of tropical parasite—finding *noth*ing—they lower their guard, relax the restrictions and decide, *"MAYbe she has peritonItis ..."* (the inflammation that occurs when one's ap*pend*ix bursts or when something perforates the intestines).

I have landed in one of those *won*derful, *ter*rible institutions known as ... a *teach*ing hospital. I recall the implications of that from Libby's birth—a long line of Looky Loos formed every time my feet went up into the *stir*rups. To a *point*, I consider it an honor and a duty to further modern science if I *can*. *Real*ly, I *do*, so *this* time I feel both blessed *and* cursed to have a never-ending parade of *eag*er, *var*iously *ed*ucated *nov*ices shining lights into *ev*ery ori*fice*, taking notes on every *breath* and sticking cold and clumsy fingers ... where the sun don't *shine*. I'll take one for the team ... if I *must*.

Once the *top* docs decide I *may* have perito*nit*is, they send in a gaggle of *ba*by docs to in*vest*igate. They test for perito*nit*is, *first*, by applying pressure to my already-tender *ab*domen and asking whether it hurts more when they *press* or when they re*lease*. I tell the *first* rookie it hurts more—*much* more—when he re*leases*. They murmur among themselves, exchange knowing glances and scribble in their *note*books.

The *sec*ond rookie steps up. Same question, same answer.

"Does it hurt more when I PRESS or when I reLEASE?"

I *wince. "When you reLEASE."* More murmuring.

Third time is *not* a charm. *"Does it hurt more when I PRESS or when I reLEASE?"* He presses. He releases.

"Ugh! When you releeeeeese," I groan.

By the *fourth* exam, with at least 4 *more* students still in *line*, my husband slaps the hand of the resident away from my abdomen before he can *touch* me and says, *"It hurts more when you reLEASE! Why do you have to TORture her to get the SAME answer OVER and OVER?"*

The attending physician steps in to de*fend* the *drill* by saying, *"They NEED to know what it FEELS like ... each ONE of them. It's not eNOUGH just to SEE it; they might have a patient down the ROAD who can't TELL them which hurts MORE, so they have to know by TOUCH."*

"Let 'em go touch someone ELSE for a while. You're FINished here." The attending physician seems inclined to press the argument *and* my *ab*domen, but my husband shoots him down and shuts him up with a withering I-*DARE*-you stare. [MENACING SNEER]

"Thank you!" Even on my near-*death*bed, people-pleaser to the *core*, I wouldn't have de*fend*ed myself. I'm glad and grateful my husband steps in to draw the *line*.

The rookies who *did*n't get a turn frown like dejected little kids who *just missed* the ice-cream man. Then they *all* file *out* of my room for an animated, audible comparing of notes just outside my *door* with the ones who *did* take a *turn*.

"Did you FEEL that?" ... "I KNOW." ... "Cool, HUH?!" ... "What about her BOWel sounds?" ... "BiZARRE!"

Note to doctors in training: don't *do* that. I hope HIPAA (the relatively new privacy standards in hospitals) put an end to *most* of that, but few patients would appreciate hearing you and your colleagues high-five over how *sick* they are. Take it to the *locker* room. [PAUSE]

Another day, during rounds, one of the medical residents amazes his *peers* with one of my *stats*:

Standing at the foot of my bed, he announces, [ENTHUSIASTIC] *"SHE has HAD ... 90 bowel movements today! That's unPREcedent-ed!"*

"What does he MEAN?" I wonder. *"Unprecedented HOW? ... Are we talking unprecedented in all of human HIStory? Just how wide a circle are we DRAWing here?"*

He makes his announcement as if I'm not lying *right there* ... as if he's speaking at some frequency I can't *hear*. He says it with an *isn't-that-cool ... what-a-freak* tone in his voice ... as if I'm a monkey in a *zoo* or *some*thing. B*e*l*ieve* me ... if I had had any *one* of the day's 90 within *reach* and even an *ounce* of *strength*, I might, like a *mon*-key, have *flung* it at him.

I have to ad*mit* that the statistic *does* qualify as re*mark*able—90 bowel movements in *one* day?! ... Well, my parents always *wanted* an over-achiever. ...

"Tah-dah!"

[PAUSE, THROW ARMS IN AIR]

CHAPTER 38

STANDING in Hospital Hell ...
Surrounded by Angels and Demons ...

Weeks earlier, when I arrived, my nurses welcomed me to the floor with great fanfare and no small amount of curiosity.

"Don't take this the wrong WAY," one nurse begins. *"I mean ... I'm REALLY sorry you're so SICK, but it's kind of NICE to have you WITH us. We don't EVer get ANYone YOUR age on THIS floor."*

"REALLY?"

"Yeah, I think the youngest patient I've had all YEAR was 70. You have a blind woman in her 80s next DOOR and a man who's almost 95 on the OTHer side. This'll be FUN for a change."

She's very sweet, and I know she *means* it in the nicest *possible* way. *Still,* I would rather *not* provide this par*ti*cular kind of *novelty,* and, al*ready,* I can tell I don't *share* Nurse *Nancy's* definition of *"FUN."*

"Tell me THIS," I ask, half *jok*ing. ... *"Do the people on this floor get BETter?"*

She smiles and tilts her head as if to say, *"SOMEtimes."*

In *truth,* over the following weeks, we *do* manage to eke out a few *tiny* glimmers of *fun,* talking about our *kids,* catching glimpses of *very* early Oprah episodes and decorating my *room* ... for *Easter.* I mourn when Nancy isn't there and find I *brace* myself for her days *off.* You can feel *so* vulnerable in a hospital. When you *click* with someone on the *staff,* you *sleep* better, you *eat* better ... you *get* better.

*Some*times, especially at *night,* I feel particularly uneasy. My husband always leaves a few quarters in a little cloth box at my *bed*side so I can buy a newspaper the next morning if I feel up to *read*ing one. I keep a stack of cassette tapes and a cassette player on my windowsill, too ... and my Bible ... and some pens, note cards and a few postage stamps—nothing valuable. I know better.

At about 2 o'clock one morning, I hear someone rustling around in my things, [HUSHED] v-e-r-y quietly, opening the lid of the box with the coins, silently shuffling through my stack of get-well cards, opening each envelope. I open my eyes but intentionally don't move. She has on a pair of scrubs—the uniform kind, not the kind they wear in the operating room. She has a laminated badge clipped to her hip pocket, but I can't see it—too dark and too distant. For a long time, she doesn't realize I'm watching her. She moves v-e-r-y s-l-o-w-l-y, opening everything, including my Bible, invading every inch of my space.

It creeps me out. She has her back to me, and when she has slunk almost to the end of my shelf of belongings, she turns to look at me over her shoulder. Her eyes meet mine, and I know immediately why she's there. She knows I know. She hopes to find something worth stealing, and she knows I couldn't stop her if I wanted to.

That's the part I find most chilling: when she realizes I'm awake and watching her every move, she doesn't flinch ... or jump ... or bolt out of there or raise her eyebrows ... or express any surprise or remorse at all; she just glides out as slowly past my stuff as she glides in. That tells me she is quite a pro ... good at her game. It makes me fear for the blind woman next door and the almost-95-year-old man on the other side.

Uncharacteristically, I feel afraid. Adding to my sense of isolation, the hospital assigns me to a private room, even though my insurance doesn't cover it. They conclude any roommate would understandably object to sharing a space with me, modern-day leper that I am—the bathroom monopolizer. With that, my universe shrinks to a space about 8 feet long by 3 feet wide—the distance from my hospital bed to the toilet.

I have so many tubes and needles tangled around me, connected to my arm and my chest and, eventually, up my nose that I can't navigate even that short distance quickly or well. I appreciate the reassuring stainless steel safety bar and pull chain installed next to the commode ... "in case of emergency." By now, every bowel movement feels like an emergency.

I'm sorry; I *know* this is revolting. In *some* ways, I wish I could paint a prettier picture, but perhaps I wouldn't appreciate *heaven* as much if I hadn't gone through *hell*. Fear *not*; you'll have a front-row seat for the Bright Light *soon*, but, as an *"embedded journalist"* in the war against death ... against General *Bucket* ... for *now*, I find myself on the *front* lines ... in a gruesome *battle*, so I *cover* it as I *experienced* it.

I sit doubled *over* on the toilet clutching the bar while *literally* shooting blood out of my be*hind*. It can take me 15 *minutes* to *finish*, wave after *unrelenting* wave, with only a few minutes in between. After every round, I lean my head against the wall. ... I breathe hard. My heart races. My stomach lurches *so* violently it sounds like someone's throwing merciless punches to my *gut*. [DOUBLE OVER; DEMONSTRATE SOUND]

I cling to the smooth surface of the stainless bar and rest my *cheek* (that's the cheek on my *face*, in case you were *wondering*) on the cold tile *wall*. I find those surfaces oddly *comf*orting, like a cool oasis. I just want to feel *something* ... *anything* ... other than the fire that now plagues my overworked sphincter. I wonder often whether I'm going to *die*. It seems *likely* ... and *imm*inent.

CHAPTER 39

STANDING around with My Panties Down ...

Eventually, I become *so* weak from my solo performance in ... *"Cirque de So Embarrassing"* my nurses fear I'll *faint* on my way to the *bath*room, so they bring in a *bed*side com*mode*, thereby shrinking my universe to an even *tini*er patch of the planet. *Then*, when I can't even make it *that* far without an accident, they confine me to my *bed*.

I have almost *no* control of my bowels, so, for a couple of *days*, until they start feeding me through a central line in my *neck*, instead of by *mouth*, I have to sit on a bedpan *constantly*. It digs *deep* ridges into my *bum* ... and ... into my *dignity* ... since there's *no* way any nurse can keep up with my every-6-minute pooping schedule. I just have to *lie* there, with a soiled, stinking bedpan under my bottom for *long* stretches at a *time*. [PERKY] De*light*ful!

*Some*how, I manage to make the *best* of it by rigging up a makeshift *desk* against my *thighs* so I can write *notes* while I wait for the next painful wave to *hit*. In a *way*, it feels worse than the *worst* contractions of *child*birth ... with*out* having a child to *show* for it—certainly *not* the kind of ... *"multiple births" any*one would launch a *rea*lity show to *capture*. [REPULSED FACE]

My bedpan and I become the ... K*eleph*ant in the *room*. Visitors don't know where to *look*. Some make in*cong*ruous comments at my *bed*side. My über-sweet, über-modest *sist*er arrives to find me sitting atop my personal ... stainless *steel* Johnny on the *Spot*. I can *tell* it makes her un*com*fortable. She *cring*es. There's no *good* way to disguise my pre*dic*ament. She chats *nerv*ously, politely pretending not to *see* my legs splayed a*part* and my body arched at an *odd* angle ... balancing on the *bed*pan *und*er the *cov*ers.

This isn't Cathy's *"thing."* She's *so* modest—always *has* been. When she needs a bra in junior *high*, she can't *bring* herself to say the *word* "bra." Instead, she tells our mom she needs ... [SHIELD MOUTH W/ BACK OF HAND, WHISPER] "top underwear" and then blushes at the mere thought.

I'm a little more ... out there. In first grade, I come home from school one day to find my mom playing the piano. I announce, [EXCITED, HIGH PITCHED BUT W/ AUTHORITY] "Mommy, from now ON, I'M going to wear JUMPers on GYM days, because, THAT way, I can take OFF my jumper ... and STILL have my shorts and BLOUSE on ... so no one can see my TITS."

With that, my mother strikes an extremely non-musical chord on the piano. That word goes over so well, in fact, I think this may be the first time I've used it since then. In any event, clearly, better my bum on a bedpan than Cathy's.

Back in my hospital room, on my bedpan, I poop. The violence of the contraction and the groan that goes with it unsettle my sister. I ring for the nurse and hope she can come quickly but already know she can't come quickly enough. My quest for the call button shifts the sheets on my bed, so Cathy catches an unobstructed view of my panty-less perch under the covers. ["HOME ALONE" FACE, GASP]

She earnestly observes, "I bet the WORST part of this ... IS ... having to go without [WHISPER] UNderwear." [EMBARRASSED CRINGE]

I laugh. [SARCASTIC] "Yeah, Cath, THAT'S the worst PART. [SERIOUS] ... Actually, NO, the WORST part is ... fearing I won't live to see Libby grow UP ... [SILLY] but the underwear thing ... THAT'S a bummer, TOO."

CHAPTER 40

STANDING around Filled with Guilt (*NOT* the Catholic Kind) ...

I'm *grate*ful to Cathy for providing an unin*ten*tionally amusing per*spec*tive. Our talk about underwear (or *lack* thereof) underscores a stark reality I can't ig*nore*. While the doctors and nurses try to take care of *me*, *I* must take care of my *fam*ily. *Some*times, I consider it more difficult for *them* to be be*side* my bed than for *me* to be *in* it. *They* can only *guess* how I feel; I *know* how I feel. I don't want them to *know* how terrible my *nights* are ... how terrifying my test results are ... how terri*tori*al Dr. Dolt has be*come*, simultaneously re*lish*ing his *"interesting"* case *and*, I su*spect, fear*ing his colleagues will discover his in*com*petence.

I just have to focus on sur*vival*—*"One Goal"*—like my precious *Black*hawks in pursuit of a Stanley *Cup*. My *fam*ily members, on the *oth*er hand, have to keep their lives going in *and out* of the hos*pital*—*many* goals.

They struggle. My *"sole-breadwinner"* spouse has to arrange care for Libby, keep his 6-day-a-week business running, monitor my *care*, make his own *meals*, pick up his own *shirts*, do his own *laun*dry, clean our house, and keep *my* family and *his* family in*formed*. He tries to visit me twice a *day*—usually on his way *to* work and then a*gain* on his way *home*. We can't af*ford* to have him sit at my side 24/7; his straight-commission salesman status means ... if he doesn't *work*, we don't *eat*. His mom comes to *help*. Neighbors bring meals. Still, with no *end* in *sight*, it's too ... *much*.

I do what I can from the hospital to help, lining up play dates and babysitters when my husband has client meetings. At *first*, he assures my family that they don't need to *come*. *"She'll be out in a few days."* Eventually, they can't *stand* the long-distance updates, so Cathy and my mom come to see for them*selves*.

It's almost *Easter*, and I need help to pull off the caliber of celebration I hope Libby will remember—the kind of celebration I remember from my *own* childhood. She needs an Easter dress ... and an Easter hat ... and Easter *shoes*. The Easter Bunny needs to gather all the familiar elements for her *basket* ... *not* something I can accomplish from my *hospital* bed. Those qualify as *perfect* errands to assign to my sister and my mom. They want to *help*, but it terrifies my mom to *see* me like this.

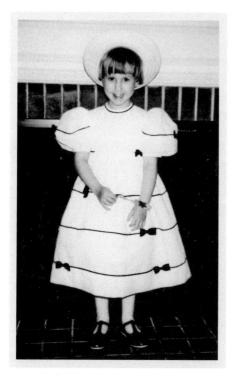

Libby at Easter 1990.

I feel so *guilty* when they visit me in the hospital ... guilty for not getting *better* ... guilty for putting them *through* all this. They *love* me, and every time a doctor or nurse asks me a *question*, they have to hear me describe my *excruciating*, deteriorating condition in details *they* clearly find painful to *hear*. I want to pro*tect* them. I struggle with my *new* role as care *getter* versus care*giver*.

When I speak to cancer-support groups, patients tell me *they* feel that guilt, *too*. I urge them *not* to do what *I* did ... *not* to add guilt to the *existing* hardships of *treatment*. *Some* of us get sick in the *first* place because we try to take care of everyone *else* without asking for or acknowledging what *we* need. We park our pain *in*side our bodies, and, *eventually*, it works its way out as *cancer* ... or co*litis* ... or canker sores. What*ever*!

Back in 1990, I don't have the benefit of hindsight, so the guilt goes *on*. My spouse and my mother (and, of course, Libby) have always *trusted* me to take *care* of *them*. I can't *do* that from my *hospital* bed. Feeling like I'm letting them down hurts *almost* as much as my unrelenting *symp*toms.

At *one* point, my mom falls *so far* into den*i*al she doesn't *recognize* me. She and Cathy have just arrived at the hospital from St. *Lou*is. My mom gets on an elevator where I'm al*ready* lying on a gurney and headed for *tests*. She stands there, chatting somberly with Cathy, and glances distractedly at *me*. I try to smile and flutter my fingers in a faint wave. Sur*prised*, Cathy says, *"It's Kelly!"* My mom looks hard at my horizontal form and blurts out, *"That's not Kelly."*

Cathy and I *both* say, *"YES, it is."*

I see the same vacant look flood my *mom's* eyes I had seen in *Lib*by's eyes the morning the paramedics came—immobilizing *shock*. I go on my way in the elevator to the *lab*. Cathy and my mom head to my floor ... to *wait*. App*ar*ently, when my mom steps off the *eleva*tor, she takes 2 wobbly steps, stumbles back against the *wall* and just slides in *slow mo*tion to the floor in shock—dazed, disbe*lieving*, unable to process what she has just *seen*: her 29-year-old *"baby,"* so pale, *so* weak, *so* obviously near *death* she cannot *fath*om it.

I've lost 14 *pounds* in a *week*, even *more* in the month since my mom last *saw* me at a family *wed*ding. I know I look *bad* but, surely, *not* so bad as to be unrecog*nizable*. Recalling it *now*, my mom describes my image on the elevator as *"gray and SKELetal."* I weigh 96 pounds, down from a healthy, *ro*bust 134. My mother can *see*, once a*gain*, I have brought her face to face with her greatest *fear*— the fear she will out*live* one of her *child*ren. She refuses to take it *in*; her psyche won't *let* it in.

CHAPTER 41

STANDING between Awful and Awe-Filled ...

[MOCK CELEBRATORY TONE] *"As long as we're havin' a PARty, let's invite ... EVeryone!"*

Beside my *fam*ily members, the people I welcome most warmly through my door are my *pastors*. Yes, I said, *"pastors" ... plural*. Because, leading up to my illness, I have attended 2 churches, I have 2 congregations and 2 teams of *clergy* members sending me *notes*, coming to *visit* and cheering me *on*.

When my *favorite* pastor visits but doesn't find me in my *room*, he tucks messages into my *Bible*. (Perhaps one shouldn't *have* favorites among clergy people, but I confess I *did*.) *Some* pastors can pull off the *pastoral* side of their job descriptions better than the *pro*phetic side; this guy nailed *both*—great in the *pul*pit, showin' us how to *live*, even *bet*ter in a *crisis*, helpin' us when we *die*.

He didn't leave those notes for me as a *test*, wondering ... *judging* ... [HOLIER-THAN-THOU] *"Will she turn to GOD in this? ... Is she PRAYing enough? ... Is she spending enough time in ... the WORD?"*

No, he *knew* I was digging *deep*, scouring as many pages of my third-grade Bible as I *could* ... between nurses and needles and nausea (*Oh, my!*). ... He *knew* I was starving for any scrap of *relevant* wisdom I could apply to my circumstances, not out of *fear* but out of a desire to under*stand* ... understand *what*, I'm not *sure*.

"Help me make SENSE of this," I would beg. *"What am I supposed to DO? ... How am I supposed to FEEL? ... What does God ASK of us in cases like this?"*

To his *credit*, he admits he has never *seen* a *"case like THIS."* He urges me not to worry so much about what *I'm* supposed to *do*; rather, he urges, try to see what God/the Universe/our church can offer *me*—love, peace, hope, community, comfort.

An avid, early recycler and fellow member of the *"Styrofoam-Cup Task Force,"* this pastor/friend writes his notes on the backs of cards that come with a never-ending stream of *fl*ower arrangements sent by friends and family. Returning to my room to find one of his notes feels like a sustaining, spiritual *scavenger* hunt, with handwritten clues pointing me toward helpful *verses* and healing thoughts. I still *have* his notes.

His most *powerful* pastoral nudges lead me to:

Romans 5:3-5: *"Rejoice in your sufferings, for suffering produces perseVERance ... perseVERance produces CHARacter ... character produces HOPE, and hope does NOT disapPOINT us. ..."*

Hmmm. *"Persevere!"* Where have I heard *that* before?

... *and* ...

Matthew 6:31-34: *"... do not be anxious ... Seek first the Kingdom of God."*

Those verses will loom large as I head into the Bright Light. ...

One verse I find decidedly *un*helpful is the 23rd Psalm. Lesser but well-meaning pastors and hospital chaplains trot out that familiar standard, but I wonder whether they *realize* that, at 29, I do *not* find it *comforting* ... to *think* about ... the *"valley of the shadow of DEATH."* I'm trying *not* to die. I don't want *"STILL waters"*; I want *raging* rivers. Based on my experience *in* hospital beds *and* beside them, I can say with au*thor*ity, *ge*nerally speaking, *save* that Psalm to comfort people at *fun*erals ... people left behind when *oth*ers die, *not* to comfort the dying them*selves*.

Nearly *every* day of my 5-week hospital incarceration, I receive 10 to 15 get-well cards, many from people I've never *met* but who pray for me nonethe*less* ... because they *hear* about me at *church*. They take the time to buy a *card* ... to write an encouraging *line* or two ... to look up the hospital's *address* ... to slap a stamp on an envelope and drop it in the *mail* ... just for *me*. I *mar*vel at that. I had no i*dea* so many people care about us ... about *me*.

I find *all* the attention pro*found*ly humbling ... *and* heal*ing*. If you think a get-well card doesn't *matter*, think a*gain*. It's *no small thing*. When I open each one, I can actually *feel* each sender's healing intentions wash over me. Over the *years*, *oth*er patients with *oth*er conditions in other *hosp*itals tell me they've had the same experience. Hallmark is *on* to something: open a card; close a wound. [PAUSE]

As I descend toward *death*, my senses seem to in*ten*sify. [CALM-LY, SLOWLY] I can *hear* things and *feel* things and *smell* things I couldn't be*fore* and haven't *since*. As a kind of unscripted *rit*ual, when a card ar*rives*, I hold it open in *front* of me, close my eyes and *breathe*. [HANDS IN A *V*, CLOSE EYES, BREATHE] With *each* card a few inches from my *face*, I swear I can actually *smell* the people who *sent* them ... smell their *homes*, their *kitch*ens, their *gar*-dens, their soap and sham*poo*. After nearly 5 *weeks*, I *cling* to those smells as a rare and wonderful link to the outside *world*.

In *spite* of my condition (or perhaps be*cause* of it), I make it my *miss*ion to send a *hand*written note to *every* person who visits and everyone who sends me cards and *flow*ers. *Some*how, that *disc*ipline gives me a sense of con*trol* when, in all *oth*er areas—bowels espe-cially—I have *none*.

At *times*, it seems my *body* ... is at *war* ... with my *brain*. With all my *phys*ical systems shutting *down*, I feel my *men*tal faculties rev-ving *up*. It's a*maz*ing! It's awesome, and I *don't* mean *"awesome"* in the over-used way we hear that word spoken so often to*day*. My mother raised me with an appreciation for precision in language. ... I mean *"awesome"* as in *truly* breathtaking, unfathomable, deep and *fear*some. Just when I need to weigh huge, life-altering, potentially life-*end*ing decisions, my brain rises to the oc*cas*ion. It seems my synapses almost *crack*le, firing *far* faster *even* than to*day's* Face-book posts or *Twit*ter feeds.

I just wish I could say the same for Dr. *Dolt*. When will *his* brain cells perk up? It looks like I may *die* waiting for *him* to pull his head ... out of his *bum*.

My heart—my intu*ition*—works at peak performance, *too*. I know who's trustworthy. I know who *isn't*. I don't have to ask my pastor any more questions. In each *moment*, I *know*, clear as a *bell*, what I need to *know*, what I need to *do* and what I need to *say*. If only I had this power in Mrs. Schneider's *second*-grade *math* class; instead of that D she dished out for my *near* failure to grasp *fractions* ... the one grade that sent me hiding behind my grandmother's *shower* curtain in shame ... if I could have harnessed the power I feel *now* ... back in second *grade*, I could have knocked cranky old Mrs. Schneider's *squeaky* orthopedic *shoes* off.

For *some* reason, in the midst of all this new-found (but, a*las, tem*porary) *bril*liance, I experience intermittent blindness in one *eye*. The room spins as if I've had ... *10* too many *cock*tails. I *think* they blame my wildly fluctuating blood pressure and continuing blood *loss* for *those* symptoms. Several times nurses break Procardia under my tongue to keep me from stroking out.

They use Procardia for what they call *"hypertensive emergencies."* I have *sev*eral. I start flailing in my bed, with my blood pressure suddenly through the *roof*, so nurses rush in with Procardia. On the *plus* side, used sublingually (under one's tongue), Procardia causes an im*med*iate drop in blood pressure—no more flailing. On the *mi*nus side, by 1994, the FDA declares that kind of emergent use of the drug *dang*erous, even *dead*ly, so hospitals stop *us*ing it that way.

"Man, if my COlon doesn't KILL me, my MEDicine just MIGHT." [PAUSE]

Still, almost *fiend*ishly, I crank out my *thank*-you notes. *Some*times I have to secure the note card to my makeshift desk with a rubber band so I can write with my *right* hand while I cup the palm of my *left* hand over my left *eye* ... to keep my hand steady and to stop the *room* from *spin*ning.

I have samples of my *hand*writing from those days; they're re*mark*ably *leg*ible. *Al*so re*mark*able, my thoughts come out ... [QUIZZI-CAL] *cus*tomized and co*her*ent. I remember people's names, their *child*ren's names, their *pets'* names and what they were *do*ing the last time we *spoke*. In the notes I write to each visitor and each card-sender or flower-sender, I inquire about *their* health and *their* goings-on with specific *int*erest. I make *jokes*.

"How is that POSSible?" I wonder. Looking *back*, I attribute it to sheer force of will ... and a desire to have *both* the con*nec*tion and the dis*trac*tion writing provides. One of my husband's colleagues sends me the Dr. Seuss book *Oh, the Places You'll Go!*—a surprisingly *great* book to read when you're dying. ... Even with my pants *down*, reading and writing keep my *spir*its *up*.

CHAPTER 42

STANDING in Line
at the Blood Bank ...

In 1990, hospitals urge families of patients who need a lot of *blood* ... to line up what they call *"designated donors."* In light of the AIDS crisis and fears about blood-supply contamination, reserves fall to a precarious *low*.

I can re*late*; my *pers*onal blood bank is running on empty, *too*. I need *6* trans*fus*ions. My family scrambles to find donors with compatible blood types on short *not*ice. My dad rolls up his sleeve, but they rule him *out* for *some reason*. *Cathy* rolls up *hers*. They tell us they can't *use* my hus*band's blood ... in case we want more *child*ren. I need *more* ... a *lot* more.

Talk about Divine inter*ven*tion. ... Get *this*! ... Be*cause* my husband in*sist*ed I change denomi*nat*ions, in the 2 years leading up to my *ill*ness, I faithfully attend 2, count 'em, 2 churches ... churches *full* of people ... red-blooded, big-hearted *people*. *So*, when the word goes out that I'm a quart *low*, God-fearing folks from *both* congregations flock to the *hos*pital ... with sleeves rolled *up*, veins standing *by* and hearts willing to meet the de*mand*. They keep me a*live*.

I *rea*dily ad*mit* ... in the *end* ... what I saw as my husband's un*reas*on-able demand that I change where and *how* and with *whom* I worship ... *saves* ... *my* ... *life*. The Universe sees fit to use what I *once* saw as a perverse in*jus*tice ... for *Good*. Hmmmm. ... *Another case of "If you don't get what you WANT, find a way to love what you get ANYway."*

"Yes, God, I GET it. AGAIN, I GET it. The circumstances I rail against MOST often turn out to bring my greatest BLESSings ... in the END."

I'm not sure *what* that says about my hus*band*, but I think it says something pretty wonderful about *God*. Simply, God is *Good*. ... No matter what each of us intends indi*vid*ually, *I* believe, col*lect*ively, as a *whole*, the Universe is ... wired for *Good*. As human beings, we're gonna step in some poop (me more than *most* people, perhaps), but I believe God uses it *all* for ... ferti*li*zer. ...

I'd call *that A Po*sitive (which just happens to *be* ... my *blood* type)!

CHAPTER 43

STANDING at Walgreen's ... Searching for the Perfect "Going-Away" Gift ...

So now we're up to April of 1990, less than 2 years after that disturbing question from Ginny in the *park* that day. I've been in the hospital for almost a *month*. The weather outside has morphed from dead of Chicago *winter* to first blush of *spring*, not that I feel *any part* of that happy tran*si*tion.

My veins have started to collapse from all the *needle* sticks. My arms, now skinny and fragile, have turned a deep yellow black from the bruises that go *all* the way from my wrists to my *arm*pits on both *arms*. I joke that the *least* they could *do* is offer hospital gowns in a color that wouldn't clash with my *bruises*.

Something's wrong with my *blood* sugar, so they come in to prick my fingers several times a day as if I were a dia*betic* and then they adjust my IVs ac*cord*ingly—all 4 of my IVs. With my adrenal system shutting down, they have to give me high doses of IV steroids. *That's* always fun.

I don't take anything by mouth anymore so my gut can *"rest."* Yes, it *needs* a vacation. I'd like to send it a*way* somewhere. All this *time* ... I keep *begg*ing them to take out my *colon*. Each argument ends with another *theo*ry ... another *test* ... another puzzling re*sult*.

I've seen Libby only once in 4 weeks. I miss her *terribly*. We decide it would *scare* her too much to *see* me ... with my sunken eyes, discolored arms and *so* many tubes and beeping devices keeping me among the living—*barely*.

Dr. Dolt doesn't know what to *make* of me—his long-awaited *"interesting case"* has him *stump*ed. Be careful what you *wish* for, Doctor. He arrives one morning with 2 colleagues.

Without emotion, he says, *"We've tried EVerything we can THINK of. We don't know what you HAVE, and we don't know what to DO about it. At THIS rate, you have about 2 DAYS to LIVE."* [PAUSE]

I find it absolutely *mind*-boggling that they choose to *tell* me this ... with no one *else* in the *room* ... no spouse, no family member, no chaplain at my *side* ... *no* one to help me *process* it. Just, *"BOOM!"* There it *is. "You have 48 hours."* [PAUSE] I didn't *doubt* it.

They urge me to say my good-byes to my husband and my daughter ... my 3 ½-year-old *daugh*ter, who, if I *die*, will remember *noth*ing a*bout* me. [PAUSE]

I think, *"Say my good-BYES?! ... SAY my good-byes?! I can't SAY my good-BYES. Libby won't remember ANYthing I SAY; I'll have to WRITE them."*

How ir*on*ic: I had tried to prepare *oth*er parents for this ... *un*likely possi*bil*ity ... with the articles I wrote a year *ear*lier ... and *now* ... I have to prepare my*self* for this ... *very* likely ... *proba*bility. [SLIGHTLY SHAKE HEAD IN DISBELIEF]

My husband comes to see me later that day, and I give him the grim news. We hug. We cry. We look at each other for a long moment, as if searching for an answer ... a way *out* ... in each other's *eyes*.

I break the silence and try to lighten the *mood*. *"I'd like you to do me a FAvor,"* I say.

"ANYthing!" he says, looking at me ex*pect*antly for his as*sign*ment, probably assuming I want him to *call* someone—my *par*ents, my *pas*tor. I sur*prise* him with my re*quest*. At *this* point, I become abso*lute*ly single minded—laser-sharp focus on *one* person, Libby, and *one* mission, to tell her in a few *hours*, quickly and co*her*ently, everything I had *plan*ned to tell her over the next 70 *YEARS*.

"I want you to go to Walgreen's for me."

[CONFUSED] *"What? ... WALgreen's?!"* [DOUBTFUL] *Oh, Kell ... I don't think WALgreen's has anything that can help you NOW."*

"No, I KNOW. It's nothing like THAT. ... I want you to get me one of those black and white speckled composition notebooks. ... You KNOW, the kind with the black fabric binding down the edge. [PAUSE] *If I'm*

gonna write my LAST words, I want to write 'em in something PERmanent and DIGnified looking. I want one of those black and white speckled NOTEbooks."

"Okaaay." My husband's *mouth* says *yes*, but his *feet* say *no*. His shoes seem stuck to the *floor*. There's that *look* again ... that traumatized "I-can't-take-this-IN" expression I have seen ... in my *daughter's* eyes ... in my *mother's* eyes ... and *now* see in my *husband's* eyes.

"HURry," I plead, not sure how accurate Dr. Dolt's time frame might be, given his *in*accuracy about nearly *everything else*.

That *has* to qualify as one of the *saddest* trips to Walgreen's anyone has *ever taken*. I can't *imagine* how surreal it must feel ... [ZOMBIE-LIKE] getting in the *car* ... going through the *motions*, walking into the *store*, finding the *school*-supplies *aisle*, waiting in *line* ... checking *out* ... *all* the while holding what he *knows* will contain his *dying* wife's *last* words. Geez! As I imagine the scene from my hospital bed while waiting for him to re*turn*, I know *mine* isn't the *only* gut wrenching today.

He re*turns* ... with a notebook he won't *show* me right away. He holds the cover flat against his chest, but I can *tell* it's *not* a composition notebook. It has bold *purple* logos splashed all *over* the back *cover*.

[CONFUSED, AMUSED] *"What have you DONE?"* I ask. Could it be Walgreen's was *out* of those iconic black and white notebooks?

He turns the notebook a*round* to reveal an almost-neon-colored tropical scene with what ap*pears* to be Safari Barbie ... wearing a loin-cloth, *ani*mal-print bi*ki*ni, swinging on a *vine*—her make-up and jewelry im*pec*cable. [PAUSE] My eyes *pop*. He *laughs*.

I sputter. Here I *was* ... being what *I* thought was ... *I* don't *know* ... appropriately *somber*, and *he* shows up ... with *this*?

[MOCK SCOLDING] *"What part of ... DIGnified ... did you not underSTAND?"*

He takes a long, slow, deep breath as if to *brace* himself. [STRONG] *"If you're gonna DIE,"* he says, lower lip quivering and jaw clenched the way men's do when they're trying *not* to show emotion. He holds the notebook out toward me, his hand *shaking*, tears in his eyes. He shakes it off and begins *again. "If*

My 1989 Lisa Frank "Designer Collection" notebook.

you're gonna DIE ... you're gonna DIE the way you LIVED—with a SMILE on your face. ... ANYthing you have to SAY to us, you can say in THIS ... SaFARi Barbie ... NOTEbook." [LONG PAUSE]

CHAPTER 44

STANDING between a Doctor and His Nobel Prize ...

I spend the next few hours carefully filling 9 single-spaced pages with things I want Libby to know about me ... *and* about her*self* ... and about her *ancestors* ... if I don't live to tell her my*self*. My task feels both urgent *and* effortless at the same *time*.

Had Ginny not asked her *question* ... had *I* not taken it *seriously* ... had I not written *all* those thank-you notes and said what I wanted to say to *everyone* ... had I not felt so guided and *loved* ... pro*tected by* ... con*nected to* ... and *part of* ... *God* ... my *whole life* ... I might have felt less peaceful than I *did*. I had had brushes with death be*fore* but never this*close* and never with *so* much at *stake*.

Dr. Dolt returns mid-*af*ternoon, with a bit of a spring in his step, it appears to me. Does this *man ever* display an appropriate de*mean*or? I *wonder*.

"I'd like you to consider an experimental TREATment," he begins.

"Treatment for WHAT?" I ask. *"We don't know what I HAVE, DO we?"*

"Well, I'm inCLINED to think—and have been saying all aLONG— that you have Crohn's disease."

"What?!"

This is the first I've *heard* of this *theory*. Isn't this the guy who was *"sure"* 8 months ago it was *nothing* ... then *"sure"* it was hemorrhoids ... then *"sure"* it was my big, full-*term ba*by who had messed up things *"down there"* ... then *"sure"* it was a bug I picked up in *Mex*ico and then *"sure"* it was not *HIS fault*, whatever *it* was ... but ... seemingly *un*sure about *every*thing *else* ... ex*cept* that I had 2 days to *live*??!

In *fact*, a few weeks *ear*lier at my *bed*side, when one in the gaggle of baby docs tosses out Crohn's disease as a possi*bil*ity, I very distinctly hear Dr. Dolt declare Crohn's *un*likely ... because my disease (whatever it is) has attacked my colon *first*, my *large* intestine. Crohn's usually starts in the *small* intestine, he tells his im*pression*able protégés. *"PLEASE, God, DON'T let them follow TOO closely in his FOOTsteps ... or ... MISsteps, as it were."*

It doesn't *matter what* he said back *then*; he's sticking to his story *now*. He has brought papers for me to sign to authorize this experimental *treat*ment. He presents the disclaimers about how high risk and *un*tested this approach is ... not yet FDA-approved ... but *"very promising"* ... very cutting *edge* ... possibly *lethal* (let's gloss over *that*) ... and ... the papers he *hopes* I'll *sign* say neither *he* nor the *hos*pital nor anyone *else* in the whole flippin' *un*iverse will be responsible (morally, legally *or* fin*an*cially) if anything goes *wrong*.

He finishes his *sales* pitch, sets his papers on *top* of my Safari Barbie notebook, still lying open to the page I was composing when he ar*rived*. He slides the papers toward me, carefully aligning the signature line on *his form* with *my* right *hand* (my *sign*ing hand). From his lab coat pocket he extracts the *same* expensive *pen* he had tossed in the air in his *off*ice 8 months *ear*lier ... when he declared my case *un*worthy of *his* ... or of *my* ... con*cern*.

"How many people have you tried this treatment on beFORE?"

[CLEAR THROAT UNCOMFORTABLY] *"Well ... me, PERsonally? NONE, but I'm VERY well versed in the SCIence beHIND it, and I can TELL you ... [blah, blah, blah ...] ..."*

"Tell me THIS," I say. ... *"How many people in the WORLD have received this treatment ... from ANYone?"*

"Five."

"How many of them are still aLIVE?"

[DEEP BURBLING] *"Well,* [AWKWARD COUGH] *we don't like to TALK in terms of those staTIStics."* ... I *bet* you don't.

"They're all DEAD, AREN'T they?"

[MILDLY SHEEPISH] *"Well ... YES, TECHnically."*

He makes it sound like death is a technicality ... that a person can be a [HIGH VOICE] *little bit* dead. One might *argue*, in the Bright *Light*, one is only ... a [HIGH VOICE] *"LITTLE BIT dead,"* but, having *been* there, *I* would argue you're *actually* ... *"not QUITE dead."* There's a *difference*. Either way, *part* of me wants to belt out that song from *"The Wizard of Oz."* ... Dr. Dolt, those patients are ... *"morally, ETHically, SPIRitually, PHYSically, POSitively, absoLUTEly, undeNIably AND reLIably DEAD."* Why, *"they're not only MEREly dead; they're really most sinCEREly dead!"*

Dr. Dolt confirms it; they're *all dead.* I ponder that frank ad*mission. While* I'm pondering, he comes up with a perk he hopes will *sweet*en the deal enough to persuade me to *sign.*

"We could even AIRlift you by HELicopter to Rush Presbyterian, where they HAVE tried this treatment before ... TWICE."

"And the patients DIED, right? ... You just SAID so."

"Well ... YES, but ..." ... Here we go a*gain!*

I interrupt to save myself what I can *tell* is going to be a load of manure. *"How likely am I Even to survive the FLIGHT?"* I ask. I look at the clock. *"According to YOU, NOW I have ... LESS than 48 hours to live. ..."*

"I'm not sure you WOULD survive the transport, but I think we can get you STAbilized."

"REALLY? You don't seem to be able to do that HERE, on the GROUND. What makes you think you can do it in the AIR?" Clearly, I'm losing my *patience* ... and *finding* my *voice. "ANYway, I don't want to fly aWAY from my FAMily ... with SO LITTLE TIME left."*

In an offensively bright tone, he counters, *"They can MEET you there. It's NOT FAR."* He acts as if we'll all have a happy little gathering over tea and scones ... or ... a *Ferris* wheel once we *get* there.

[PRESSING] *"The treatment IS promising. I really hope you'll conSIder it ... in the interest of medical SCIence. ..."* His voice trails off. I finish his thought in my head, *"... you're gonna DIE ANYway."* [PAUSE]

What do you know?! Here's a*noth*er *rat* wanting me to fly all over town to generate *head*lines for him. You can dress up a user in a *lab* coat or in a journalist's *jacket*, but he's *still* a *rat*. Years *lat*er, I figure out *why* I keep attracting these scoundrels, and I develop some effective rep*ell*ent, but that's a*noth*er *story* ... another *book,* perhaps.

Dr. Dolt stares at me with a syc*oph*antic ex*press*ion that turns my st*om*ach (which doesn't take much, considering my con*d*ition). I can *tell* ... he *thinks* he's winning me *ov*er. He's practically *drool*ing. He knows what *any* experienced salesman knows at *this* stage of a negotiation: *"The next person who talks ... loses."*

I decide not to say a *word.* I just slide his papers back toward him, *un*signed.

This makes him *vis*ibly *an*gry, but he's not *quite* ready to give *up*. He chooses to lose by speaking *first. "You know, Kelly, we ALL want to win the NObel PRIZE."* [LONG PAUSE]

The Nobel *PRIZE*??! ... I *seethe.* He's leaning in toward me al*ready,* so I take advantage of his proximity. Using every ounce of strength I *have,* I reach up with my *right* hand and take hold of his stethoscope and a fistful of his lab coat *fab*ric. I twist the wad *clock*wise in my *fist,* pulling *his* face closer to *mine* ... using *his* weight to pull my *own* weight up off my *bed.* ... [RISING ANGER] The Nobel PRIZE? ... The Nobel *PRIZE*??!

Practically nose to *nose,* I say, *"No, doctor! Some of us just want to live long enough to send our DAUGHters ... to KINdergarten! ... GET OUT of my ROOM!"*

On my last *syll*able, I push him *back*ward, releasing my grip on his *chest,* too weak to give my push any *real* momentum ... much as I wish I *could* knock him off his *feet.* My eyes ... could burn *holes* through him. [INTENSE, NARROW EYES] He takes a stunned step *back*ward, absently adjusts his lab coat, his mouth gaping open, as if he's about to re*spond.*

"GET OUT of my ROOM!"

He hastily gathers his papers and his precious *pen,* turns and scurries out into the hall like the toxic little rodent he *is.* [PAUSE]

How *dare* he suggest I should hand *over* what's left of my hope and my *life* ... to become his own personal *lab* rat! [SOFTER] If I didn't feel he was *personally* responsible for *so much* of the trouble I face ... if I thought I were dying because of some mysterious *bug* and *not* his in*competent caregiving*, per*haps*, this close to *death*, I WOULD take one for the medical team ... help find a cure for ... *something*. Not a bad legacy, I'll ad*mit*. But *this* ... *this* feels out*rag*eous.

The cynic in me (and she doesn't come out to *play* very often) wonders whether Dr. Dolt *wants* me to die as part of this experimental treatment so *no* one will *ever* find out what (or *who*) *really killed* me.

Ex*haus*ted, I fall back on the bed ... my heart pounding so hard in my chest I can see the thin fabric of my hospital gown bouncing to its beat. And *yet*, in *some* ways, I feel *bet*ter, more peaceful than I have in *weeks*. I got *that* off my *chest*. I positively tingle with the satisfaction of having said pre*cis*ely what I wanted to say pre*cis*ely when I needed to *say* it. [PAUSE]

I assume I've seen the *last* of Dr. Dolt ... but *no*. Maybe 30 minutes *later*, I see him *right* outside my *door*, where he whispers conspiratorially to a man I don't *recognize*. When he *realizes* I can *see* him, he shifts one step down the *hall*, so *all* I can see is a sliver of his *lab* coat. For lack of a better *name* (since I don't re*mem*ber his *real* one), let's call him ... Dr. Pawn (as in, used by Dr. Dolt to make his *move*).

Dr. Pawn knocks, doesn't wait for a response (most doctors *don't*) and then introduces himself as a psy*chi*atrist whom Dr. Dolt has asked to ... *"look IN on"* me.

OK, *now what*? Am I *crazy* because I won't play a*long* with Dr. D's *un*requited am*bi*tions?

Dr. Pawn says, *"Dr. Dolt TELLS me ... he's afraid you're NOT considering your medical OPtions ... CLEARly."*

[CALMLY] *"REALLY?"* I say. ... *"Hmmm. ALL ... right. Let's reVIEW. ... My doctors can do NOTHing, and I will DIE within 48 HOURS. [PAUSE] My doctors can fly me across town for an experimental treatment that has never worked on ANYone in the WORLD ... and I will DIE, probably in LESS than 48 hours. [PAUSE] ... OR ... They can let Dr. Larsen give me the coLOStomy I've been asking for since I GOT here ... and I MIGHT live, although even THAT'S a long shot because they've let me linger here SO long I'm no longer FIT for surgery.* [PAUSE] *Would you SAY I am ... 'considering my medical options CLEARly,' Dr. Pawn?"*

[COMPASSIONATELY] *"Yes ... I guess I WOULD."*

"If you're aware of aNOTHer medical option—one I've over-LOOKED—I'd LOVE to HEAR about it."

I begin to think *may*be I have an ally in Dr. Pawn. *May*be he under*stands* why *my* priorities don't mesh with Dr. *Dolt's* priorities. I remain *skep*tical. Good *thing*, because, with the next words out of his *mouth*, Dr. Pawn tips the scale from *possible do*-gooder to *im*possible *doo*fus. He stands there thinking for a long moment before he takes out what ap*pears* to be a pre*scrip*tion pad. He starts scrib*bling.

"I'd like to GIVE you something," he says, without looking up from his *pad, "to help you SLEEP."* [PAUSE, STRAINED EXPRESSION]

*Dumb*founded, I say, [EVENLY, INCREDULOUS]*"DOCtor, if someone told YOU ... you had 48 hours to LIVE ... would you want to spend ANY of them SLEEPING?"*

He stops writing mid-stroke. [ASHAMED] *"No. ... No, I supPOSE I WOULDN'T."*

I nod as if to say, *"Of COURSE you wouldn't."*

[FIRM WITHOUT ANGER] *"Get out of my ROOM."*

CHAPTER 45

STANDING in the Bright Light ... Emerging with a Semicolon ...

Once I refuse to sign Dr. Dolt's permission slip, essentially, he throws in the towel. He loses interest, which gives the faithful, long-suffering surgeon, Dr. Larsen, his opening (no pun intended) to save the day ... and save my ass, literally. Still, I have to endure one last test at the hands of the dreaded Dr. D.

He agrees it can't hurt at least to consider a colostomy, though he grimly predicts I won't survive a surgery. He does nothing to conceal the fact that he couldn't ... care ... less. He says, before any surgery, I'll need a sigmoidoscopy to see just how extensively my colon is involved. Again, he predicts I might not survive even the test.

On that happy note, they put me on a gurney, and I bid a rather hasty but heart-wrenching farewell to my spouse, both of us wondering whether we've come to the end of our ... "as-long-as-we-BOTH-shall-LIVE" vows. [PAUSE]

They wheel me from my room to a fairly small, harshly lit exam room on a distant floor of the hospital. Dr. Dolt tells me I will find the test extremely painful, worse, probably, than anything I have felt up until now.

"How is that even POSSible," I wonder. On a pain scale of 1 to 10 ... I'm already at "eleventy BILlion," as Austin Powers's nemesis, Dr. Evil, might say.

More bad news ... my own "Dr. Evil" can't give me anything for the pain this procedure will certainly inflict because, if he perforates my colon (which seems likely given its delicate condition and his ham-handed approach to the practice of medicine), I'll need emergency surgery. Since that's the case, they don't want any pre-procedure pain-management drugs to interfere with any medications or anesthesia I might require during *surgery*. [MOCKINGLY CHEER-FUL] *This* just gets *bet*ter and *bet*ter!

They tell me to lie on my *left* side. We have a few minutes to kill while, be*hind* me, the medical team sets up the equipment for my *test*. Dr. Dolt will step in when they have everything in *place*. In the *mean*time, he has to stay out of their *way*. There's no room for him be*hind* me, so he stands on *my* side of the gurney, both of us face-to-face for the *first* time since I ruffled his jacket and, pre*sum*ably, his *feath*ers, by ordering him out of my *room*. ...

That leaves a sort of awkward *zone* between us. ... We have time for a little small talk in our cramped *quar*ters. [SARCASTIC] *"Oh, GOODy!"*

Softening a little, Dr. Dolt apolo*get*ically ob*serves* that I may not have to *grin*, but I will just have to *bear* it—the *pain*, that is (and *bare* my be*hind*, for *that* matter).

"You'll just have to bite the BULlet," he says.

"OK," I say, extending my palm through the rails on the gurney. *"WHERE'S my BULlet?"*

He laughs, seemingly taken aback by my *hum*or under *fire*. He looks at me for a long moment ... right in the *eyes* ... for what I *real*ize may be the first time *ever*. Judging by the *look* on his face, it seems to strike him as an *absolute epiphany* that there might be *more* to me ... than a con*found*ing colon ... *or*, we're about to find *out* ... a *semi*-colon.

"You KNOW, Kelly," he says ... *"I think, under OTHer circumstances, you might be a really entertaining WOman."* [PAUSE]

"That's FUNny, Doctor, because I think, under ANY circumstances, you would still be a BAD doctor." [PAUSE]

I hope I *actually said* that and didn't just *think* it. I'm *al*most certain I *did*. It's funny, though, when I feel well enough to record my whole *"Bright Light"* experience in a journal on my 30th birthday (4 months *later*), I don't include that *line*. I think I left it out because it struck me as too ... *mean*. I don't like the way it makes me *sound*, but it *was* true. I *did* think that ... under *any* circumstances Dr. Dolt would be a bad *doc*tor. I was be*yond* the point of filtering *any*thing for *any*one by then.

I must have said *some*thing because I remember Dr. Dolt taking a sharp breath *in*ward, not offended or *haugh*ty, more *hum*bled, it seems. I don't *say* it to be *mean*. I say it because it's *true*. I say it because he needs to *hear* it. I say it because, if he's the *last* person I will *ev*er speak to (and they have *told* me that might be the *case*), I want to leave him with some self-a*ware*ness, some insight that might help someone *else* ... maybe even help *him*. He could be a better man ... a better *doc*tor. He *knows* it. I just hold up a *mir*ror.

Granted, it might *not* be the brightest strategy to in*sult* the man who's about to shove a scope up your bum, but I'm be*yond* worrying about such things. I have some dying (or sur*viv*ing) to do; I don't know *which,* and I trust a higher Power to pre*vail* here. Dr. Dolt's an M.*D.* ... *not* an M. Deity. He hasn't killed me *yet.* [PAUSE]

The technicians finish preparing the room. Dr. Dolt moves into po*si*tion. I'm already in a tre*men*dous amount of *pain* as it *is*. Without a bullet on which to *bite*, the *only* thing I can *think* to do to pre*pare* myself for *more* pain is ... pray. Pray *very, very* hard, something I've *been* doing since before I left my *room* (and for most of my *life,* in *one* form or a*noth*er, though not *always this fer*vently).

Dr. Dolt decides to use a *ped*iatric scope for the procedure, smaller than those typically used on a*dults,* so less risky ... less likely to perforate my *col*on. I feel cold while clinging to the stainless steel rails on my gurney. I wrap my knuckles tightly around the top rail ... to pre*pare* for more in*tense pain.*

Right a*way,* it becomes sheer *tor*ture, *so* painful I can't even pray a whole *pray*er. I *try* to say just the *phrase,* "*Seek first the Kingdom of God*" ... "*Seek first the Kingdom of God*" ... over and over and over. Eventually, I can't even say *that* much. I have to cut it down to *2* words: "*Seek God*" ... "*Seek God*" ... "*Seek God.*"

I had read those words for the *first* time in *Freedom of Simplicity,* a book by Richard Foster. They o*rig*inated in the *Bible* (Matthew 6:33), but I hadn't ever had them put into *con*text (nor perhaps ever even *heard* or *read* them) before encountering them in Foster's *book. La*ter, my pastor points me to a *long*er version of the *same* passage (Matthew 5-7) in one of the *"scavenger-hunt"* messages he leaves in my Bible at the *hos*pital. I *love* that kind of serendipity—receiving the same wisdom from several *sep*arate, persuasive sources *al*most at *once*.

The verses have to *do* with ... not being *anx*ious ... with seeking the Kingdom of God ... in *all* ways at *all* times ... with *re*cognizing that God is *with* us *al*ways. As I head into this un*pre*cedented *pain*, this strikes me as a *most* appropriate time to ... *heed* that ad*vice* and to remember that *teach*ing. I don't have to be anxious. ... I am *not* alone.

"Seek God" ... "Seek God" ... "Seek FIRST the Kingdom of GOD" ...

Al*ready*, I begin to feel a sense of *calm* ... or ... calm doesn't really describe the sense I have; it isn't an *"earthly"* feeling, so earthly words don't do this experience *jus*tice. I have the sensation of al- most *weight*lessness (maybe the term *"out-of-body"* fits better, but I a*void* that term because, to *me*, it makes the experience seem too ... *car*nival, too unreal, and this experience produces the *most* real feelings I've ever *had*).

"Seek God" ... "Seek God" ... "Seek first the Kingdom of God" ... "Seek God" ...

As Dr. Dolt prepares to insert the scope, I have a sort of quivering feeling in my *chest*—quick shudders that make my prayer sound *shak*y to me, as if I'm speaking through chattering *teeth*. I don't know if, as I *pray*, I'm actually *say*ing the words out *loud* or merely *think*ing them so hard it only *feels* like I can *hear* them.

The boundary between my insides and everything *out*side of me becomes *blurred*. On a *spiri*tual level, it begins to feel as if my skin is ... e*vap*orating ... no longer *nec*essary. I'm not separate from *any*- thing anymore. I'm still uniquely *me*, in terms of my *con*sciousness, but it seems I'm shedding my earthy *"PACK*age" ... my *"wrap*per," if that makes sense. *Brie*fly, I wonder whether the doctors and techni- cians can *hear* me (a preoccupation that flashes through my head for no more than a *frac*tion of a *second*).

I find time *so* hard to gauge. At *first*, it feels as if I'm traveling be- tween 2 *worlds*—between the world I *know* (earth) and the one I believe exists but could never have described be*fore* (not exactly *heaven* but a world or a realm *"this SIDE of heaven,"* if that makes sense).

I *vaguely* hear someone tinkering with the equipment be*hind* me. I'm still clutching the gurney rail ... *or* ... not so much *clutch*ing anymore. My hands still *rest* there, no longer holding on for dear life as be*fore* ... more like letting *go* for a ... *dear*er life ... *if that* makes any sense.

As the procedure be*gins*, I become less and less a part of the *one* world (earth) and more and more a part of the *oth*er (this heavenly place).

"Seek God" ... *"Seek God"* ... *"Seek God"* ...

As I *say* it, I get an overwhelming *feel*ing ... a com*pul*sion ... an *ur*gency telling me I *must* follow the Source of this ... *"other world."* Someone or something *beck*ons me. It starts up above my *head*—a Light—a Light unlike *any* light I have *ever* seen on *earth*—not a *hal*ogen or a high-watt *bulb*. It feels warm, *not tem*perature-*warm* but warm as *in* ... *wel*coming. It seems to *say* ... without *words* or *ges*tures or *move*ment, really ... it seems to *say*, "I Am HERE. FOLlow Me."

The *"Light"* starts *out* slightly above my *head*, at *one* end of the gurney, [SOFTLY, SLOWLY] and then It travels slowly past my *face* toward my *feet*, where It settles at the other *end*. As It passes my *face*, I feel as if I lift *out* of myself, *off* the gurney. I move *with* the Light and *fol*low It. I have the sense my body hasn't moved at *all*, but my *self* (perhaps my *soul*, if you will) has been transported ... drawn *out* of me ... to *join* the Light at my *feet* ... to become *part* of that Light.

The Light creates ... or ... is *framed* by ... a sort of box or cabinet into which I feel com*pelled* to *go*. It feels like I'm *gently glid*ing into the *Light*. The space with*in* the *"cabinet"* seems *small*, but, as I enter, I can see be*yond* it to the most ex*pan*sive, most in*credible "place"*—not really a place at *all* but a *feel*ing, a feeling of profound calm ... and safety ... and protectedness—an inde*scrib*able place.

This *"indescribability"* presents a *chal*lenge to me. As an *"embed-ded journalist"* reporting from this un*familiar front*, *how* do I find words to describe the inde*scrib*able? The ones I choose can't *help* but be in*ad*equate. It feels *strange* not to have the right words,

equipped as I have been since *birth* by an unparalleled editor mother, *later*, an outstanding *jour*nalism school *and* a lifelong love of
*lan*guage.

Words are what I *"do."* For words to fail me *now* ... seems ironic at
best ... but also necessary and *na*tural. After *all*, I experience this
heavenly *"place"* not as a place to *"DO"* ANYthing. Rather, I experience it as place to *know* and to *be*. A*las*, I must admit and la*ment* my
limited vocabulary and carry *on*. ... [PAUSE] Perse*vere*!

The *"cabinet"* has definite *walls*. I'm framed *in* by it on my *left*, my
right, over*head* and *und*er*neath*. I feel sort of like I'm crouching inside, but I'm *not cramped*. I feel awe-struck, not unlike the moment
in *The Secret Garden* when the children peel away the overgrowth
and peer into the *gar*den for the first time ... *or* ... like emerging from
a *cave* and letting your eyes adjust when you encounter bright sun-
light, but with*out* the harsh *glare*.

This isn't a light that hurts your *eyes*; in *fact*, I feel certain even
blind people could see this Light.

The box or cabinet has no front and no back. I can look *for*ward and
see the beautiful place—the incredible, calm Light—but I can *tell*,
with*out* looking *back*, the box or cabinet is *o*pen be*hind* me. The
doctor and technicians carry on in *that* world ... be*hind* me. I know
they're *there*, but I'm not really aware of what they're *doing*.

And, *most* miraculously, I feel absolutely *NO* PAIN. For the first
time in *8 months* ... I feel NO PAIN, even though I *know*, *out*side this
"cabinet," my *bod*y is in the worst pain of its *life*.

The Light or the Source ... *God* ... tells me, without *words*, to look
toward the Light ... to look toward It*self*, *not* to look *back*. If I had a
physical *face* in this *set*ting ... in this *space* ... in this *non*-physical
realm, it seems God would rest the *chin* of that face ... right in God's
own *hand* ... letting me *rest* there ... in*vit*ing me but not *for*cing me
to look toward the Light ... and *not* to look *back*.

It isn't a *phy*sical force. It's a still and very *real* but *spir*itual force—
stronger than any earthly force I have *ever* en*coun*tered. It's as if
sheer *will*—God's will, I think—compels me *in*to the *"cabinet"* and
keeps me facing the Light. But I have *free* will there, too.

As strongly as I feel compelled to *enter* the box, I feel *equally* strongly compelled not to go be*yond* it ... *into* the *Light*. In*stead*, somehow I understand I am invited to stay *right here* in a sort of archway—an archway, *I* believe, between ... *life* and *death*. I am cer*tain*, as I huddle in my *"box,"* that God does not intend for me to die at this moment. God al*lows* me, enables me, per*mits* me to escape the *pain*—pain that I am certain I could not en*dure* if I stayed ... *"in my body."*

I think God *knows* that. Also, *I* know ... I will not die *now,* and I will *never* leave Libby, not even *when* I *die. Noth*ing can separate us—*ever.* I learn that in the Light. [PAUSE] I don't learn it because I see people in the Light whom I have loved and lost. I *don't.*

Later, when people *ask* me about *that,* I admit I don't see any dead relatives during my time in the Light, which makes me think one of 2 *things:* either *my* relatives didn't *go* there (which, for *some* of them, seems a distinct possi*bil*ity—just *kid*ding!) ... *or* ... I didn't go *"far enough IN."* I consider the latter more *like*ly.

This *"place"* doesn't *have fences.* You can agree or di*s*agree, but, as an embedded journalist, from what I ex*per*ienced, *I* don't think this *"place"* turns *any*one away. I'll say a little bit more a*bout* that in my conclusion, titled *"OutSTANDING Lessons Learned in the Light."* [PAUSE]

[AWE-STRUCK EXPRESSION, LOOKING OFF IN DISTANCE] I linger in the Light for ... I don't know *how* long. It seems like several *min*utes maybe, but I have *no* sense of time or space while I'm ... *"aWAY."* I just soak up the *energy.* [SOFTLY] I *wit*ness it ... let it wash over me, *into* me. Awe-struck by what I see and feel and know, I feel as if I'm standing on heaven's front porch. In the Light, I have the answer to every question I have *ever pon*dered—complete clar*ity, amazing grace, unlimited, all-encompassing love.

All joy. No judgment. All peace. No panic. All healing. No hurting. All calm. No chaos. All kindness. No cruelty. No worry. No prob*lems. No sadness. Just one ... big ... *"YES!"* to everything Good.

In the Light I understand *every*thing and *every*one. Un*fortunately* (and ap*propriately, I suppose), I don't get to carry that perfect clar*ity and understanding back *with* me when I come *out* of the Light, but I retain the vivid *memory* of it. *In* the Light I feel connected to and I feel a *part* of ... every *good* thing, from *every* time and place ... on a cellular level ... no ... even deeper than *that*. ... *What's deeper*? Atomic level? ... *Quantum* level? Whatever you *call* it, I feel completely connected to, imbued with, saturated by, part of ... this unfathomable Light. And I don't have to *work* at that understanding; I just *have* it. It's *mine*, effortlessly. This may not make *sense*, but I become a part *of* that understanding. I AM the understanding. This is where, in an *earthly* story, I might say, *"I guess you had to BE there."*

To call the experience *"amazing," "astonishing," "awesome"* or *"miraculous"* invokes such *in*adequate adjectives. It fits *all* of those descriptors. Still, they don't do It ... *justice*. They're not *big* enough, not *quiet* enough ... not ... *enough*. Still, they're the best I can *do*. My time in the Light was, at the *same* time, the most *thrill*ing experience of my life (and near-death) *and* the most incredibly calm and reassuring experience of my life.

When the procedure *ends*, I hear Dr. Dolt and the technicians urgently asking, *"Kelly, are you all right?!"* ... *"Kelly, can you HEAR me?!"* ... *"Kelly?"* ... *"Are you all RIGHT?"* Apparently, they've been trying to bring me around for a long time. *How* long, I don't *know*.

When I return, my *"spirit"* whooshes out of the *"box."* My eyes glide *"back into my HEAD,"* so to speak, and my *"self"* takes up residence back in my *body* ... back to the pain. Nothing has *changed* ... and yet ... *EVERYTHING* has changed.

As I exit the box/cabinet/archway, I actually *back* out and *back in* to my *body*. At the *time*, this strikes me as significant and still *does*, though I'm not en*tire*ly sure *why*. Throughout the *"journey,"* I feel God *"telling"* me, *"Don't look back. Follow Me."*

The whole time I feel *willed* not to turn around, and, a*gain*, I think the fact that I come out of the box *facing* the *Light means* something. But I don't know *what*. By the time I'm coming *OUT* of the Light, I'm already losing my grip on the clarity and the *"perfect understanding"* I had *IN* the Light. As I said, I don't get to bring back *samples*—like moon rocks or something. I emerge with SOME answers I didn't have be*fore* but not with ALL the answers to *every*thing, like I had ... in the *Light*.

I have the feeling that, had I looked *back*, I would have *died*. In other words, I couldn't look back on this *earthly* world unless I were going to *stay* in that *heavenly* one. I had a *choice*. No One *forced* me to stay facing the Light. No One and noThing *forced* me to return. I had the sense I could go the *rest* of the way *in* ... if I *chose* to. I thought about Libby and never *seriously* considered leaving her be*hind*.

Libby playing pilot in a plane constructed by her Great Uncle Herb.

While in the Light I think, *"I can ONly look BACK if I decide it's MY time ... to DIE. It ISn't."*

I feel that so *clearly*; I'm not going to die in *this* moment, nor am I going to die in the *hospital* (at least not *this* time). That sense stays with me into my eventual surgery (which I *still* have to beg Dr. Dolt to al*low*). It stays with me through my re*covery*. This won't kill me. Dr. Dolt won't kill me. The pain won't *crush* me. *Some*how, I know I'm going to survive, even though the results of the sigmoid*oscopy* don't tell Dr. Dolt all he says he needs to *know*.

Funny and fitting, isn't it, that now *he's* the one digging for a pony in *my* pile of manure? [PAUSE]

Since that experience, among many *oth*er conclusions I have drawn from it, I am not afraid to die. I am certain I have seen life as it exists after death, and it's a beautiful—inde*scrib*ably beautiful—*"place."* This experience has confirmed something I have always believed—that death is a *lot* worse for those left be*hind* than it is for those who *die*. I am *cer*tain. That doesn't mean I'm in a hurry to get *back* there any time soon, but I am *not* afraid to *die*.

Some scientific/medical folks suggest I hallucinated, or they describe what I experienced as my brain's *"chemical reaction"* to the pain I couldn't en*dure*. I'm OK with that. ... Who's to say what happens *af*ter this life *isn't* one of those phenomena? Why do we anthropomorphically as*sume* or in*sist "heaven"* has to be a *"place"* when it could be (in fact, *is, I* be*lieve*) an *experience* in a realm we cannot fully fathom this *side* of it?

CHAPTER 46

STANDING 10 Centimeters from a Dead Animal ...

We knew going into the sigmoidoscopy that merely inserting the pediatric scope might put enough pressure on my ailing colon to perforate its delicate wall, akin to a ruptured appendix. Eventually, Dr. Larsen discovers that's exactly what I've had for the past several weeks, if not the past several *months* ... not a burst appendix but, essentially, a burst colon.

He opens me up to find what *should* be a sterile environment—my abdominal cavity—polluted with blood and stool and all manner of bacteria because the walls of my colon—almost *all* 5 *feet* of it— no longer exist. They find my colon shredded beyond recognition. In fact, the remains of my colon qualify as *such* a putrid *specimen* I'm told they send them off to some high-level colon consortium in Canada with a note that I imagine says something like, *"Take a look at THIS!"* to which *I* would add, *"She walked around with THIS in her belly for 8 months, and, yes, her doctor STILL gets to practice MEDicine! Can you BELIEVE it?!"*

No *wonder* I lost so much blood. No *wonder* I had so much *pain*. No *wonder* I didn't respond to any *treat*ments.

And why didn't Dr. Dolt *find* it? *Simply*, he didn't *find* it because he didn't *look*. When he performs the flexible sigmoidoscopy in his office in *Aug*ust—re*member*, the dis*tracted*, obli*ga*tory, per*funct*ory chore he considers a waste of his *time* ... because he jumps to the conclusion I haven't brought him an *interesting case?*—he spends barely 5 *minutes*, when a *typical* exam takes 10 to 20 minutes. I didn't *know* that *then*. Dr. Dolt looks *only* at the first 10 centimeters of the approximately 40 centimeters of my sigmoid colon.

My dis*ease* ... the dis*aster* ... as it turns out, begins at 15 centimeters—less than 2 *inch*es farther up my personal ... *pipeline*. *Clearly*, I got *hosed*.

I realize, at *this* point ... perhaps at *several* points in my story, you might say to yourself, *"This woman seems dumber ... than a roll of toilet paper, and I DON'T mean the plush, TRIPLE-ply, get-'er-done-in-STYLE ... kind. I mean the see-through, single-ply, dissolves-in-your-HAND ... CAMPsite kind. Why did she stick with that CLEARly inCOMpetent doctor SO long?"*

Before you *judge*, ask yourself, *"Have I ever stuck with something or someone longer than I should have? ... an investment, a friendship, a lover, a JOB ... even a joke I keep telling that no one but ME finds FUNny anymore?"*

If *not*, good for *you*. You and I must be *wired* differently. That's OK. It takes *all* kinds. Maybe I need a little more of *you*. Maybe *you* could use a little more of *me*.

If you *have* over-stayed and over-trusted as *I* did, I'm willing to bet you lingered longer than you *should* have for some of the same reasons *I* did; you allowed yourself to be blinded by what you wanted to be*lie*ve was true—blinded by ex*ter*nals or by expired notions about yourself and/or the other factors or folks in*volved*.

We can see *so* clearly when someone *else* should cut bait, but we drag around our *own* baggage—*bad* relationships, *bad* investments, *bad* memories, *bad* decisions, *bad* doctors—as if it's a *life* preserver. I don't think I'm a*lone* in that boat.

In *some* ways, the sicker I get, the *less* able I am to see and to fight Dr. Dolt's missteps. I ig*nore* my intuition and trust the ex*ter*nals—*his* dip*lo*mas ... *my* doctor's recommen*da*tion, his assurance that Dr. Dolt is his *"go-to gastro guy."* ... I see the eager, awe-struck looks on the residents' faces when he barks at them at my *bed*side. ... I count on my long-ago instilled belief and memories that doctors *help* people ... that they know what they're *doing*. All that conspires to keep me tied to Dr. *D*. ... until the *end*, when something drastic happens to snap me out of my com*pli*ant, al*most* code*pen*dent coma.

I think it was Mark Twain who said, *"The only people who go looking behind DOORS are those who have hidden there themSELVES."* I trust *others* because *I* am trustworthy. I don't tend to look behind doors because it would never oc*cur* to me to *hide* there my*self*.

Don't hear me saying I'm perfect—not by a *long* stretch. I AM a work in progress and always will be, but I AM trustworthy.

Why did I stick it out *so* long with Dr. Dolt? Because I trusted that he was what he ap*peared* to be. *Why?* ... Because *I* AM what *I* appear to be. Also, from very early *on*, I learned to look for the *good* in people ... to see *God* in them. I believe we all *have* It; we just don't all choose to display It in helpful or healthy *ways*.

Just like my health and my strength slip away *so* gradually I don't *notice* ... (to the point that I can't even lift a cardboard *Golden* Book!) ... back *then*, at 29, when I *trusted* someone, unless they did something *obvious* and horrific early and *often*, my *trust* dissolved *so* gradually I didn't notice *that*, *either*.

Now, at 51, I'm a *lot* better at listening to my intu*i*tion, trusting that *"still small voice"* and surrounding myself with people who *do* have my best *interests* at *heart*. I used to be *so* intense about being and doing and giving what everyone *else* wanted me to be and do and give, but I felt so *un*loved a lot of the time. I did *part* of that to MY-SELF. I thought making oth*er* people happy would make *me* happy. I misca*lcu*lated. For a long time, I attracted people into my life who didn't know how to *give*, in part, because *I* didn't know how to *take*. Like it or *not*, if you want to be healthy, you *have* to do *both*.

It's *funny*; when I stopped pursuing what I *thought* I *wanted*—to make everyone *else* happy—what I *really* wanted came to *me*: happiness ... joy ... balance ... peace. I had to change the way I think of my*self* so I could attract kinder people and better, *health*ier experiences.

Some of us stick with investments, eating habits, arguments and, *yes*, *do*ctors and *lovers* ... *long* after we realize (or at least start to see *glimmers*) that they're not *good* for us. That doesn't make us thick as a roll of Cottonelle *Ul*tra; it makes us ... *human*—*all* made in the image of *God*, I believe, but walkin' around in some pretty *un*godly dis*guises* some*times*.

When I arrived at the hospital and doctors told me, *"Your colon is trying to KILL you,"* I didn't realize that, left un*checked*, Dr. Dolt's *twist*ed combination of in*dif*ference, incompetence and *arrogance* would *al*most al*low* my ... errant *organ* ... to get *away* with ... *murder*.

Members of the surgical team tell me, *"From the LOOK of it, your colon must have been disintegrating for MONTHS! ... Weren't you in a LOT of pain?"*

"Yep."

"How did you STAND it?"

I joke, *"My maiden NAME is Standing. I've been Standing my WHOLE LIFE."* Yuk, yuk, yuk. In truth, in *this* case, I don't find that very *funny.* [PAUSE]

The sigmoidoscopy tells Dr. Larsen I *must* have the surgery, and, with those results in *hand*, he pretty much steps in and overrules Dr. Dolt about any further de*lays. "Hal-lay-LOO-yuh!"*

Now, I'm *so weak* it becomes a race against *time* to beef me up for surgery before I die from the *lack* of it—a bi*zarre* catch-22. [PAUSE]

*E*verything changes once Dr. Larsen takes the reins. I make it past the 48-hour mark ... still not *dead.* Ideally, he'd like about a *week* to fatten me up and to cool down my colon. He knows he may not *have* that long. T.P.N. helps (the IV system that fed me through ports just under my co*ll*ar-bone). I make it past 72 hours ... *still* not *dead.*

In a silly moment, I briefly wonder whether I'm getting more time because I ... *"did my HOMEWORK."* I had *fi*nished my *"assignment"* in my Safari Barbie notebook be*fore* the due date, so, of *course*, they didn't call off school. They *never* call off school when you *haven't* done your homework, *right*? I couldn't af*ford* to be the *"procrastinating perfectionist"* I had tended to be in the *past* ... about *this* batch of *writ*ing.

I make it into day *4* ... still a*live*! Not feeling *great* but enjoying the surge of energy that comes from having a new *game* plan—one that won't earn *any*one a Nobel *Prize* but ... one that *might* get me back to my *kid*let.

Surgery goes on the schedule for the next *morn*ing. They send in what they call an *"ostomy nurse"* to explain what the surgery will ac*co*mplish *plumb*ing-wise and to show me the mechanics of attach*ing colostomy bags ... changing them, cleaning them, deodorizing them. Shew!

Despite my professional familiarity with colostomies, courtesy of my icky job 5 years earlier, I start to get overwhelmed. After all, I wrote about other people's colostomies but never imagined I'd need one of my own. I fear I'll forget some key detail.

[RAPID-FIRE, PANICKY] *"Do the bags ever fall OFF?"* … *"Will people SEE it under my CLOTHES?"* … *"What happens to my … you know … RECtum … if I don't ever USE it again? Do they sew it shut or something?"* … *"How many people HAVE these?"* … *"Are any of them MY age?"* … *"Will I be able to get PREGnant?"* … *"Will my husband even want to LOOK at me?"*

My inquiring journalist's mind wants to *know*. The nurse couldn't *be* more patient. She assures me we'll go over everything *many* more times and practice *all* the finer points before I leave the hospital. She's wonderful. I *half* expect to see angel wings peek out from under her bright purple sweater as she heads down the *hall*.

She tells me the Ostomy Association offers lots of support, *too*. I had forgotten what a great resource the association had been during my PR days. The nurse even finds someone in the hospital (a patient) who already serves as a kind of *"ostomy ambassador."* He comes to visit me the night before surgery. I welcome his tidings of first-hand reassurance.

I begin to think, *"I can DO this."*

Dr. Larsen? Well, *he* just wins the hearts of everyone who *loves* me. He explains things clearly, honestly and patiently, looking me right in the eye. When he visits, he very purposely crosses the room to sit casually on the window sill. He puts *down* his clipboard to give me his *full* attention. His posture tells me he has *nowhere* else he'd rather *be*. What a stark comparison to Dr. Dolt, who always stands with his arms across his *chest*, barely *in* the door, ready to dash out, seemingly too important to give me more than a few seconds of his precious *time*.

For a few *days*, when Dr. Dolt became particularly hard to pin *down*, my husband and I started timing the lengths of his visits during rounds—36 seconds *one* day, 47 seconds another. If he stayed for more than 2 *minutes*, it usually meant he was showing off for his colleagues or protégés, in which case he might not even acknowledge *me* at *all*—instead going directly to my chart at the end of my *bed* and talking in ... *med*-speak, with*out* *both*ering to translate for the science-im*paired.*

Once I have Dr. Dolt in my rearview *mir*ror, I see his habits *so* much more *clearly.* If I wanted to waste *any* more energy on *him*, it might really make me *mad.* ... Like *him*, I have more im*port*ant things to do. I handle Dr. Dolt, my a*dult* "*ruiner*," the way my dad helped me handle Danny *Beck*ett, my *child*hood "*ruiner.*" I choose to look ahead, not back. I look for the Good and re*fuse* to be blinded by the *bad.* It may sound *trite,* but life's too short. I know that all too well ... especially in *this* moment.

Dr. Larsen lets me ask *every* question, even follow-ups, repeats, tangents and say-it-agains. He's *everything* Dr. Dolt *isn't.* He and the ostomy nurse come in with a Sharpie marker and help me decide where I want to locate the *"stoma,"* the hole in my abdomen where I'll attach the colostomy bags from here on *out.* They draw some very e*lab*orate dotted lines to diagram my *surgery* (and *"DRAStic lifestyle change"*) to *come.*

Before they wheel me down to *pre*-op, Dr. Larsen takes my *hand,* squeezes it and says, a*gain,* looking *right* into my *eyes,* [SOFTLY] *"It's been a LONG road, hasn't it? Let's get you WELL."* [SWOONY SIGH] If I weren't already married, I think I could *love* this man....

The next thing I re*mem*ber, it's about 2 o'clock in the *morn*ing. I'm in the IC*U*, and 2 nurses have come in to give me the most *heav*enly thing hospitals have to *off*er ... a *sponge* bath. The warm, soapy *water* and their *own* fresh, *fem*inine, soapy scents *fill* my room with ... re*cov*ery. If recovery has a *smell, that's it.* [SLEEPY] Up until this middle-of-the-*night,* no one has *ever* *given* me a *sponge* bath ... not as an a*dult,* anyway. It feels de*licious.* I practically *purr* ... and I don't even *like* cats.

I feel *groggy,* and my limbs feel *heavy* and *limp.* I'm half a*sleep,* half a*wake.* I feel the nurses lift my arms to *wash* them. They lean me *up,* untie my hospital gown and gently scrub my *back* ... the back of my *neck,* my *face,* into my *hair*line, so I feel *tingly fresh.*

I *love* the soothing sounds of the water trickling back into the *ba*-sins as they wring out their *wash*cloths. [DROWSY] They have this great, seemingly *un*intentional, almost hyp*not*ic, syncopated *rhy*thm to their movements ... *one* washing while the *other* rinses, so there's *never* a time when I don't feel the warmth and comfort of *someone's* soothing *touch*. [PAUSE]

[CLOSE EYES, SMILE PEACEFULLY] *"Yes, Lord, bring me more of THIS!"*

[EYES POP OPEN] Wait a *min*ute! The fresh soap *smell* fills my nostrils and suddenly af*fects* me the way the aroma of *coffee* affects a caffeine-a*hol*ic. I'm out of *surgery!* ...

My eyes pop open. [RAPID-FIRE] *"I MADE it."* ... *"How AM I?!"* ... *"How did it GO?"* ... *"What did he FIND?"*

Both nurses *laugh*. *"Well, good MORNing, Bright Eyes! ... You did GREAT. You're going to be FINE. He'll come in to talk to you in the MORNing."*

I look down at my stomach. They've only loosened my hospital gown in the *back* and haven't gotten to my girlies yet, so I can't *see* how Dr. Larsen connected the dots in the *front*. The nurses follow my line of *vision*.

One asks, *"Would you like to see your inCIsion?"*

Would I? ... I'm not *sure*, but I say, *"Mmm hmmm."*

We have a little trouble shifting me around with all the *tubes* and *wires* and ICU accoutrements, but, eventually, they remove my *gown*.

I *gasp*. [SHARP BREATH IN] *"Oh, my God!"*

I don't say that as a *swear*. I almost *never* say that. I say it as ... *what?* ... an excited *ut*terance, I guess. I can't be*lieve* what I see. What has Dr. Larsen *done*?! I look at the nurses in utter disbe*lief* while I try to search their faces for an expla*na*tion.

They look *back* at me, con*fused*, not sure *what* I'm re*act*ing to.

"Oh, my gosh!" I say in my more typical vernacular.

"What's WRONG?"

I can't *speak* for a minute. My eyes fill up with *tears.* I'm so choked up I have to swallow a couple of times because I know they won't under*stand* me if I try to *speak.*

"What's WRONG?"

The dotted Sharpie diagram is *gone.* The incision isn't where he *said* it *would* be. My abdomen doesn't look *any*thing like the photos the ostomy nurse had *shown* me.

In my own Colin Firth/King George halting *stut*ter, I *finally* manage to say, *"I don't ... HE didn't ... I don't ... have a CO-LOS-tuh-MEE."* [DISBELIEF]

"No. It turns out you didn't NEED one."

[LONG PAUSE ... SMILE, DROP JAW, INCREDULOUS]

I feel great ... im*med*iately. Later that morning I'm sitting up in a chair, as comfy as can *be,* [DEEP, HAPPY SIGH] feeling very, very *weak* but very, very much more like my*self* than I have since *Au*gust.

Dr. Larsen walks in ... beaming. I beam *back.*

"I don't have a coLOStomy," I announce, as if he doesn't *know.*

"Yes, I'm aWARE of that." He smirks.

"But HOW?"

"You have 10 centimeters of colon that looked like it wanted to hang aROUND for a while ... 10 centimeters of HEALTHY colon." He held up his thumb and index finger about 4 inches a*part,* indicating the amount of colon I have *left. "You STILL may have to have a coLOStomy ... down the ROAD, but let's see how you DO. ... That little bit of colon hung in there a loooong time; maybe it's here to STAY."*

"ME, too?"

"YOU, too."

He fills me *in* on a few more details about *yes*terday's surgery and tomorrow's re*cov*ery. I *know* I have a long road. I can't walk or bathe or ... *any*thing ... unas*sis*ted. I haven't eaten solid food in ... forEVer.

I can't lift *anything* for 6 *weeks* ... at *least*. *None* of it *matters* ... the re*stric*tions, the rehabili*ta*tion, the in*con*venience, the ex*pense*. *None* of it matters.

"I get to be Libby's mom! I get to be ... Libby's MOM!" [SHAKE HEAD BACK AND FORTH SLIGHTLY IN HAPPY DISBELIEF]

"I feel great, Dr. Larsen. How is this POSSible ... to feel SO much better SO FAST?"

"That's what it feels like to get a dead ANimal out of your BODy. You had a 5-foot-long dead ANimal in your body—your COlon. Now, it's OUT."

"You're WONderful." [EYES BRIMMING W/ ADMIRATION]

"Glad I could HELP." He nods and walks out of the IC*U*. [PAUSE]

If I had it in my *power*, this man ... this *fine*, *hum*ble, *pa*tient, *hon*est, *un*assuming, au*then*tic, engaging, skilled, com*pas*sionate, kind and *caring man* ... would have a Nobel Prize on his desk before *night*fall. [PAUSE]

CHAPTER 47

STANDING on Steroids ...

On the brink of death in 1990, my body quits making the hormones *most* people make *na*turally. It takes my body a long *time* to realize my colon didn't *kill* me ... a long time to re-start pro*duc*tion. In the *mean*time, I need pretty hefty doses of steroids to keep me a*live*. It takes my doctors 3 *years* post-crisis to wean me *off* of them.

If someone *you* know or love has to take steroids long term (or *even short* term), *brace* yourself! It probably ain't gonna be *pretty*. He or she may get cranky, even sui*ci*dal. This person may become some-one you don't *recog*nize ... *phys*ically and/or emotionally. *My* advice: dig deep. Find whatever well of compassion you have with*in* you 'cause you're gonna *need* it.

If you have to *take* steroids, brace yourself. It probably ain't gonna be pretty from the *in*side, *eith*er. You may experience a perplexing phenomenon that makes you simul*tan*eously aware you aren't be-having like your*self* ... *and* ... *fur*ious when *oth*er people notice the *same thing*. Be gentle with yourself and the people a*round* you ... *if* you can.

Steroids mess with *every*thing ... from moods to *mem*ory, even bone density and *bal*ance. A patient can balloon up ... and break out. In *my* case, my metabolism went *nuts*—sometimes roaring, *more* of-ten whimpering. That con*trib*uted to ... but probably didn't exactly *cause* ... *wild* fluctuations in my weight—from a low of 96 pounds in 1990, immediately post-*surgery*, to a *high* of 240 pounds in 2005. ... *Ser*iously, 240 pounds! ... I have the Weight Watchers' records and photographic evidence to *prove* it.

I'm not going to pretend steroids *made* me *fat* ... or ... Dr. Dolt *made* me *fat* ... or ... the *"moon being in the 7th House"* ... *made* me *fat*, to quote a '70s anthem. *I* made me fat. My *choices* made me fat. Ste-roids didn't *help*, but I own *every* pound I put *on* and every pound I, *ul*timately, took *off*.

On or *off* steroids, once I put *on* all that weight, I had to do a lot of work on *me*—on the *in*side—before I could make any *lasting* changes on the *out*side.

CHAPTER 48

STANDING on a Scale ...

I launch a *number* of attempts to trim down—*once* losing 73 pounds on Weight Watchers and keeping it off for a couple of *years* ... only to pack it back *on. My* fault, *not* theirs.

I tend to walk around with a smile on my face no matter *what* size I happen to be at any given *moment*. I don't just *seem* happy; I *AM* happy. I guess I'm good at *"compartmentalizing,"* keeping hurts from *one* side of my emotional ledger from robbing me in *oth*er columns.

Still, I endure several episodes of fairly well-hidden self-loathing and sadness, interspersed with periods of reluctant resignation to my bloated bum. I'd tell myself, *"I'd rather be FAT and HEALTHY than THIN and SICK."*

"What?!"

Don't scoff; at the *time,* I *truly* believe I have *only* those two options—fat and *healthy* or thin and *sick.* Where did I get *that* idea?

Upon my release from the hospital, doctors tell me to eat a *"high-fat, low-fiber diet"* to manage my dis*ease* ... the disease they have not yet de*fined*, mind you, and wouldn't pin *down* for several more *years.* The medical wisdom of the *time* suggests people with digestive diseases should avoid fiber and *any* foods that contain a lot of water.

"Krispy Kremes?" ... *"YES!"*

"Lettuce, tomatoes and cantaloupe?" ... *"NO!"*

That might have qualified as a recipe to keep my *taste* buds tapping and my *gut* from rumbling, but it kept my *bum* expanding, *too.* Plus, I felt increasingly miserable in my marriage, a*noth*er recipe for female bum expansion if ever there *was* one.

I have no science to back this *up*, but it seems to *me* that when a *woman*'s unhappy in her marriage, she tends to pack ON pounds. When a *man's* unhappy, he works OUT, perhaps getting in shape and hoping to attract someone who WILL make him happy, someone *not* his wife. Hmmm. I don't know. I'm speaking *gen*erally here, *NOT* suggesting that was the case under my own *roof* ... that I *knew* of ...

CHAPTER 49

Kelly STANDING Meets Elizabeth Gilbert ... in Pages, *Not* in Person ...

As I sit here writing this part of *my* story and contemplating the remaining paragraphs to *come*, I am reminded of Elizabeth *Gil*bert's story, as told by her in *Eat, Pray, Love*. Early *on*, she talks about the break-up of her *own* marriage by saying ... the reasons are ... *"too personal and too sad to share. ..."* She goes *on* to say ... much of it had to do with *her* problems but, *"... a good portion of our troubles were related to his issues, as well."* She writes, *"I don't think it's appropriate to discuss his issues in my book. Nor would I ask anyone to believe that I am capable of reporting an unbiased version of our story. ..."*

Let me be *clear*, in case there is any *doubt*: I am *not* Elizabeth Gilbert, although I confess it would *not* break my *heart* to sell as many books as *she* has. And, the story of my life *would*, I believe, make one *heck* of a good *movie*. My daughter thinks Jamie Lee Curtis, in her *"True Lies"* days, would capture my personality best. I'm *flat*tered. [PAUSE]

I respect and even ap*plaud* Gilbert's statement about the privacy of her *mar*ital de*mise* and submit that I, *too*, have clear boundaries about what I will and will *not* share, bowel movements notwith*stand*ing.

To be *fair*, however, *she* writes about the part of her life she spent with*out* her husband ... *after* her husband ... or at *least as* her husband takes on a diminishing role in her *life*. By definition, I can't tell *my* story the way *she* tells *hers*. My brushes with death ... *some* of them ... happened with my husband either just on the *outs*kirts, as with the lightning strike ... or ... in the eye of the *storm*, as in the case of the Bright Light. I can't tell what I saw, heard and felt without including at *least* a sliver of his reaction and in*vol*vement, sometimes *more* than a sliver.

Here's the deal I *hope* I have struck with *you*, Dear Reader:

I don't *ask* you to be*lieve* I am, as Gilbert puts it, *"capable of reporting an unbiased version of our story."* ... I readily ad*mit* that I have presented you with *my* version of events ... *my* Truth. I have tried to *"own"* the decisions I made and attitudes I held that didn't serve me *or* my *mar*riage *well*—the poop I flung into my *own* fan, so to speak. I have *not* tried to cast my husband as a villain; I have cast him—and my*self*—as flawed human beings, just as I believe we *all* are. I have left out or changed names to protect the guilty or the merely mis*guid*ed.

Where I have shared private *in*sights, I have done it in what I would call *"the public interest,"* in hopes that *my* 50-plus years on the planet, in some *small way*, might help others with *their* ... *next* 50 years ... or 5 months or 5 minutes, if 50 years sounds like *too* much of a *stretch*.

If *you* have been the victim of a crime ... been caught up in a natural or *un*natural disaster ... had a job you detested ... encountered a bully or been hurt by idle gossip ... struggled with your health ... or your *mar*riage ... or your *weight* ... or your *faith*, by now you *know*: *I* can relate.

I can't ... show and tell ... how I *na*vigated those waters by pretending I did it a*lone*. *E*ven Elizabeth Gilbert has several *"someones"* at her side as she eats, prays and loves in *her* book.

I have *no* wish to hurt or embarrass *any*one. Where *I* messed up, I *tell* you that. I hope I seem contrite—because I *am*. Where I conclude *oth*ers messed up, *some*times I tell you *that*, too ... or ... I let *them* tell you with their own *ac*tions (as *I* re*mem*ber them). When my stories have endings, I tell you what I learned, *e*ven from the *bad* stuff, as a cautionary tale or as en*cour*agement.

I have arrived at a forgiving, *"better-not-bitter"* place with nearly everyone I allowed to *hurt* me. No doubt you can tell where I still have some *work* to do in that regard. With all that said, let's ... *"persevere!"* [PAUSE ... DEEP, AUDIBLE BREATH ...]

CHAPTER 50

STANDING beside the Man of My Dreams ... Watching Him Become a Nightmare ...

I don't blame my ex-spouse for the *choice I* made to feel un*happy*. I didn't push *hard* enough or in the right *ways* toward marital *hap*piness. I have to ad*mit* that it may not have *felt* like a *choice*, but I ... *chose* ... to make matters *worse* by overeating. That doesn't make me a *stu*pid person or a *bad* person—but what a stupid *stra*tegy!

I*ma*gine ... my husband tells me he doesn't find me attractive any-more because a particularly un*pleasant chron*ic illness and surgical *scars* on my *stom*ach (about which I had NO choice) have *made* me unattractive. [PAUSE]

That makes me *sad*, so I stuff myself with feel-good foods that, once converted into 110 extra pounds of unsightly fat on my *bum, thighs, tum*my and *upper arms* ... make me feel worse than *ever* ... *and* ... make me *TRULY* unattractive (... by *some* cultural standards, any-way).

Never *mind* that I have the added challenge of *life*-altering, *mind*-altering, *mood*-altering *ster*oids coursing through my veins ... mak-ing me crave even *more* of the *high*-fat, low-fiber *junk* food my *doc*tors, es*sen*tially, have "preSCRIBED." By the *way* ... that ultimately un*wise "preSCRIPtion"* for a high-fat, low-fiber *diet* ... came from ... you *guessed* it ... Dr. *Dolt*. It seems he just *can't* keep his *hands* off my *health*. A*gain*, does that make me dumb as a stump or merely *obed*ient? Probably a combo platter—*with large FRIES, please!*

I have *choices* about my circumstances, and I don't *exercise* them. ... I *do* exercise, however ... walking an hour a day, even at my *heaviest*, but, thanks to drug-induced cravings and *emot*ional *eat*ing, I take *in* more than I walk *off*.

Essentially, my husband declares me ... *unlovable.*

"Ever since your illness," he says, *"I haven't found you attractive."* [PAUSE] *Ouch!*

The truth *is* ... he hadn't found me attractive from day 4 of our *hon*eymoon. I *knew* it ... *felt* it ... but never under*stood* it. *THAT* early in our *ma*rriage ... it felt as if something *in* him just ... clicked *off* that day, like a *light* switch. I never knew *what,* and he never would *say* (if he even *knew* or *no*ticed), but *some*thing clicked off. ...

I spent the next 21 ½ years trying to figure out *what* ... hoping the man I had *dated* would re*turn* and ... mesh with the man I *ma*rried. Sadly, *tragically,* he never *did.* Five years into our *ma*rriage, my illness provided just the latest in a *long* line of ex*cu*ses he concocted for the utter lack of affection in our *ma*rriage.

The *one* shining exception came during those 5 weeks in the *hos*pital. *THEN,* he seemed to *love* me ... desperately—looking *back,* almost *too* desperately, perhaps. But, after *that,* something clicked *off* a*gain* and ... *never* clicked back on. [PAUSE]

I *tried* to talk to him about it *many* times over the years. I remember *one* conversation in par*ti*cular ... over *din*ner one night, about 2 years *a*fter my surgery.

I said, *"We seemed SO close in the HOSpital. I felt like you loved me SO much, but NOW ... EVer SINCE ...* [TRAIL OFF, PAUSE] *... What HAPpened?"* I had asked the question be*fore* in various *ways,* but he *ne*ver would *a*nswer. He would just tighten his lips and declare with his *po*sture, *"Discussion O-ver."*

This time, he answered, and his response *floored* me. He said, *"I don't ever want to get that close to you aGAIN ... because ... if you DIE, it will HURT me too much."* [PAUSE]

Wow! The way *I heard* that ... it made me con*clude* ... he could love me *only* when I was *dy*ing ... and I knew, even with *my* track record of survival, I could *"almost-die"* only *so* many times. I had hoped he could love me during *or*dinary times, not just in a *cri*sis. I didn't *care* to live on the brink ... per*pe*tually ... and didn't feel I should *have* to ... to bring out his af*fec*tion.

In 1990, I imagined ... once *out* of the hospital and reu*nit*ed, we would be *happy*. I even dared hope we might end up *bliss*fully happy. Right or wrong, naive or merely *hope*ful, I felt I had *that* much *com*ing.

I spend 4 grueling months getting back on my *feet* and learning to do nearly *everything* again—walking, bathing, *parenting*. I spend 4 months losing *most* of my hair and waiting for it to grow *back*, waiting for my incisions to fade—one 7-inch-long *vert*ical scar on my *abdomen* and several small ones near my *shoul*der, where my *life*-saving central line had been ... 4 months waiting for the *deep* horizontal ridges that had formed in my *finger*nails ... to grow *out*. Ap*par*ently, that *happens* when your body shuts down the way *mine* did.

Mid-recovery, my spouse's firm transfers him to St. *Lou*is—a welcome opportunity to live closer to my *fam*ily ... but ... the firm had offered him the job while *I* was in the *hos*pital, several months earlier, when he obviously couldn't *pull up* stakes ... with *so* much ... *at* stake. ...

Before I'm all the way back to *nor*mal, but with my *whole*-hearted *bless*ing, he heads out of town in pursuit of a job they can't hold open for him any *long*er. I stay behind trying to sell our *house*, which we *think* will be a *snap*.

For *Lib*by, that means, after 8 months of missing her full-strength *mom*my, followed by 7 weeks without *any* contact at *all* (during my hospital stay and the early weeks after my re*lease*), followed by 3 months of wobbly recovery ... *NOW* ... she'll have to do without her *daddy* for 7 *more* months. *Big* picture, it makes sense. Short *term*, it takes a *toll*.

We put our beloved little white Cape Cod house on the *mark*et ... with its *perky* blue shutters, de*tached* garage, cedar deck and happy little postage-stamp of a *gard*en ... in our *pop*ular, *kid*-friendly *neigh*borhood (*some* would say *"kid inFESTed,"* with 36 children under the age of 6 on our *block*). *Yes*, we put our home on the market ... *one* day before Saddam Hussein invades Ku*wait*, thus touching off the Persian Gulf *War*. [PAUSE]

The real estate market *stalls*. It seems *everyone* ... around the *globe* (*and* in our *neigh*borhood) ... fears *this* may *mean* ... World War *III*, so *no* one considers buying a new house *now* to be [DANA CARVEY/GEORGE BUSH ACCENT] *"prudent."*

I endure 7 months of solo *parenting* ... 7 months living with*out* a car (including a Chicago winter that *forces* me to *drag* our daughter to and from [QUICKLY] the *grocery* store, the *post* office and the *library* ... bundled up in a cute-but-*cum*bersome wooden *sleigh* from Crate & Barrel. ... I spend 7 months desperately trying to sell our *house*, with a Realtor's open house EVERY Sunday, which requires me not *only* to *stage* the house ... but *also* to whisk our *now*-4-year-old *out* the door for *hours* ... with*out* wheels ... with*out* a partner and with*out* spending any *money* ... but *with* enough toys and enter*tain*ment to keep her *oc*cupied.

I spend 7 months' worth of sleepless nights obsessively tuning in to round-the-clock coverage of that first Iraq war ... because the Army sends my re*serv*ist brother-in-law to the *front*—one of the *first* to arrive and among the *last* to leave, God *love* him! To this *day*, I do what I *can* to support the USO and Chicago's Pritzker Military Library, in *part* because of *him* and in memory of those in*tense* *months* ... the nearest I have *ever come* to having someone close to me in *harm's* way. [PAUSE] My *dad* came back from Korea before *I* was *born*, and I didn't know or hear a lot about my Uncle *Herb's* Air Force missions in Vietnam until *many* years *after* the *fact.* [PAUSE]

Back on our *own* front, my husband and I spend 7 months living 300 miles a*part* and seeing each other *only* every 6 *weeks*. After all *that*, I i*magine* we'll be *as close as* ... or *closer than* ... we had been at my hospital *bed*side. ... *Not* so. SO not so.

I join my husband in St. Louis only to find him cold and distant—a*gain* and *still* ... and unwilling to *talk* about it. As was my co-dependent/people-pleasing *ten*dency, I choose not to *push*. I look for explanations that don't put him in a bad *light.* He has a new *job*. He feels pressure to impress his *part*ners. He feels over*worked*, having to do all the things for him*self* over those 7 months that *I* would typically have done: [QUICKLY] pick up his own *dry* cleaning, shop for his own *groc*eries, make his own meals on the nights when he *doesn't* have business dinners or eat with my *par*ents. Yes, *he* must feel stressed, *too*, having to live apart ... having to live with my *parents, his in*-laws, even though they have a separate apartment in their *home* that he occupies rent-*free.*

I have to ad*mit* ... *I* probably couldn't handle that well my*self*. ... I might not have felt all that close to *him* if I had endured that distance from *him* and proximity to *my* in-laws, even though we got along *fine* (ex*cept* for the Kelly's-not-Catholic thing). I e*mpath*ize. I make ex*cuses*. I try *so* hard to see his behavior in a good light and to see our world as it *could* be, not as it *is*.

When he claims, *"Ever since you've been sick, I haven't found you atTRACtive,"* I let him get a*way* with that. I don't *quest*ion it. I think perhaps *I* wouldn't find me attractive, *eith*er. I never consider the possibility that his statement says more about *HIM* than it says about *me* ... or my attractiveness.

Not helping his *case*, I had seen news stories and read feature articles about men who found their wives *more* beautiful after they emerged from comas ... or ... survived breast cancer ... or disfiguring *car* accidents. I wanted to be one of *those* wives. I wanted him to see me like *those* husbands saw *their* wives. *A*lways sensitive and apologetic about my *looks*, even be*fore* my surgery, I *still hoped* I could become *more* beautiful in his eyes.

After *all*, it had worked for Baby Pattaburp when I was 6. *Her* scars made her *more* beautiful, *more* precious, *did*n't they? My dad con*vinced* me they did. Even my husband's *own* behavior at my hospital bedside 7 months *ear*lier—his gift of the Safari Barbie notebook—made me believe ... *I* ... *could* ... *be* ... one of those *wives*. As I *said*, in*stead*, my illness provided only the *lat*est in a long line of excuses for his chronic dismissive be*hav*ior.

I don't blame *him* ... at least not en*tir*ely. If he had it *in* him to be a better man, I *have* to believe, he would have *been* a better man. *R*ecently, I heard someone say, *"Hurt people hurt people."* I'm not positive who coined that phrase *first*—perhaps Sandra Wilson, PhD, who authored a 2001 book with that title—but I think, whatever the source, that *"hurt-people-hurt-people"* statement ap*plies* here. I suspect my husband (now *ex*) qualifies as a ... *"hurt person"* (on some level, we *all* do), but he would never tell me why or how or by whom he'd been *hurt* ... if he *had*.

He knew *my* hurts. I disclosed my *"hurt history"* before we married—the whole shebang. In *retro*spect, I should have *chal*lenged him ... should have summoned the girl balls to say, *"If you've decided to find me unattractive for the rest of our LIVES, I want OUT.*

I want to LOVE ... and BE loved. If you can't bring THAT to the table, for whatEVer reason—YOUR phobias and fears or MY scars, SO BE IT. ... I want OUT while I'm still young enough to find someone who CAN love me, someone who WILL find me attractive, someone who can look PAST my scars and see my determiNAtion ... and my deSIRE ... and not just my diSEASE." [PAUSE]

That might have been a compelling *speech* ... but I never de*l*ivered it. Not *all* of it. Not then. *Not* in those *words*. I *d*idn't summon any girl balls—not *yet*, anyway. At *that* point, I didn't *want* out. I wanted to stay *in, all* the way *in.* I wanted to live up to the vows I took to the man I had nicknamed the *"M.O.M.D."* (*"Man of My Dreams"*).

What a sad joke *that* had become and so *early*—apparently only 4 *days* into our marriage for *him* and only 5 *years* into our marriage for *me*. I'm somewhat surprised his rejection didn't crush my spirit, but I think the thrill of having sur*v*ived gave me hope in parts of my life that were *h*opeless and had *been* hopeless from the *start.* I reasoned, *"If I could come back from the brink of DEATH, SURELY our MARriage could recover, TOO."*

I told myself ... I *just* had to stick it *out.*

"Persevere! Turn the other bum cheek, so to speak. Maaaaybe," I thought, *"if I preTEND I'm not sick ... pretend I never WAS sick ... if I attempt to shield my husband from the inconVENience and unpleasantness of my chronic illness, then maaaaybe he'll love me again ... like he did when we were DATing ... those rare, brief, shining, Camelot moments when he really DID behave like the 'M.O.M.D.'"*

Again, I *c*hose to see *him* ... *and* to see our re*l*ationship ... as they *could* be, *not* ... as they *were.*

Stoicism and perseverance have their *place.* Stoicism ranks as a virtue *if* you lace it with reason and logic ... *if* the outcome you seek stands a chance in hell (and even, *some*times, if it *doesn't*). Lost causes *can* turn around. For years ... *DECADES* ... I thought, believed, prayed, hoped the outcome I wanted—a good marriage, a loving relationship, growing old to*get*her—stood a *chance.* It *did*n't. I didn't *know* it didn't, and, like a modern-day Donna Quixote, I allowed 21 ½ *years* to pass pursuing that *"impossible dream."* [PAUSE]

At the height of his indifference (actually cruelty) toward me, I told my husband I wished my disease *had* killed me ... so *he* could have moved on to someone he considered more *worthy* of him ... and *I* could have *stay*ed in the Bright Light, where I *knew* I was loved.

It pains me to remember having said that now. I knew that had I *died*, I would have missed seeing Libby grow up into the amazing laugh and love factory she has be*come*. At the *time*, however, I honestly wondered whether it would have been better for *her* if I *had* died, so my husband could have found a wife who made him *happy*.

Almost *daily* he made it *pain*fully clear he considered me a bitter disappointment on nearly *every* front. He didn't do that *public*ly, *only* *privately*. He wasn't foolish enough to make his disapproval obvious to anyone but *me*. Too many people *liked* me. It would have made *him* look bad to speak ill of *me*. To *him*, it seemed, image mattered more than *any*thing, so he delivered his ridicule, verbal and *non*verbal, *only* under our *roof*. (Under*stand*, when I say *"nonverbal,"* I mean with *fac*ial expressions and *heavy*, im*patient*, disapproving sighs, *not* fists, although his *words* left bruises that could prompt a comparison to *"sticks and stones."*)

If I thought we had *problems*, he said, *"Go FIX yourself."* A*gain*, protective of his *im*age, I sup*pose*, he didn't want his firm to know when I pursued *ther*apy—saying he considered it *"a racket."* He insisted I NOT bill our insurance company for it, even though we had coverage ... *and* ... insisted I choose between $150 worth of therapy per month or $150 for a twice-a-month housekeeper for our 4-bedroom, 4-bath home plus 960-square-foot carriage house. By then, we could have afforded *plenty* of *both* kinds of sup*port*.

That makes me more per*plexed* than pissed ... and more pissed at my*self* than at *him*. I had more choices than I exercised. So did *he*. If we wanted to have a different story to tell than the one I relate in these chapters, we—*both* of us—should have chosen to live *differently*.

Thanks to my long-held practice of *"compartmentalizing,"* I managed to have a very full and happy life *filled* with wonderful friends and family and travel all over the *world*. I wrote speeches and *gave* speeches and mentored newbies in the speaking *business*. I threw myself into all *kinds* of civic causes, parent organizations, church leadership and corporate-spouse duties. I genuinely loved *all* of the outlets I had—parenting most of *all*. My friends tease me about the tears that stream down my face when I watch Libby perform—no matter how big or how small the *part*. I felt (and still feel) SO blessed to have lived to see every Brownie badge she earned, every note she sang, every punch line she delivered.

Sometimes I felt more hopeful about my marriage than I did at *oth*er times. My weight rose and fell in tune with my *e*motions. I didn't spend *much* time at 240 pounds (about a year and a half), just long enough to rock my self-esteem ... *but* ... that was *ALL* about to *change*. ...

CHAPTER 51

STANDING on a Mission ...

In January of 2005, in my second year of a 4-year master's program at ... Eden Theological Seminary, I'm considering a career change ... from speechwriting and motivational speaking into ministry or hospice chaplaincy. Given my brushes with death, especially the Bright Light, I wonder whether I might be called to help other people ... as they face death and/or grim diagnoses.

As part of my seminary coursework, I go to Guatemala and Costa Rica for 21 days on what my seminary calls an ... "OPEN-hands" or "EMPTY-hands" mission trip. That means ... unlike the more familiar kind of mission trip, on which a group of church folks head off ... loaded down with tarps, tools and building supplies intending to "improve" some impoverished area to Western standards, we head off to those same impoverished areas with empty hands, intending to hear and collect the faith stories and struggles of natives and ... further ... intending to bring those stories back to our congregations, where they might respond with interest, compassion, activism and, yes, maybe even cash.

I detect an almost smug superiority about our mission versus those of more manual missionary laborers. Leaders tell us we conduct our efforts "by invitation, not by imposition." Throughout my time in seminary, I would often hear that phrase ... a phrase I appreciated, embraced and even expanded into non-religious settings. I happen to agree that mission, evangelism, persuasion or change of almost any kind happens better by invitation ... than it does by imposition.

The same applies to weight-loss efforts. In my experience, attempts to lose weight unfold more fruitfully by invitation than by imposition, too. I don't know about most people, but if someone tells me to lose weight, my appetite grows and my mutinous bum cheeks swell almost immediately ... and against my will. On the other hand, I respond better to friendly ... "invitations."

I meet a little girl in Guatemala, 9-year-old *Wil*ma, who, by her mere and meager existence, essentially *"invites"* me to lose *weight. Further*, she *"invites"* me to *think* differently, to *live* differently, to consume the world's *resources di*fferently. I would go so far as to say ... she saves my *life*. In a language I don't speak, in a country I don't *know*, at a time I didn't ex*pect*, by invi*tat*ion versus impo*si*tion, Wilma saves my *life*. [PAUSE]

There I *am*, empty-handed on a Guatemalan mountainside, in pursuit of Wilma's *"faith story"* ... well, at least in pursuit of her *parents'* faith story ... *hers* if she can ar*ti*culate it.

How do they live? What do they EAT? How and what do they pray ... IF they pray? As a displaced farm family on a plantation taken over by an international conglomerate and impacted by changing TRADE policies, what have they enCOUNtered on the LOWest rung of their country's socioeconomic LADder? And what, if ANYthing, does that make them believe about GOD? How can we HELP? What might they want us to tell the folks back home about them?

Wilma and her mother and 4 siblings live in a shack rather ingeniously pieced together out of wood scraps and cardboard *box*es. A few chickens peck and scratch around the loosely defined compound. Several sickly looking dogs laze in the dirt with *thick clumps* of *mud* ... stuck to their patchy *fur*.

I notice Wilma for the first time as we climb up the steep dirt path to meet her *fam*ily, with me huffing and puffing under the weight of my ... *well* ... *weight*. She is mid-way up the *moun*tain, about 100 feet from our *group*, and wading *ank*le-deep in the narrow, rapidly flowing river that rushes behind the *box* she calls *home*. Although 9 years *old*, Wilma stands *only* as tall as an average American 4-year-old. *Grant*ed, Maya people don't tend to be *tall*, but guides tell us Wilma and her siblings owe at least *part* of their short stature to malnu*tri*tion, *too*.

[TENDERLY] She has the most *beau*tiful dark eyes and shiny black hair *so* clean and carefully brushed it *barely* suggests her rustic existence. She approaches our group with a shy expression, head slightly lowered, peeking out from under her hair as it falls forward, *half* covering her *face*. Someone urges her closer and shows her a digital video of herself and her brothers in the *river*. She lets out the most uninhibited *gigg*le I have ever *heard*. ... I fall *in*stantly in love with her. ... We *all* do.

She speaks *only* Spanish. *I* speak *al*most only *Eng*lish, feebly trying to recall 2 *years'* worth of *long*-forgotten college *Spa*nish. At several points, my Spanglish malaprops turn Wilma's *gigg*les into full-blown guf*faws*. Ap*par*ently, as a lesson in *"stranger danger,"* someone has told Wilma and her brothers *not* to give their *real names* if *"white people"* ... Americans ... *ask* ... be*cause*, if they *do*, they risk being kidnapped for *il*legal a*d*option. Our guide describes that as a fairly *rare* but *real threat*. I think Wilma's name really *is* Wilma, but her *broth*ers *trade* names or offer aliases to be *safe* and/ or *funny*. That leads to some silly exchanges as *they try* to keep their *own* names *straight*.

I know at *least* how to ask a person's *name* in Spanish.

"¿Como te llama?" ...

Wilma's brother responds, *"Mi nombre es Nicolas."*

Excitedly, in Spanish, I say, *"My DOG'S name is Nicolas!"* stupidly thinking he might actually ap*preci*ate the co*in*cidence and the fact that I know the Spanish word for dog—*perro*.

The little boy I have engaged in conversation must decide his *pride* matters more than his *privacy* because he bursts out, *"¡No! Mi nombre no es Nicolas!!"* [*"My name is NOT Nicolas!"*] Then he points emphatically to a*noth*er boy and says, *"¡Eso es Nicolas!"* [*"THIS is Nicolas!"*]

By *now*, I realize I have insulted *both* boys. I try to sal*vage* our rapidly deteriorating rap*port*. Turning to the *"REAL"* Nicolas, I say, *"Oh! No! No! My dog is VERY HANDsome,"* as if it might make him feel *better* some*how* ... to know I have com*pared* him ... to a *hand*some dog, not a merely *average* one ... or an *ugly* one. [PAUSE]

Geez! No one will draft *me* into diplomatic service any time soon, *that's* for sure! [PAUSE]

All of the children, *EXCEPT* Nicolas, fall on the ground and con*vulse* with laugher, chanting, *"Nicolas is a dog! Nicolas is a dog! Nicolas is a handsome dog!"* in Spanish. Yikes!

He pouts briefly but recovers when he sees himself on yet another digital-camera screen. Our guide tells us the family lives in such a remote area it may well be the first time the children have seen their own images. Somehow their mother knows and trusts our church-sponsored guide, so she doesn't object to our taking photographs and videos. Alas, my batteries are dead the day we visit Wilma's mountain, so I can only peek over the shoulders of my traveling companions.

We don't find the rest of our visit nearly as entertaining. We take turns stepping into Wilma's home (invited by her mother). She talks openly about both her dire circumstances and about her unshakable, joyful faith. I have encountered that remarkable combo platter on every mission trip I've taken. It seems ... the more simply people live, the more joy they possess. That doesn't mean they find their circumstances easy by any means, but I've noticed they often have a peace and joyfulness about them that more prosperous folks lack.

During my visit with Wilma's mother in their cardboard home, I stand, and she sits ... on what may be the family's only chair. At one point, Wilma shyly peeks in from outside, politely waits for a sign of permission from her mother and then quietly moves onto her mother's lap. This time, carefully choosing the right Spanish words to convey my thought, I tell her I think Wilma is one of the most beautiful children I have ever seen ... because she is.

After I say it, I hope that doesn't make either of them fear I plan to kidnap her. How sad that "stranger danger" plagues even their remote mountain, along with poverty.

I believe I am beginning to have the kinds of revelations an "empty-hands" mission means to provoke. ...

Wilma seems almost to glow from within. She strikes me as an "old soul," wise in her eyes, so to speak, as if she arrived on the planet knowing more than most of us will learn in a lifetime. She seems to possess a balance of curiosity and timidity I find charming ... and admirable in someone so young, having rarely mastered the "balance thing" myself ... and almost never even attempting the "timid thing." I am many things; timid isn't one of them.

Wilma's mother asks me whether I have children. I tell her I have one daughter, by then 10 years older than Wilma.

Photo by Rev. Jerry Amiri

Wilma, second from right.

[SURPRISED] *"¿No mas?... (No more?)"*

[SAD BUT RESIGNED] *"No mas."*

She seems incredulous and asks, *"Don't you WANT to have more children?"*

I explain, through a *trans*lator, that I would have *liked* to have had more children—1 or 2 more—and, in fact, had *tried* for a while but encountered some ... *health* problems, so ... *"No mas."*

She said, *"I am very SAD for you."*

Wow! *She* is very sad for ... *me*! This woman who lives in a cardboard *box*, with no *in*door plumbing ... no plumbing at *all* from what I can see ... and no obvious way to feed her children or improve her *pros*pects ... this *w*oman ... feels sad for *me*.

I tell her God gave me a good one ... my very *own* beautiful *"Wilma"* but blonde and *very* tall, comp*ara*tively. I hold my hand up high above my own head to indicate my daughter's 5'10" inherited height (inherited NOT from me, obviously, at 5'4").

"If I had more money, I would have more CHILDren ... MANY more," she says, *"but it is very difficult to FEED them."*

We have a very *personal* conversation, Wilma's mother and I, examining the universal pangs of motherhood across 2 cultures. We seem *so alike* ... and so obviously *different*. We agree about feeling blessed by our children.

At one point, while another member of our group talks to her *mother*, I smile at *Wi*lma. My hand hangs loosely at my *side*, and she reaches out and strums my fingers several times as if they are loose *harp* strings. I *FEEL* her energy. Her *small* gesture leaves a *lasting* impression.

When Wilma thinks no one is *watch*ing, she seems to go about life with innocent, giggly, *un*bridled *joy*. In *that* respect, she reminds me of my*self* ... be*fore* all the poop hit my teenage *fan* ... and even *since*. I *AM* ... *full* of joy ... *most* of the time, almost re*gard*less of my circumstances. In 2005, in a powerful *way*, Wilma's countenance re*minds* me of that ... reminds me of a version of myself I haven't seen in a *long time*. [PAUSE]

I had participated in *countless* hands-*on* or hands-*full* mission trips be*fore* I head to Guatemala, but, for *me*, this *emp*ty-hands version has a far greater *im*pact. I believe ... *too of*ten, the good-intentioned people who go on mission trips ... go intending to change *oth*ers (at least to change their *cir*cumstances and, *u*sually, to change their the*ol*ogy, often without even knowing or *car*ing what theology they might al*read*y em*brace*). As *I* see it, the *great*er value of that kind of travel may *well* reside in how and how much it changes and challenges *us*, the *mis*sionaries. [PAUSE]

One of my fellow sem*in*arians, a man in his mid-40s from an impoverished African country, observed, [AFRICAN ACCENT & CADENCE] *"MANY times ... missionaries would come to our village intending to introduce us ... to a God they thought we did not KNOW."* Simultaneously a*mused*, dis*mayed and* in*sult*ed, he said he and his fellow citizens watched and listened to those am*bitious ev*angelists and concluded, [AFRICAN ACCENT & CADENCE] *"Often, by the end of their visit ... we felt CERtain ... we knew that God ... far better* *than THEY did."* Then he provided the memorable line that stuck with me well beyond *seminary* ... *"One should conduct evangelism by invitation, NOT by imposition."* I a*gree.* (When *he* said it, with his smooth African accent and cadence, it sounded like, *"EEN-VEE-TAY'-SHUN, not EEM-PO-ZEE'-SHUN."* I still *hear* it that way in my *head.*)

Don't get me *wrong*; I consider the *house*-building, *well*-digging, *med*icine-bringing brand of mission worthy and imp*or*tant—essen-tial, in fact. *So* did my African *co*lleague, but, like *him*, I haven't always *seen* that kind of mission trip change the *participants* for

good ... nor for *long. Some* people even return puffed up and proud, brushing off their hands and re-turning to their creature com-forts with a clearer *con*science but, *sad*ly, in *my view*, with no greater *con*sciousness about their *im*pact on or obli*g*ation to the world beyond their own *reach.* That strikes me as decid-edly NOT what *"J"* would *"D"* in the *"W.W.J.D.?"* (What would Je-sus do?) *equ*ation. I feel blessed to have gone on *both kinds* of mission trip.

In *any* event, there I stand, at 240 pounds, watching malnourished little Wilma revel in the *sim*plest pleasures—water rushing be-tween her *toes*, jokes she shares with her *broth*ers, sticks and rocks used as *toys.* There *I* stand, at 240 pounds, watching Wilma *smile* despite the rumble in her own tummy (which we took steps to ad*dress*, by the *way*, albeit in-a*de*quate and *temp*orary steps—*pur*chasing the woven goods her

Me at 240 lbs. in 2004.

family made, *leaving* money for *food*, *a*lerting a local *a*gency to their *needs*).

But Wilma changes *me* more than I change her *c*ircumstances *or* her the*o*logy. Wilma's image *haunts* me ... in a *good* way. From that day *f*orward ... *she* takes up *residence* ... in my *heart*. On the bus ride back from Wilma's *v*illage, I have a *huge*, *u*nsettling *insight*, "*Holy SHINE-OH-LEE! I'm a HYPocrite!*"

"*What am I DOING??!! Who am I KIDding??!! As a seminarian or future PAStor, I can't step into a pulpit and urge OTHer people to make the life-altering changes THEY need to make ... when my BUM ... is the size ... of a BUS!*"

I realize, at 5'4" tall and 240 pounds, if I urge people from the pulpit not to *lie* or *gossip* or any of the *o*ther things Jesus *wouldn't do*, they'd be well within their rights to say, "*I'LL stop lying and gossiping and all that OTHer stuff, Kell, when YOU stop cramming your face full of KRISPy Kremes.*"

This ranks as another monumental revelation for me, the kind of monumental revelation I think mission trips *should* inflict on their participants. I had settled comfortably into the self-deceptive lie my doctors had *told* me ... and which I found easy to be*lieve*: "*I'd rather be FAT and HEALTHY than THIN and SICK.*" Wilma invites me to wonder whether I have *o*ther options. I'm not *sure*, but, a*gain*, I know I can't, in good *c*onscience, step into a pulpit and urge *o*ther people to make the life-altering changes *they* need to make when *I* haven't made the most *o*bvious life-altering change *I* need to make. I know I need to set a better example. I need to start with my*self*.

Don't take that to mean I think pastors *are* or *should* be *p*erfect—nor neces*s*arily *thin* and *fit*, for *that matter*. I *don't*. Pastors sin, swear and suck just like the *rest* of us. Even though I believe we're *all* made in the image of *God*, on a *h*uman level, from time to time, we *all* suck. At that point, in January 2005, overeating was *my primary vice*. Oth*er* people, other *p*astors have *o*ther virtues and *d*ifferent vices. Wilma spoke to *mine* and invited me *out* of it.

I return from Guatemala de*term*ined not just to *eat* differently but to *live* differently. I decide I can't be such an *o*bvious over-consumer of the world's resources when that beautiful little girl doesn't have enough to *eat*. I trade in my gas-guzzling SUV (a Toyota 4-Runner) for a tiny little peanut of a car (a Scion XA) that gets 36 miles to the *gal*lon.

Without fanfare and without the ceremonial *"last supper"* that characterized *pre*vious weight-loss efforts, I *qui*etly dedicate myself to losing weight (well, as quietly as I do *any*thing).

Thanks to what Weight Watchers *used* to call its *"Core Plan"* (*now "Simply Filling"*)... and ... thanks to walking an hour a day 6 days a *week* ... gradually *in*creasing my *pace*, I lose *96* pounds in 13 months. *Then,* I have 2 medically necessary *sur*geries—*one* to remove 8 pounds of excess *skin* (gag!) *and* a *long*-overdue breast reduction that takes me from a hellish DDD cup size to what I *wel*come as a heavenly C–D size.

Smaller, healthier, happier me in 2010.

All told, I lose 110 pounds. As of the writing of this book, I've beaten the odds and have kept the weight off for almost 6 *years* (with *one* 25-pound relapse-and-recovery following a surgery that restricted my exercise for *12* weeks; I didn't adjust my appetite *fast* enough when I had to curtail my *work*outs, but I'm back in the saddle again, with*out* any lasting saddlebags, I'm happy to re*port*, thanks, *this* time, to Weight Watchers' *"Points Plus"* program).

I keep the weight off one day at a time, one step at a time, one bite at a time, and I tell myself the ancient Weight Watchers wisdom: *"Nothing TASTES as good as THIN FEELS."*

My friends call me *"The Biggest Loser,"* in spite of the fact that my weight loss happened TV-*free*. I joke ... (and it *is* a joke) ... that I also lost 240 pounds of unsightly *hus*band in the process. Seriously, though, *that* may have been at Wilma's unwitting invitation, *too*, but I'll leave *that* for another *time*.

CHAPTER 52

STANDING in Front of a Mirror ... and ... a Plastic Surgeon...

People ask me all the time how I lost the weight and why I think I managed to *keep* it off *this* time.

My plastic surgeon, Dr. Patricia McGuire (best in the Midwest), takes one *look* at me, hears the abbreviated clinical version of my *story* and says ... with absolute *certainty*, *"You'll NEVER put that weight back on. I can TELL."*

I love Dr. McGuire *instantly*. I believe her. She's *right*. I knew it *then*, and I believe it *still*.

*Af*ter I lose the weight, even be*fore* my surgery to remove the ex-tra *skin*, I look like a fairly *tiny person*, in *spite* of my oversized *boobs*. Some*how*, my almost freakishly narrow shoulders provide helpful *camou*flage. I *also* know how to dress to disguise the girth of my *"girlies."* When Dr. McGuire sees me fully *dressed*, during the getting-to-know-you part of the exam, she says she doubts insur-ance will *cover* my breast reduction because she *has* to remove at least a *pound* of breast tissue for insurers to consider it *"medically NECessary."*

"I won't know for SURE until I see you in your little paper CAPE," she says, *"but you look AWfully small."*

She says that doesn't mean she *can't* im*prove* my *"girls,"* but she fears insurance won't *cover* the procedure, whatever she does.

Her prediction doesn't *throw* me. I think to myself, *"You ain't seen NUTHin' YET."* She leaves the examining room. I take *off* the indus-trial-strength bra I wore, the one that *lit*erally came with instruc-tions on how to *"load it"*—how to hoist the girls into place and align disobliging *nip*ples.

She re*turns*, with the don't-get-your-hopes-up expression still planted firmly on her *brow*. Clinically, dis*pass*ionately, she opens my paper cape, surveys my feminine *land*scape and, losing *all* her professionalism, exclaims, *"OH, MY GOSH!!"*

I have to *say*—that's really the *last* thing you want a plastic surgeon to utter when she checks out your naked bod for the first time. Dr. McGuire acts *almost giddy*, downright *gleeful*.

"Oh! We can get a pound out of THERE Eee-Zee!" she sputters.

Once I have my *regular* clothes *off* and my paper gown *on*, she keeps touching my skin, almost *knead*ing it as if she can't be*lieve* what she's *feel*ing. She says she can tell I have lost weight *"the right way."*

"What do you MEAN?"

She says, [GUSHING] *"I can TELL you've been eating lots of LEAN MEATS and FRUITS and VEGetables. Your skin feels SO HEALTHY. You're gonna heal SO well!"* She adds, *"I LOVE it when someone comes in and I know I can HELP them. I KNOW ... I can help YOU."*

I almost *cry*. I think my voice rises 3 ex*cited octaves above *normal*, *"REEEEAlly?!* [PAUSE]

My friends and family, ex*cept* my husband, had encouraged me throughout my weight loss, but Dr. McGuire provides the first, most in*formed* cheer for my a*chieve*ment. In her of*fice*, I realize for the *first* time what a remarkable thing Wilma and I have done. I almost feel her tiny little hand high-*fiv*ing me ... *right there* in Dr. McGuire's office ... *all* the way from Guate*mala*. [LONG PAUSE]

CHAPTER 53

STANDING at Weight Watchers ...

Still talking excitedly, Dr. McGuire says, *"MOST people who come to me having lost this much weight have had gastric BYpass to DO it. Their skin is malnourished. Malnourished skin doesn't HEAL as well,"* she explains. *"But YOU! You've been eating the GOOD stuff—red meat, LEAN red MEAT!*

"That Weight Watchers is a GOOD program! If you can DO it, THAT'S the way to DO it," she says. Everything she says makes me feel like a *hero* ... and sounds like a commercial for Weight Watchers, I realize, but *she's* the *doctor* and *that's* what she *said*. Nobody *paid* me to say *any* of this (although maybe they *should*). ... Hmmm.

Most of my Chicago friends never knew me as a heavy person. They find it hard to believe I *ever* weighed as much as my Weight Watchers record book *says* I did. In *some* ways, it feels unbelievable to *me*, too. Thank God for *photos*. Thank *God* for my friends and family in St. Louis, the members of the congregation I served, my colleagues in professional speaking, the members of my Toastmasters club and my Weight Watchers class, along with my fellow seminarians and professors who *watched* me take off the weight and can attest it happened just the way I describe, *boobs* and *all!*

To lose the weight, I walk every morning from 6 to 7 a.m., rain or shine ... *snow* days included. *"No excuses!"* I don't pay much attention to the other people who go about their business at that hour. I begin and end my walks on a busy street ... with a technical high school at the end of the block ... and a *steady* stream of school buses and commuting parents coming and *going*. It never occurs to me that *any* of them would notice *me* out there.

One crisp but sunny morning in March 2006, almost 15 months after I met *Wil*ma, when I had *reached* my Weight Watchers *goal* and had moved on to *main*tenance mode, a heavy-set woman in a white minivan pulls up across from me on that busy *street*. She rolls down her window and literally stops *traffic* to talk to me. She says,

"Excuse me! I just have to TELL you: I have been watching you for more than a YEAR, and ... YOU ... ARE ... PHENOMENAL!" [PAUSE]

Wow! I choked up just typing that memory on the *page*. I found her im*prompt*u congratu*lat*ions one of the most humbling moments of my *life* ... and one of the most ex*hila*rating. She doesn't say another *word* ... just pulls a*way*. I stand there *stun*ned with a smile *so big* ... it might rival one of *Wil*ma's. I think I even *gig*gled.

CHAPTER 54

A STANDING Invitation ...

Why have I been able to keep the weight off *this* time when I couldn't be*fore*? I think I succeeded because I made it what I would call a *"theological imperative."* In the *past*, when I lost weight, I made it all about *me* ... about how I *looked* or how my *clothes* fit or what other people *thought* of me.

This time, it *wasn't* a*bout* me. I made it about *Wil*ma ... and *God* ... the Universal guiding Force that met me in the Light. I didn't know at that point whether I would become an ordained clergy person or a chaplain or whether I might return to my professional speaking ca*reer* ... or ... *try* something else en*tirely* (finish my *book*, *may*be— WINK), but I knew, *way* back on that Guatemalan *moun*tainside, at 240 pounds, I couldn't *be* what God had created me to be. At 240 pounds, I couldn't have the *im*pact God wanted me to *have.*

I'm *not* suggesting people *can't* express their God-given talents at whatever size they happen to *be*; they *can*. In *fact*, I like what Nordstrom calls its plus-size department— *"Encore,"* meaning *"more of a good thing."* That can be *true*—being plus size *can* be *"more of a good thing."* It just wasn't true for *me.*

As a person who used to squeeze herself into too-tight airplane seats and who, once a*gain*, makes her living in front of *audiences* by urging them to take stock and to make the changes *they* need to make, I had to make a few my*self.* I wasn't an emotionally *healthy* 240 pounds. Food replaced af*fec*tion for me. I think, on *some* level, I packed on those pounds to insulate myself from a marriage I thought I would *never* leave and a man I knew would *never* love me a*gain.* I had to get healthy, *in*side and *out.* E*ven*tually, my husband made it im*pos*sible for me to *stay, and*, thanks to *Wil*ma, by *then*, I was already *thin.*

Those times when I had made weight loss about *me, sure*, the weight came off, but it came off tempo*rar*ily. When Wilma in*vit*ed me, prompted me to make weight loss a *"theological imperative,"* the weight *came* off and *stay*ed off ... *per*manently. It wasn't about *me*. [PAUSE]

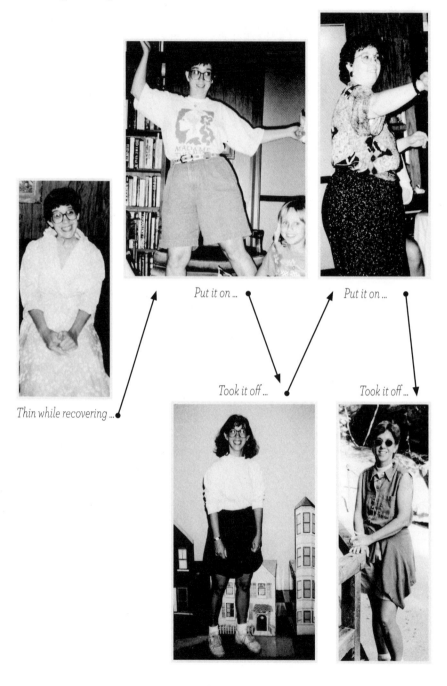

Put it on ...

Put it on ...

Thin while recovering ...

Took it off ...

Took it off ...

Put it back on ...

On again ...

Off again ...

Off for good!

■ ■ ■

[DEEP, BRACING BREATH ...] A year *later*, Hurricane Stan roars through Central America ... roars through Guate*ma*la ... roars across Wilma's *moun*tain ... and causes *massive mud*slides. Rescue workers try frantically to save the people trapped there, but they barely have *hand* shovels, much *less* adequate machinery or technology to find sur*vivors*. After 6 days of *dig*ging, they give *up* and declare Wilma's village a di*saster*. They declare it a *sacred* burial ground in honor of the more than 630 people Hurricane Stan leaves *bur*ied there.

Wilma *died*. The little girl who had saved my life ... who changed me forever ... *died*. Even if I *had*n't known for sure that I would keep the weight off be*fore, that* news makes it official.

Brace yourself. I'm about to unleash the motivational speaker in me. My ad*vice*? Whatever self-discipline you lack ... not just about your weight but about *ANY*thing that holds you back ... what*EV*er self-discipline you lack ... find ... *your* ... *Wil*ma. Whoever you are, *where*ver you are, whatever you *bat*tle, whatever stands between *you* and your *"greatness"* ... between you and your *finest self, DEAL WITH IT!* There's someone (some*thing* ... or some *cause*) out there ready to in*spire* you. Open your *eyes. Find that per*son ... that *some*thing ... that *cause*. Find ... your ... *Wil*ma. *Hon*or that person ... that inspir*a*tion, and, *if* you believe in *God*, honor that God ... by becoming the *best* person you have *in* you.

Hmmm. Does that sound more like invit*a*tion or impos*i*tion? I don't know, but I *do* know, in Wilma's honor and in her memory, I will *never* put that weight on again. I *can't*. In her honor and memory, I strive *every day* to be what God created me to *be* ... what the Universe *needs* me to be. And, if you see me *slack*ing, living casually or taking even *one* day for *granted*, like *Wil*ma, I *"invite" you* to ... KICK ... MY ... BUM!

OutSTANDING Lessons Learned in the Light ...

*Re*cently, my now-26-year-old daughter didn't seem to *share* my *opin*ion about a topic we had under dis*cuss*ion. *Fool*ishly, pressing her to defer to my *"superior wisdom,"* I said, *"I know a thing or 2 about a thing or 2."*

From the expression on her *face*, I'd say *her* jury's still *out* about that. That's as it *should* be. She's a *"grown-ass"* woman, as the *not*-so-delicate saying goes, and she *should* have her own opinions about *every*thing, and like my parents be*fore* me, I expect her to be able to defend those opinions thoughtfully, vigorously and articu-lately. She can and does. Be*lieve* me.

I lived to send her to kindergarten ... and beyond!

So, as it relates to *my* life and this *book*, I *ask* myself, *"What DO I know … a thing or 2 about?"*

What do I know … post–Baby Pattaburp … post-Steinway … post-car accident … post–teenage angst …post-Pope's … post-lightning … post-surgery … post-Light … post-*Wil*ma?

I KNOW … what it's like to *die*—to have complete peace, hope and *clarity*—to have the answer to every *question*, solutions to every *problem*—perfect under*stand*ing, freedom from *fear, worry, pain, all* earthly con*cerns, ab*solute con*nection to everything *Good*. I don't still *have* that peace … *this* side of death … but I know it *exists*, and knowing it brings me peace on *earth*. I don't believe I or *anyone* (any *person* or any denomi*nation*) has an exclusive lock on that *"place"*… *or that peace.*

I KNOW … I am not afraid to *die*. … I'm not in a hurry to get *back* there, but I *do* hope I have a return *ticket*.

I KNOW … I was *right* not to sue my *doctor*. … You might disa*gree*. Despite my attorney friend's after-the-fact observations about my *case*, we never seriously considered suing Dr. Dolt. After *all*, I came out of it *"still Standing."* I told my incredulous *friend, "When you come as close to dying as I did, you don't want to spend even one MINute of the life you have LEFT in a courtroom living the nightmare all Over again."*

It would have been a hard case to *prove* given the timing of our trip to Mexico and how *sick* our fellow travelers felt when they re*turned*. The *"tropical-bug"* theory would likely have prevailed. Did I leave other patients at *risk* by not shutting *down* Dr. *Dolt*? Probably, and that pains me to this *day*, but *I* wasn't in the best position to spot and correct Dr. Dolt's incompetence. He didn't practice medicine in a *vacuum*. I like to think Dr. Larsen and others set him straight *out* of my *ear*shot.

I KNOW … how *useful, com*forting and enter*tain*ing it can be to look back on *journals*, particularly things I wrote to help Libby know herself and me. I won't share exactly what my 9 deathbed pages to Libby con*tain*. That's between Libby and *me*. That's *right*; I will *tell* you about every bowel movement I've ever had the *mis*fortune to deposit, but *some* things are sacred. This is *one* of them. Get your *own* damn Safari Barbie notebook, and start scribbling in it … not 'cause you might *die* but to capture all the Good—all the characters, all the laughter, a few of the losses, *all* the *lessons*, all the love—you experience *this* side of the Bright Light.

I *will* say, in 2000, when Libby and I read those pages to*gether* ... on the 10th anniversary of my *surgery*—what we *now* call my *"re-birth day"* ... it a*maze*s me how many of the things—changes, choices, challenges—how *many* of the things I tried, in that notebook, to pre*pare* her for ... had *a*ctually come to *pass* over the intervening *years*. Cool! An even *more* compelling reason to start *writ*ing. What would *you* tell the significant others in *your* life if you thought you had only 48 *hours* to *live*? What legacy do *you* hope to leave behind?

For my*self* ... **I KNOW** ... I be*lieve* ... whatever you choose to *call* It, there's an Intelligence in the Universe that knows and contains every *pos*-sible implication of every *possible* thought or action in every *pos*-sible moment for *every* person, *every* day, forever ... *but* ... since *we* (*each* of us—*you*, me, *Lib*by, Danny *Beck*ett, Lee *Woods*, *Lucky* Pen-ny, Ginny, Dr. *Dolt*, Dr. *Lar*sen, Kip *Stand*ing, *Lo*is Standing, Cathy Standing *Dunk*in, Elizabeth *Gil*bert and everyone *else* past, present and yet to *come*) ... since *we* get to *choose* how we re*act* ... or choose *not* to react to *each* tiny *in*crement of *every* single *day*, it appears to *me*, not even that massive In*tel*ligence knows or *dic*tates what's com*ing* ... in the par*ticular. Rath*er, I believe It *contains* what's com-ing, but It doesn't direct or in*flict* what *comes*. [PAUSE] And, as you know by *now*, I believe It's *all* wired for Good, no matter *what any* of us in*tends*. [PAUSE]

This is heavy theological *ter*ritory, I *realize*. We could (and I *will*) munch on this forever. That's my *choice*. You may choose *differ*-ently. If you *do*, I hope you'll write about it in *your* book.

In *my* view, Jesus had *per*fect understanding of this Universal, shared con*undrum of human *con*sciousness. Also, in my *view* (and I'm not asking you to a*gree* with me), he's not the *only* person in human *his*tory who did or *does*. In *fact*, he came right out and told us *we* can do ... what *he* can do ... if ... we just ... be*lieve* ... we *can*. We just tend not to believe ... e*nough*. Jesus said over and over again, to people whose afflictions miraculously disap*peared, *"Your faith has healed you."* One of my *favorite* Bible characters is a father who asks Jesus to cure his troubled, convulsing son. Jesus says, *"Every-thing is possible for him who believes."* The father says, *"I believe;*

help me overcome my unbelief!" (Mark 9:24, NIV) I think, like that *father*, a lot of us *get* it, but we *don't* get it. We be*lieve*, but we struggle with our *un*belief.

I believed I could regenerate my *colon*. To this *day*, I often close my eyes and imagine my colon com*pletely* re*stored*. In my *mind's eye*, I see it working *per*fectly, doing *all* the things colons are sup*posed* to *do*, just the way they're sup*posed* to. From day *one*, *after surgery*, my colon—my itty-bitty 10 centimeters of Little-Engine-That-Could colon—functioned *nor*mally. And ... over *time*, it grew, and it grew, and it grew, and it grew.

"I think I can. I think I can. I think I can. I think I can."

Now, I have 57 centimeters of what appears to be brand-spankin'-new baby colon, more than 5 TIMES the colon I had after Dr. Larsen stitched me *up*. I'm a regular colon *factory*!

You should *see* it, although I'm guessing you'd rather *not*. *I* stay awake during my yearly colonoscopies *just* to *see* it—pink and healthy as the day I was *born*. Not only *that*, when my doc gets his camera up to the a*nastomosis* (the surgically created connection Dr. Larsen made to connect what was *left* of my *large* intestine— the *health*y part, the 10 *cent*imeters—to my *small* intestine), you can *see* that my *small*-intestine cells have actually ... *morphed* into *large*-intestine *cells*. They function the way colon cells do. Pretty a*maz*ing!

I **KNOW** ... God is *so* good. The Universe has such mi*rac*ulous, healing Intel*l*igence. To an ex*tent*, beyond our ability to *fath*om it, our bodies can *change* and a*dapt* to be and do what we need them to *be* and *do* ... even if it seems like *all* is ... *lost*. I'm living *proof*.

I **KNOW** ... mindfulness made a *diff*erence in how well pre*pared* I felt for the wrenching difficulties I faced in 1989 and 1990. My ad*vice*? Pay at*ten*tion when the Universe nudges you with *unexpected insights* or disturbing *questions* like the one Ginny posed to *me*, *es*pecially when they come with *visceral*, *phys*ical reactions—shudders, goose bumps, gasps, jaw drops, *eye* pops—and/*or* when they come from more than one *source* (Source) almost simul*tan*eously.

I **KNOW** ... I can go back into the Bright Light in *prayer*, *medita*tion or *imag*ination any time I *want* to. It took me a LONG time to *real-*

ize that, an even *longer* time to DO it. *Still,* I consider it almost *too* sacred to intrude *too often.* I have probably *robbed* myself of much peace by restricting my re*turn* ... *"visits."* If there's a place *you've* been that soothes *you,* guess *what?* ... You have an *automatic* open-ended re*turn ticket* built right into your *brain.* You can re*turn.* Just close your eyes ... and *"Go!"*

And *now* ... a word or 2 (... or 654 words, to be exact) about psycho-*therapy* ...

Once I have a bad experience with something, I generally like to see whether I can find or create a better one—no more vodka mixed with orange soda from McDonald's, for example ...

I knew the unfortunate experience I had with the therapist in 1977 could not be representative of the field. Otherwise, people wouldn't speak so highly of the results they achieved.

What follows may qualify as elementary psychology, but I'm gonna say it anyway. ...

I believe too many of us ignore our own histories. We may mistakenly think THAT particular branch of science—psychology—doesn't apply to us. That strikes me as ludicrous or at least short-sighted, as if, somehow, we can decide which Laws of Nature apply to us. ...

If that's the case ... Hey! Sign me up! If we CAN opt out of the science of psychology, I want to opt out of the more-obvious physical sciences like gravity and aging, too. Would that we could ... our faces and bums would stay firm for life!

Some people think of "introspection" and "therapy" as dirty words, but here's the deal: If you hear yourself refusing to think about or talk about certain issues repeatedly, even in "safe" environments or with "safe" people ...

or ... If you know certain topics or situations or environments produce familiar physical symptoms for you—a racing heart, sweaty palms, hives, irritability or an inability to focus your eyes or your mind ... and you've never let yourself explore why ...

or ... If you repeatedly find yourself in unsatisfying, lopsided, difficult or short-lived adult relationships ...

...spend a little time reviewing what you witnessed, what you put up with and what you dished out in relationships ... as a kid. Patterns take root early, and they can leave an internal invisible scar, just like a skinned knee or stitches under your chin can leave an external visible one.

Sometimes ... a scar becomes a good thing—a badge of honor that tells you ... every time you notice it ... that you encountered something difficult ... it changed you ... and you lived to tell. You may even live differently because you have that scar. You may live smarter. On the other hand, if we choose not to see our scars, not to acknowledge our patterns ... that may become a bad thing, dooming us to repeat and pursue the same unsatisfying roles for which we always settle ... or ... dooming us to inflict the same kind of pain that hurts the people we love and, ultimately, drives them away.

If you're like me, you may take the same hit over and over again, giving yourself the proverbial "I-coulda-had-a-V-8" head clunk because you don't see it coming ... again! But maaaaybe, eventually, by applying the science of psychology (instead of dodging it) —by getting some therapy with a qualified therapist (they're OUT there; you gotta shop around) and/or consulting with a skilled spiritual director, you'll learn to recognize your patterns or behaviors. You'll learn to define them and to step out of their way.

I'm not suggesting you have to pick at every psychological scab. Ick! I'm not suggesting we should use anything we find out through introspection to assign blame to parents ... or playmates for the bad habits we developed or the bad choices we made later. Past a certain point, YOU become the one who hurts you or heals you, so I'm not suggesting we adopt anything like a victim mentality or a make-'em-pay mentality. I'm merely suggesting we spend some quality therapeutic (and perhaps guided prayer/meditative) time with the little kids we used to be ... to see what they might tell us about the grown-ups we are and the human beings we hope to become—not wallowing, just wondering and celebrating the infinite choices we have ... to create even better lives than we imagine possible.

I began the chapters about my *closest* brush with death—in 1990—by likening *that* part of my life ... to fighting a *war*. At times it *did* feel like a *war*. I felt like a *soldier* of sorts, but, instead of fighting *to* the death, I fought death its*elf*.

I went in *so* well *armed*. I had *"conventional human weaponry"*—my *heart* and my *head*. After *all*, when poop hits the fan, don't *most* of us try to think and/or *feel* our way *out* of it? My *head* helped me understand what was happening *"on the ground,"* in my *body*. My *heart*—my *intuition*—helped me understand the *bigg*er picture: my family, my future and the consequences to *their* universe, to *my* universe and to ... *THE* ... *Uni*verse if I didn't *win* this *"war."* My heart told me how to re*spond* to all the intelligence my head was gathering about our common *enemy—"General Bucket."*

I had some *un*conventional weapons, *too*—what you *might* call Weapons of Mass ... Pro*tec*tion: my *faith*. I had wired *that* defense system right into my head and heart a *long* time ago and had put it to the test *many times*.

*Ob*viously, I won the *war*. ... *How?* ... *First*, I fought like *hell*. My head (and my body and my doctors) told me I was *dy*ing. They were *right*. *No doubt*. The odds felt stacked a*gainst* me, and the stakes felt im*possibly high*. I was waging a war ... to retain the *right* ... to keep on being Libby's *mom*. This war wasn't about *me*. It was about *her*.

The pain was *so* unre*lent*ing, the treatment *so* in*va*sive and my prospects *so bleak*, were it not for Libby and my desire to see her grow *up*, I might have thrown in the towel, laid down my weapons and sur*ren*dered to Gen. Bucket a lot *soo*ner.

That's how I won my war. I fought, and I fought, and I fought, fast and *fu*riously, for a *long* time. And *then* ... in an ex*cru*ciating moment ... on a gurney ... in a *hos*pital gown ... in the middle of *Am*erica ... in the middle of an ab*bre*viated *prayer*, [SLOWLY] I sloooowed down, the world stopped *spin*ning out of con*trol* and *I* sur*ren*dered.

I hung out in the Light, apparently *just* long enough to escape the *pain* and to gain the perspective I needed for the rescue and recovery to *come* but *not* long enough and not far enough *in* ... to *die*.

When *I* let go, Gen. Bucket put down *his* weapons, too. *He* called a cease-fire and *let* me win. Gen. Bucket could af*ford* to be *pa*tient. He knew he would prevail ... *event*ually.

In the *end*, in *my* case, death waged a profoundly *peace*ful *"war."*

I KNOW ... when I emerged from the Light and the surgery that *fol-*lowed, with *months* of difficult recovery a*head* of me, my dad leaned down to me on what we had *thought* was going to be *my* deathbed, and he whispered to *me* what *his fath*er had whispered to *him* from *his* deathbed, *"Persevere!"*

Acknowledgments

"It's a sign of mediocrity when you demonstrate gratitude with moderation." — *Roberto Benigni*

I have no wish to practice *"moderation"* in my gratitude to the many, many people who helped bring this book out of my head and my heart and into the ... Light, so to speak. And, for that matter, I have no wish to be mediocre. This book took me 51 years to write. No one dodges the bullets I have and remains *"STANDING"* all that time without a lot of help.

"Gratitude is one of the least articulate of the emotions, especially when it is deep." — *Felix Frankfurter*

I fear I will live up to (or down to) Frankfurter's prediction of *"inarticulateness"* here because I feel so deeply grateful ... but I'll persevere ...

Thank you, Lois Standing, Kip Standing and Cathy Standing Dunkin — the *"core family."* We have something magical, and I thank you for being so brave and supportive ... for encouraging me to tell my story ... our story ... all of it ... in an honest way, even shining a light on my/our not-so-magical moments. *"Lots of good love,"* now and always.

Thank you, Libby. You are so smart and so funny and so kind and creative. I get to be your mom! Blessings don't come any bigger than that. *"MGC AOTLAY RYB/QCO EEFC!"*

Thank you, Dean (Rob) Briscoe, unparalleled business partner, gifted guru of all things technological, landscaper, woodworker, handyman, hero and, most especially, a love worth waiting for ... You are the "Someone to Watch Over Me" ... 70% of the time. [WINK] I'll handle the other 30.

Thank you, Mary Edele. You personify friendship. I love you every day of my life. You saw this book coming better and sooner than I did.

Thank you, Linda Henman, for urging me so often and so well to pull my head out of my ... um ... *"bum"* and for all the other collaborative encouragement you provide so generously.

Thank you, Patti Allen, inspiring, encouraging, smart and funny ... and a phenomenal cook!

Thank you most of all, Roger Thomas — loud, opinionated and hilariously funny, fiercely loyal, fearless, smarter than almost anyone I've ever known and brutally honest. You and your *"child bride,"* Pat, have a better sense of what matters in this life than any two people on the planet. You kick my bum when I need it, hold my hand when I need that and always offer me a *"soft place to fall."* This book would not exist were it not for your unremitting encouragement, your frequent hospitality and your generous, insightful attention to my countless drafts. In many ways, I'm *"Still STANDING"* because of you. Thanks, Rev, more than you will ever know.

Thank you, friends, colleagues & collaborators ...

Editor: Marcia Kramer of Kramer Editing Services — fast, fantastic and funny!

Readers/Encouragers: Patti Allen, Paul & Annette Cardosi, Don Catherall, Kevin Doyle, Cathy & Carter Dunkin, Steve Durham, Mary & John Edele, Sue Graff, Linda Henman, Janet Koren, Jody & Mike Noble, Michael Norman, Pat Stapleton Oaklief, Cassia Overk, Sally Park, Dorothy Pirovano, Jackie & John Popravak, Lois Standing, Pat Thomas, Roger Thomas, Darla Temple, Beverly Mundy Weable & Trent Weable, Ryan Yantis.

Additional Encouragers: Elynne Chaplik-Aleskow, Jerry Amiri, Mary Baim, Carole Barner, Karen Bark, Sue Black, Joan Briscoe, Jan Burggrabe, Ray Clouse, Frank Daly, Judy & Maury Fantus, Sandy & Jenny Frederich, Patty Frost, Regina Galllagher, Susan Gebarowski, Gene & Mary Haberstock, Karen Hale, Jackie & Greg Harris, Bob & Cathy Healey, Aurora Hirit, Barbara & Bill Hollenbeck, Mary Holloway, Chuck & Caroline Hoppe, Kara Kaswell, Margo Knuepfer, Charlene Krombeen, Kathy Kuna, Peter Lopatin, Julie Layton, Jeanne Mastin Manley, Erica Matagrano, Diane McFarlin, Kathy Mertes, Nancy Helfert Moore, Kerry Obrist, Lesley Pearl, Tim & Char Pearson, Sue Pfeifer Carothers, Gene Rhodes, David Rubin, Phyllis Russell, Ethel Russell-Ajisomo, Dennis Sanders, Katrina Schmitt,

Teri Schoenberg, Julie Sharpe, Dallas Smith, Vickie Shrum White, Gail Spreen, Damian Szulga, Jim Walker, Linda Walker, Rhonda Wassell, Rhonda Marberry Whiteman, Joan Zimmermann Ces.

Supportive Colleagues: Read Bradford, Roger Breisch, Brian Burkhart, Bob Chesney, Conor Cunneen, Lois Creamer, Nancy Depcik, Peter Glon, Shep Hyken, Tom Lee, Toni McMurphy, Maureen O'Brien, Kevin O'Connor, Mark Partridge, Kathleen Passanisi, Blaine Rada, Sue Roupp, Leslee Serdar, Steven Steinberg, Carol Weisman, Cheryl Woodson.

Memorable Teachers/Mentors: Jennifer Ayres, Kathy Bade, Doris & Grady Balthrop, Russ Doerner, John Bracke, Elizabeth Caldwell, Anna Case-Winters, Jeanne Eichhorn, David Esterline, Christopher Grundy, Julie Jennings, Michael Kinnamon, Deb Krause, Joretta Marshall, Joe Marting, Clint McCann, Deborah Mullen, Holly Nelson, Mrs. Neville from third grade, Mr. Richardson from junior-high social studies, Don Ranly, John Riggs, Martha Robertson, Jim Sandfort, Ken Sawyer, Ron Schafer from high-school speech & debate, Mary Beth & Michael Speer, Peter Strening, Karen Tye, Christine Vogel, Peggy Way.

Publishing Mentors/Consultants: Jack Canfield, Carter Dunkin, Arielle Eckstut, David Henry Sterry, Blythe McGarvie.

Jenkins Group Team: Yvonne Fetig Roehler, Jerry Jenkins, Jim Kalajian, Leah Nicholson, Devon Ritter, Heather Shaw.

Design/Photography: Alex Ha of Alex Ha Photography, Flaviu Mitar of Flaviu Photography, Chris Scavotto of Scavotto Design, Jørgen Pedersen of Bare Bear Productions.

Legal/Financial Consultants: Steve Albart, Jordan Arnott, Ken Block, Jim Campbell, Nancy Chapman, Craig Morris, Mark Partridge, Matt Sallaberry, Nick Thomas, Vitaliy Tsymbaluk, Richard Weiss.

Image/Hair/Make-Up/Wardrobe: Sanford Barr, Cora Buckle at Bloomingdale's, Jojo Kazarian and Olita Soblinskas at Red Door Spas Chicago, Lynne Herbstritt, Lauren Nathan and Marie Williamson at Nordstrom, Nolen Levine, Patricia McGuire.

I'M STILL STANDING: How One Woman's Brushes With Death Taught Her How To Live offers a one-stop adversity shop of sorts. Kelly Standing covers nearly every kind of mishap one can face — bullying and idle gossip, violent crime, career woes, health challenges, death and dying, relationship hiccups, parenting practices, crises of faith, tight finances and even a successful weight management strategy — all in a single lifetime and in a single volume. The author provides a philosophical road map that helps readers laugh, persevere and even thrive through and beyond those landmines.

To book Kelly Standing for a speaking engagement, a book signing or book discussion and to see video clips and more, visit
www.ImStillStandingBook.com